Treasures of Ushaw College

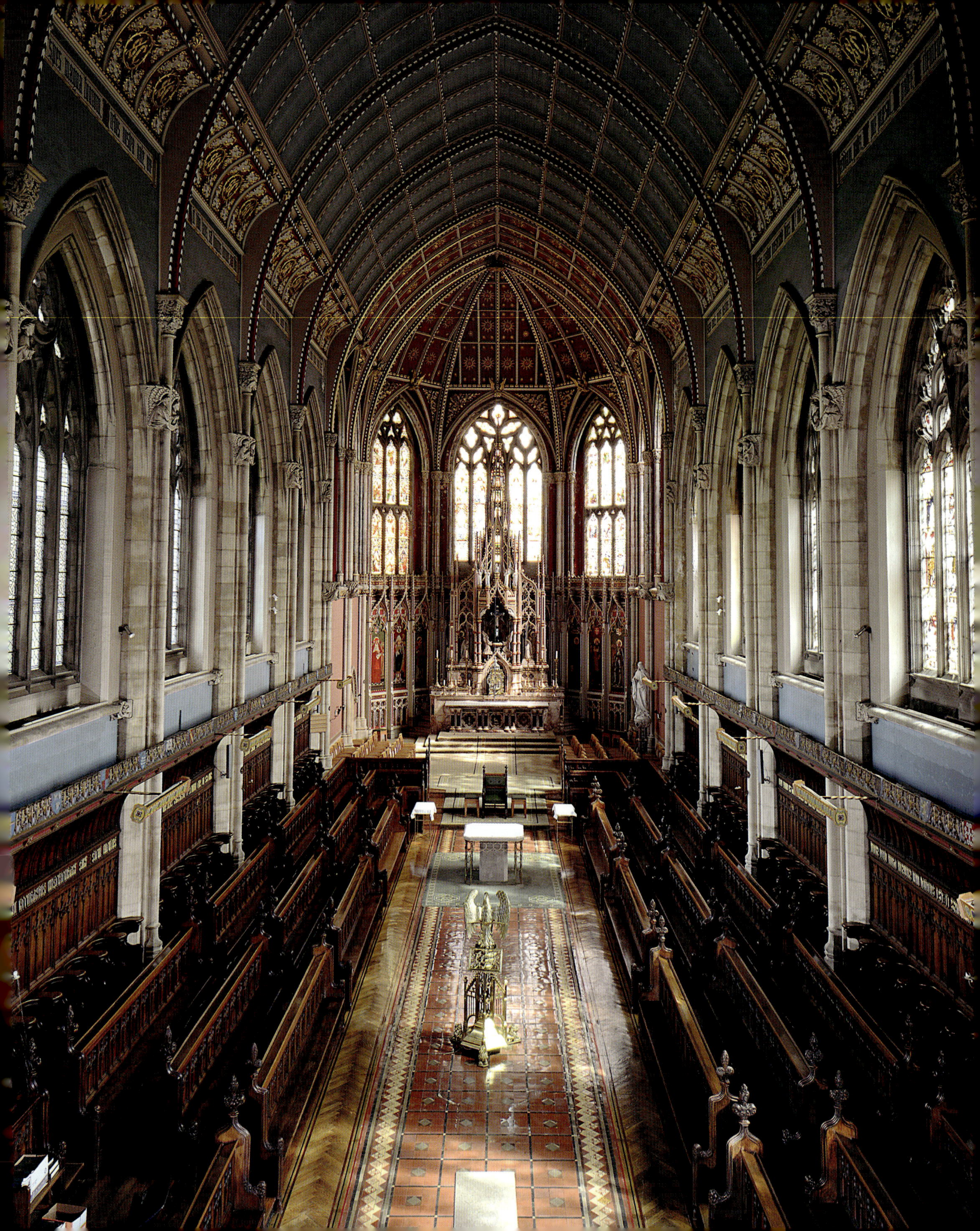

Treasures of Ushaw College

Durham's Hidden Gem

Edited by James E. Kelly

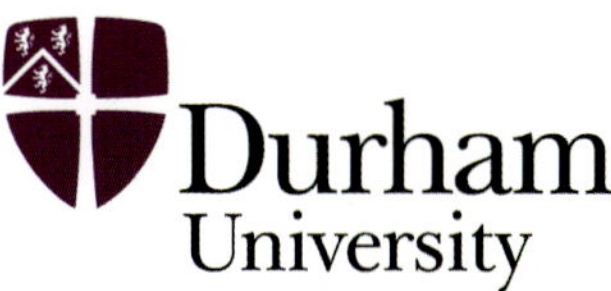

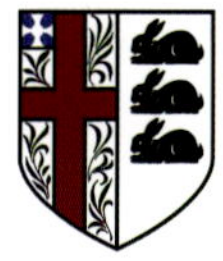

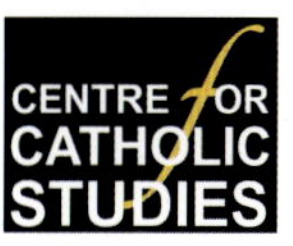

SCALA

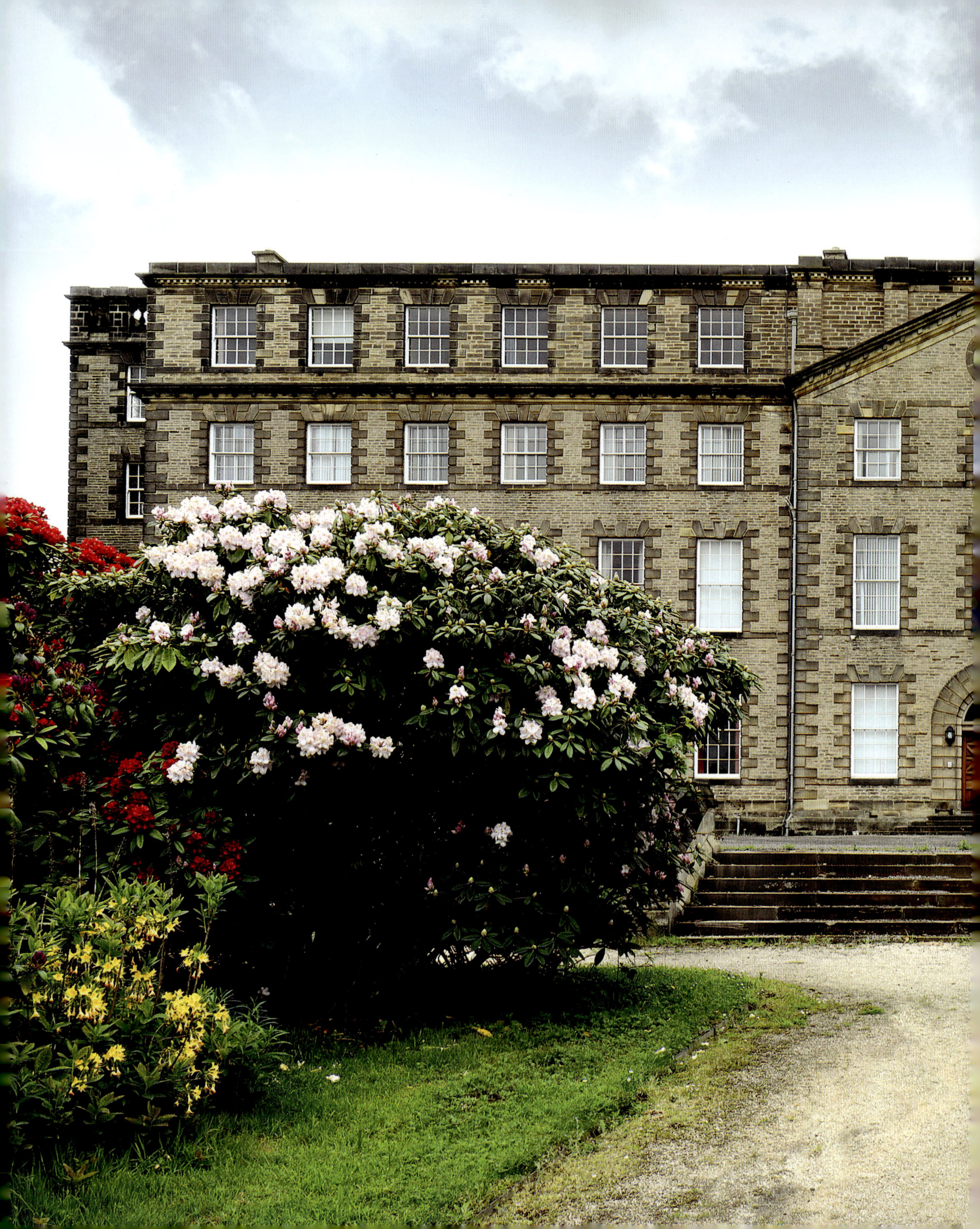

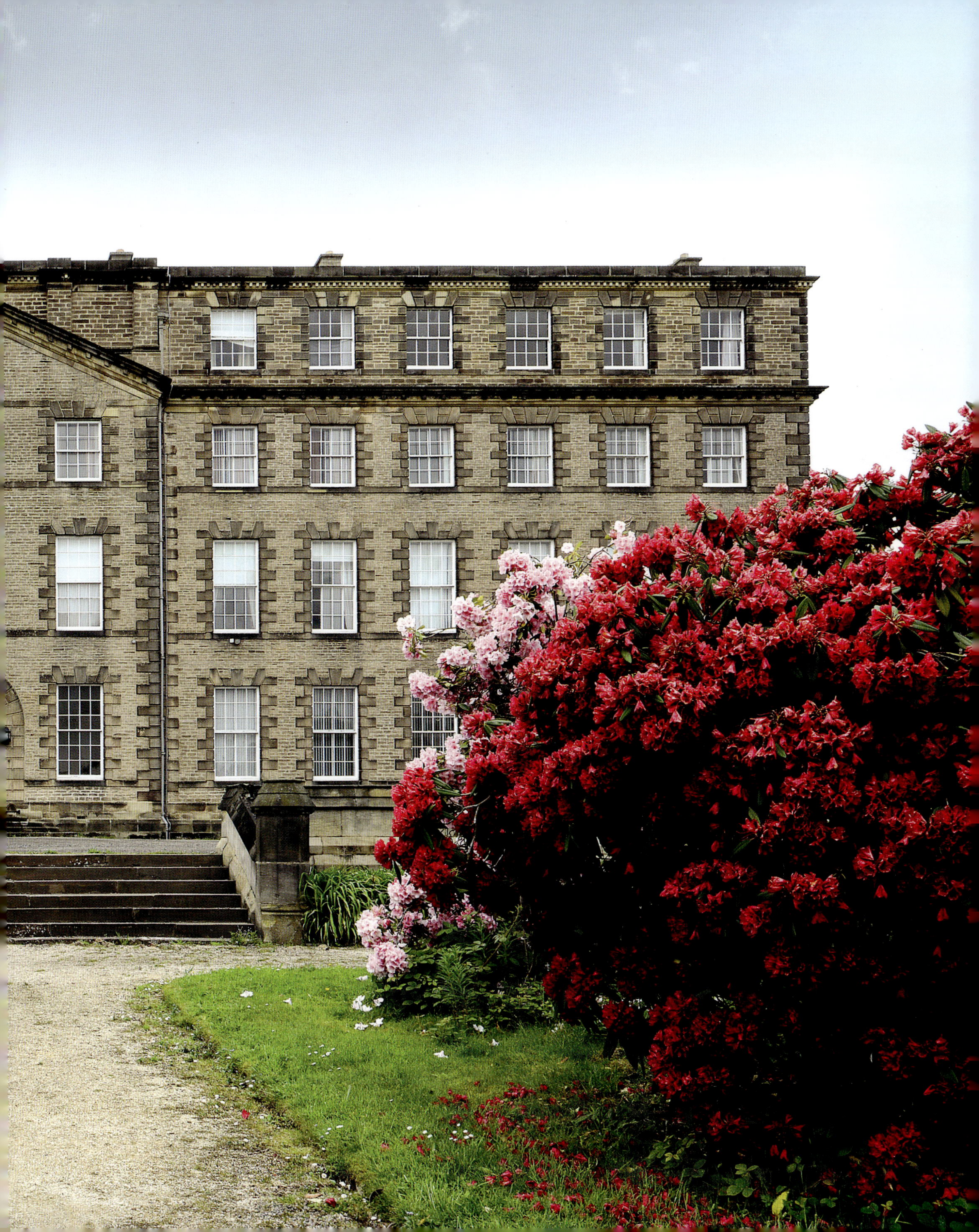

First published in 2015 by
Scala Arts & Heritage Publishers Ltd
10 Lion Yard
Tremadoc Road
London SW4 7NQ, UK
www.scalapublishers.com

In association with
Durham University
Stockton Road
Durham
DH1 3LE

ISBN 978-1-85759-934-3

Copy-edited by Jenny Lawson
Designed by James Alexander at Jade Design
Printed and bound in China

10 9 8 7 6 5 4 3 2 1

Inside cover: Detail from a photograph taken during the 1951 celebrations at Ushaw College to mark the thirteenth centenary of the death of St Aidan.

Frontispiece: St Cuthbert's chapel.

Opposite: French Book of Hours, *c.*1450–1500.

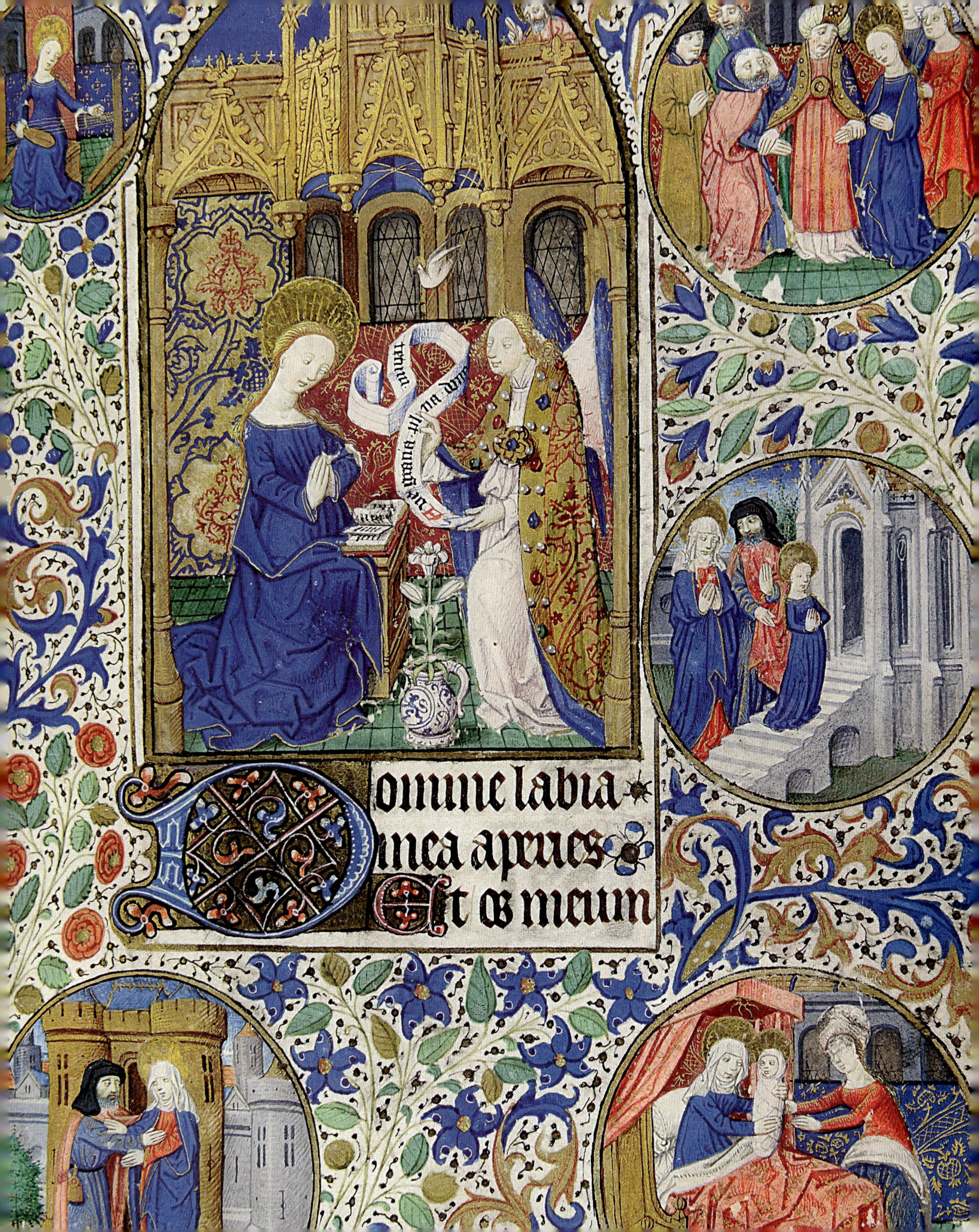
Domine labia
mea aperies
Et os meum

The Treasures

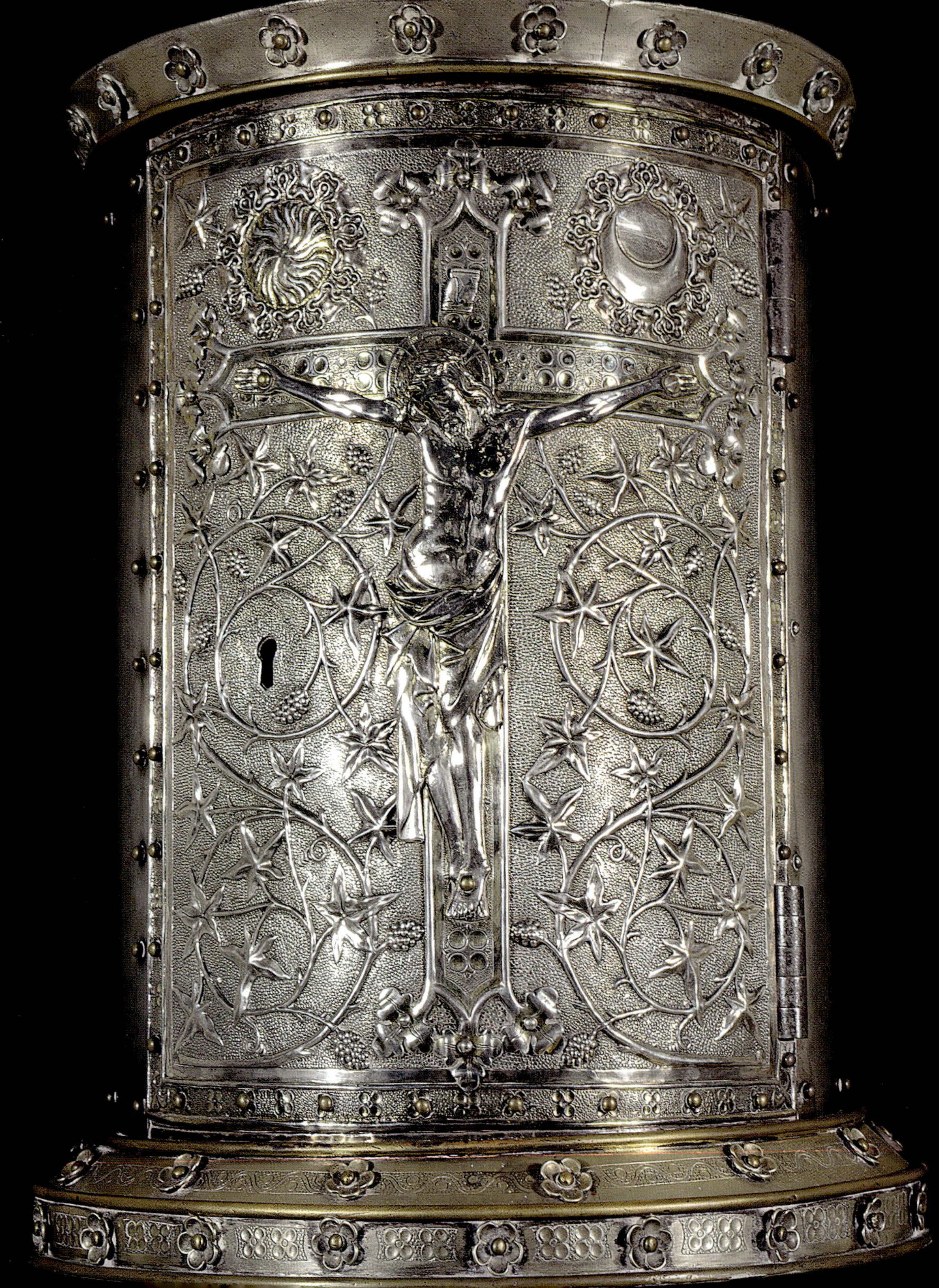

Foreword

In the sixteenth century, the future cardinal William Allen founded the English College at Douai to become an Oxbridge in exile. More than two hundred years later, the college transferred to England, its northern representatives finding a home at Ushaw College. Not only did a number of the Douai College treasures come to Ushaw, but it also became a repository for items that had survived, frequently hidden, during the years of England's Reformation.

These few lines give a clue to the richness of resources to be found today at Ushaw College, in its archival and library holdings. They are highly significant even if not widely known. Indeed for 200 years the treasures of Ushaw have been known only by those who attended the college during its time as a seminary. It is not widely known, for example, that the college's Big Library includes the only known copies in the world of several books.

The publication of this volume, *Treasures of Ushaw College*, is therefore warmly welcome as it begins to put before a wider public a remarkable story and a store of hidden gems. What is revealed here is not simply a Catholic memory but a profoundly English one. The content of this book invites us to travel carefully along the storyline of so many events and people that form part of our national and religious identity. This includes, of course, a gateway into our continental past, not just for Catholics but for the whole nation.

The first Cardinal Archbishop of Westminster, Nicholas Wiseman, was an alumnus of Ushaw. So too were many other important figures, including poets, musicians and the revisionist historian John Lingard. They will rejoice in heaven, we pray, at the publication of this book, which enables its readers to learn more about their college and some of the jewels that have been treasured there for centuries.

I congratulate all concerned with this publication, especially its editor James E. Kelly. May it contribute significantly to the future role of Ushaw College where, we trust, these treasures will continue to remain in expert custodianship for centuries to come.

+VINCENT CARDINAL NICHOLS
ARCHBISHOP OF WESTMINSTER

The tabernacle in St Joseph's chapel, designed by E.W. Pugin.

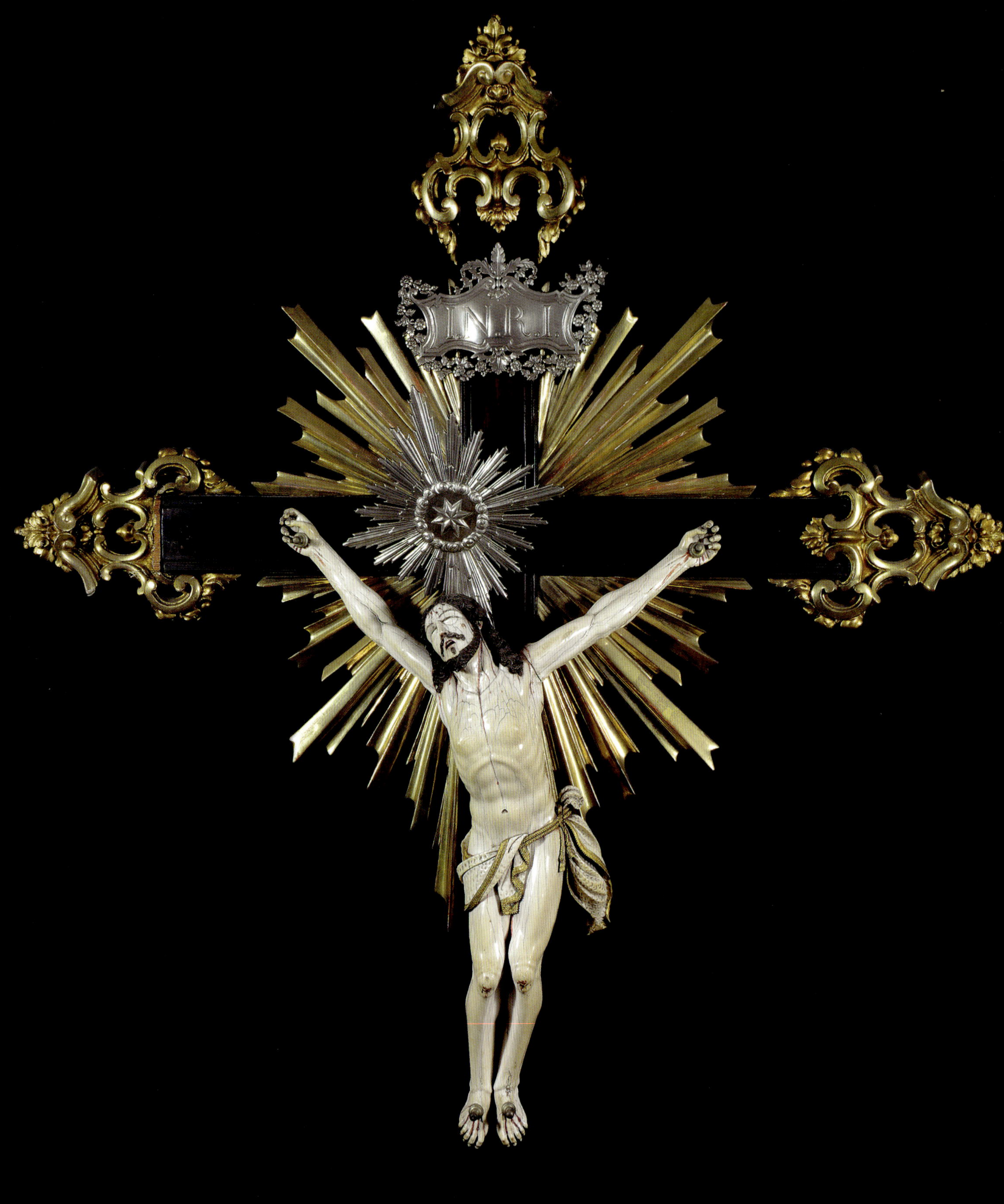
I.N.R.I.

Preface and Acknowledgements

It is rare in the twenty-first century to feel that one is entering unexplored territory, but that is the feeling when visiting Ushaw College. It might be just a few miles from Durham's famous cathedral, yet the college really is a hidden gem. From the archival and library collections to the very architecture itself, Ushaw College's treasures are largely unknown to all but the select number who at some stage resided there.

The design of this book is to bring some of those treasures to the wider national – and even international – audience that they deserve. Of course, when the choice is as dazzling as that at Ushaw, selection comes down to pressures of space and editorial judgements. Thus, among the items not included as detailed entries (though they may be mentioned at some point in the texts) are Richard III's Book of Hours; unbound copies of the first issue of John Henry Newman's *Apologia Pro Vita Sua*; several first editions of Charles Dickens's works; a first edition of Thomas Hobbes's *Leviathan*; and even a first edition of W.G. Grace's *Cricket*. There are sure to be other items not listed above that alumni of the college will recall; the wealth of material held at the college simply cannot be understated.

Equally, items are still being 'discovered' by Durham University's cataloguing team. A facsimile of an important draft poem by Lord Byron is at the final stage of verification, while two continental-made crucifixes from the seventeenth and eighteenth centuries have just been found in the week that I write this preface.

In any effort such as this, there are a number of people who deserve the grateful thanks of the editor. Claire Marsland and Jonathan Bush, who are cataloguing the artefacts and the archives of the college respectively, have handled regular requests from the editor with great patience. In particular, Claire Marsland has been committed to the effort throughout.

Kate Weightman's fantastic photography has done justice to the items and has helped ease the process. Jon Purcell, Craig Barclay and Sheila Hingley were helpful sources of advice during the planning stages, while Laura Lappin of Scala Arts & Heritage Publishers and Jenny Lawson have made the project less stressful than it easily could have been.

Of course, I am truly grateful to all the contributors for their time and efforts in supporting the publication and sharing their expert knowledge. One of these, David Knight, wishes to thank Alison Morrison-Low of the National Museum of Scotland, Edinburgh, for her advice on the orrery. Equally, I am grateful to all the speakers at the Ushaw Lectures series and the 'Treasures of Ushaw: Secular and Sacred' conference, as well as to all those who have attended and supported these events.

As anyone who has undertaken a project such as this will testify, their families always get dragged into the process somewhere along the line. Thus gratitude is due to my wife, Diane, who has been ever willing to look at different photographs, whilst my daughters, Maeve and Bridget, have never been short of opinions, as only those aged under three are. Thanks are also necessary to my mother and father – Linda and Des Kelly – as well as my brother, Joe Kelly.

The opportunity to work at Ushaw has been a huge privilege. Mgr John Marsland, Rev Dr Michael Sharratt and Peter Seed allowed me into their 'home' and made me feel welcome: an act that should never be underestimated. Paul Murray, Andrew Harston and the Congregation of Jesus UK province helped manufacture the opportunity for this project. Perhaps the biggest debt of thanks, though, is to the members of the St Cuthbert's Society of Ushaw, whose generosity and support, not just to the college but to me personally, has been immeasurable. It is to them and all who have worked to preserve Ushaw and its collections – and will continue to do so into the future – that this book is dedicated.

JAMES E. KELLY

The eighteenth-century crucifix, which was a central feature in the chapel of the English College at Lisbon.

Contributors

Sophie Andreae, Patrimony Committee, Catholic Bishops' Conference of England and Wales
Mary Brooks, Dept. of Archaeology, Durham University
Jonathan Bush, Archives and Special Collections, Durham University
Stefano Cracolici, Dept. of Italian, Durham University
A.I. Doyle, Honorary Reader in Bibliography, Durham University
Eamon Duffy, Faculty of Divinity, University of Cambridge
Alastair H. Fraser, Archives and Special Collections, Durham University
Richard Gameson, Dept. of History, Durham University
David Gehring, Dept. of Theology and Religion, Durham University
Brad S. Gregory, Dept. of History, University of Notre Dame
Margaret Harvey, Dept. of History, Durham University
Simon Johnson, Downside Abbey
James E. Kelly, Dept. of Theology and Religion, Durham University
David Knight, Dept. of Philosophy, Durham University
Katherine Krick, Dept. of History, Durham University
Claire Marsland, Heritage Collections, Durham University
Thomas M. McCoog, SJ, Fordham University
Susannah Monta, Dept. of English, University of Notre Dame
John Morrill, Faculty of History, University of Cambridge
Tessa Murdoch, Victoria and Albert Museum, London
Roderick O'Donnell, Fellow of the Society of Antiquaries of London
Peter Phillips, Dept. of Theology and Religion, Durham University
Frances Pritchard, Whitworth Art Gallery, University of Manchester
Stephen Regan, Dept. of English Studies, Durham University
Susan Royal, Dept. of Theology and Religion, Durham University
Chris Seddon, St Cuthbert's Society of Ushaw
Michael Sharratt, Dept. of Theology and Religion, Durham University
Lucy Underwood, Dept. of Theology and Religion, Durham University
Jonathan Wright, Dept. of Theology and Religion, Durham University
Bennett Zon, Dept. of Music, Durham University

The mortuary chapel, designed by E.W. Pugin.

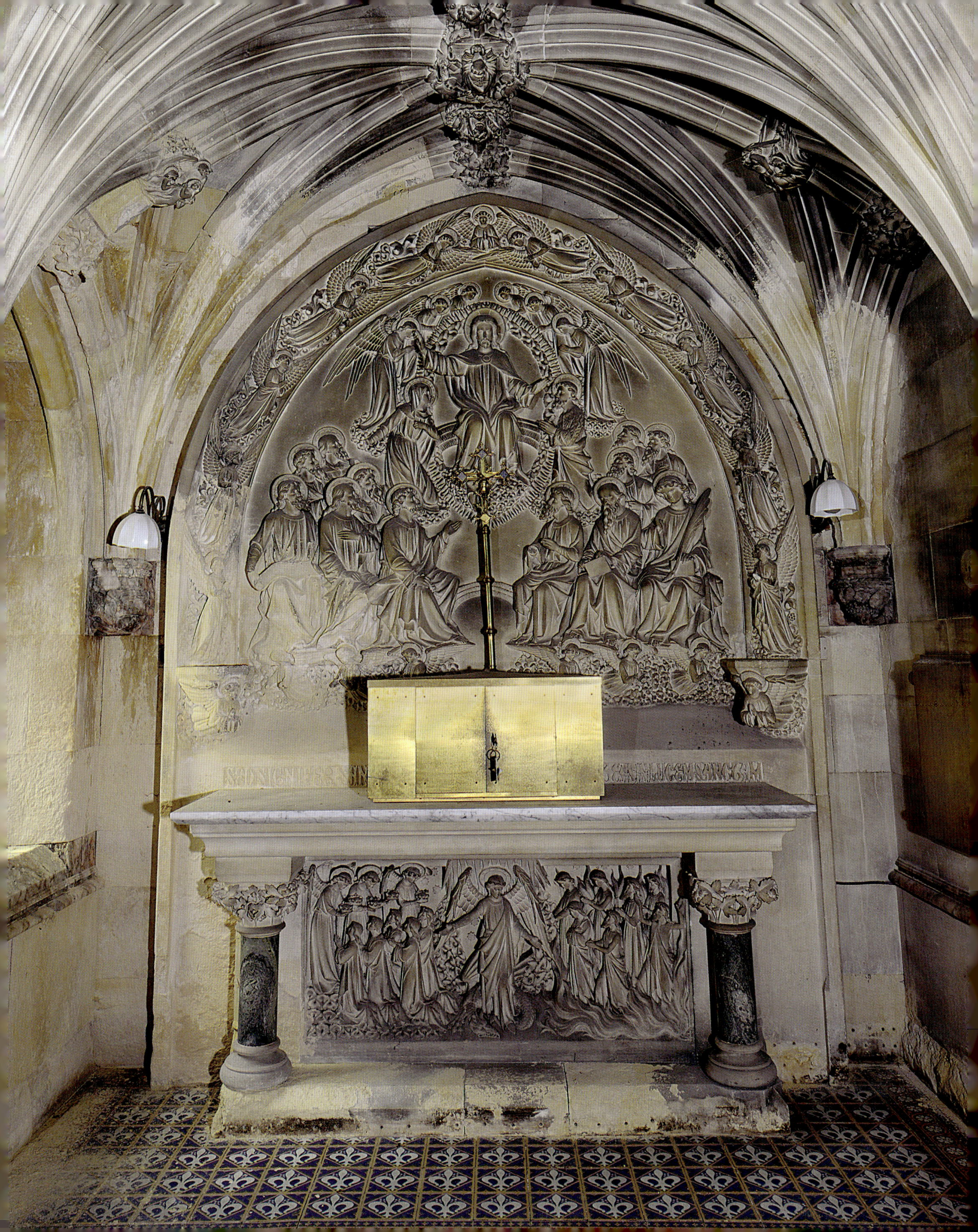

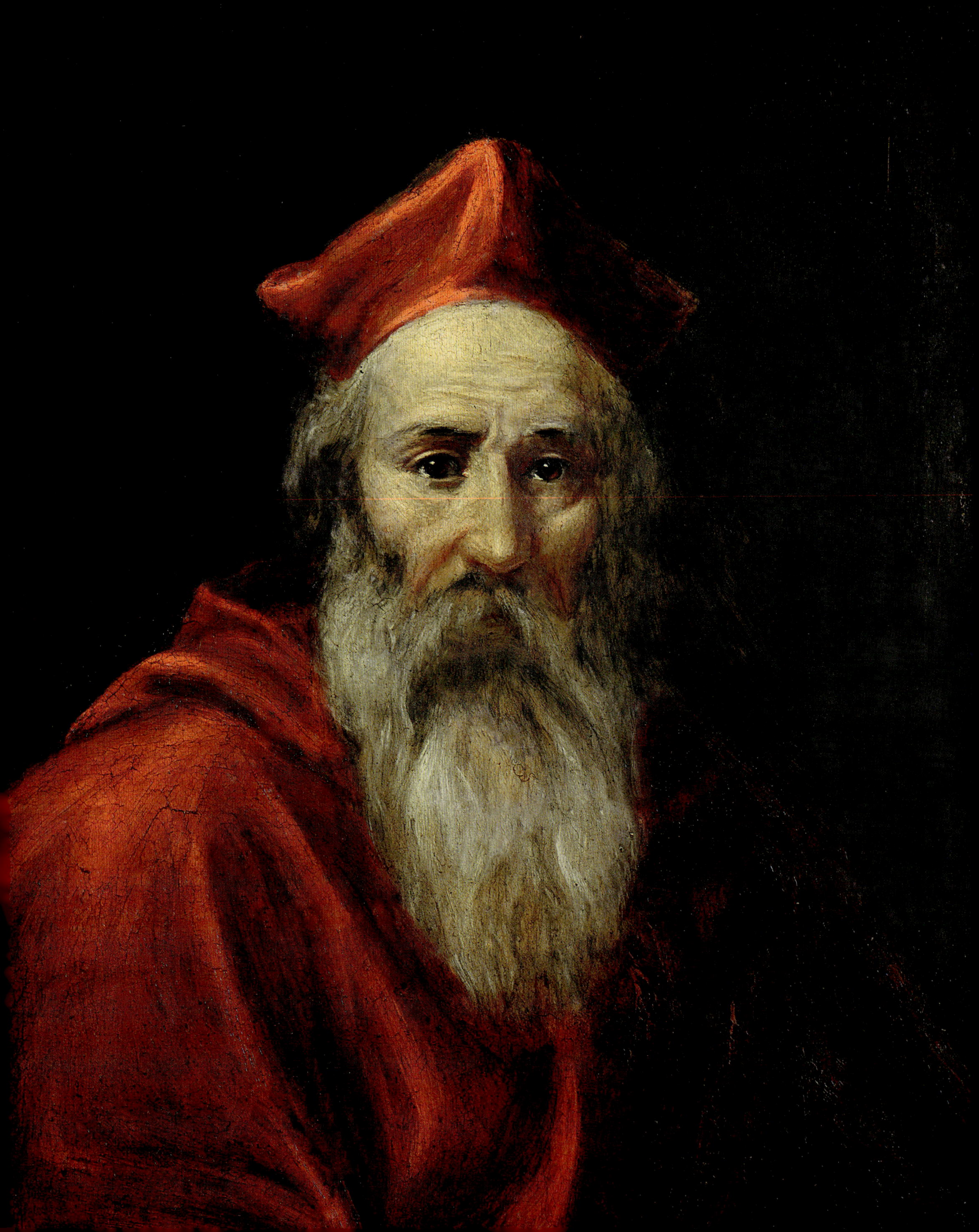

Introduction: Historical

Ushaw College trained men for the Roman Catholic priesthood for more than two centuries, from its establishment in 1808 till its closure in 2011. For much of that time it also functioned as a boarding school for boys as well as a seminary for men destined for the priesthood. This unique system of educating lay and clerical students alongside each other was at odds with both the spirit and the letter of the seminary legislation of the sixteenth-century Council of Trent, which aspired to create a separate clerical caste free from worldly contacts, lay ambitions and lay habits of life. Ushaw's mixed system was inherited from the English Roman Catholic colleges established in Europe, above all Douai College (originally part of the Spanish Low Countries, later incorporated into France), of which Ushaw was the northern descendant.

Douai had been founded in the reign of Elizabeth I by a Lancastrian refugee Oxford don, William Allen, to provide an institution for Catholic scholars driven out of Oxford and Cambridge by the Queen's new Protestant establishment. Allen's college at Douai is often described as the first Tridentine seminary, but the special circumstances of Catholics in England demanded that it be more than a training centre for aspirant priests. Due to English schools and universities being closed to Catholics, recusant gentry sent their sons to be educated in the English Catholic foundations abroad, of which Douai was both the first and the most important. For two centuries Douai provided both Catholic priests and lay gentry with the schooling forbidden to them by the laws of their own country. However, in 1792 its staff and students returned to England in flight from the secular persecution of the French Revolution.

The English College at Douai, of which Ushaw is the northern descendant.

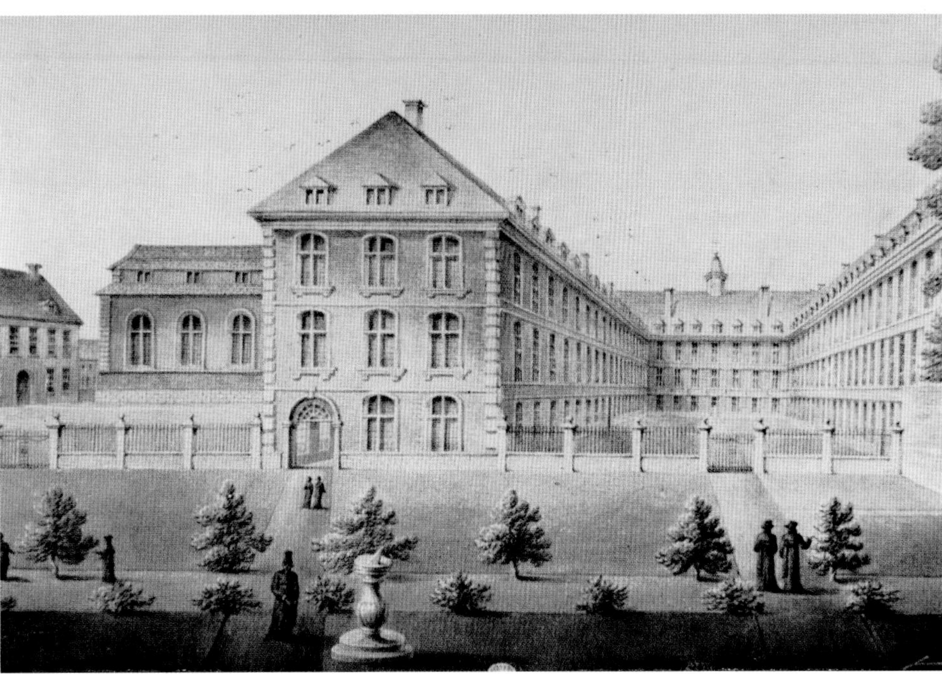

Cardinal William Allen, founder of the English College at Douai.

It was, at first, not clear that the departure from revolutionary Douai was to prove irreversible and, when realisation did dawn that the return to England was indeed to be permanent, the Catholic authorities at first hoped that Douai's work and traditions might be continued within a similar single institution on English soil. But the cantankerous vicar apostolic of the Northern District, William Gibson, himself a former president of Douai, wanted his own establishment to train priests for the north. In any case, regional differences and rivalries, once repatriated to England, soon asserted themselves. In 1794 a group of Lancastrian students training alongside other Douai refugees at the Old Hall Green Academy in Hertfordshire staged a rowdy practical joke, in the course of which they dragged one of the southern students backwards into a pond. As luck would have it, the superior of Old Hall Green – the vicar apostolic of the London District, John Douglass – was a Yorkshireman. He overreacted, raging against these 'low, vulgar fellows ... a parcel of Lancashire blackguards'. The entire northern contingent walked out in dudgeon and the die was cast for the emergence of two separate seminaries, each claiming descent from Douai.

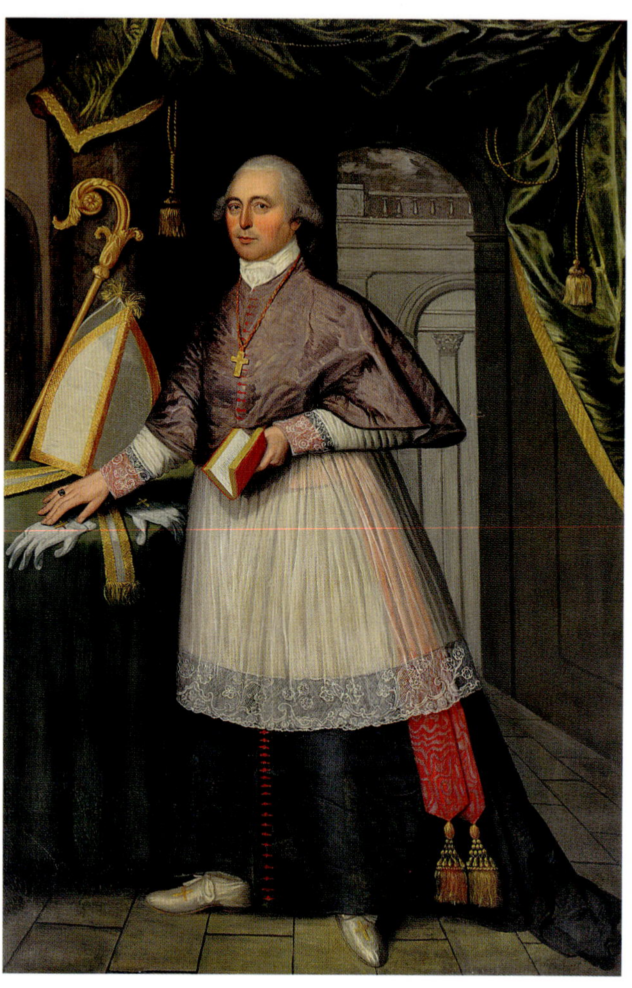

Bishop William Gibson, vicar apostolic of the Northern District from 1790 to 1821.

After several migrations, Douai's northern colony established itself at Ushaw, in the purpose-built and austerely handsome Georgian building, which still forms the core of the present site. Thus began another two centuries of immensely fruitful work. The Catholic community in the north was then on the brink of political emancipation and would soon experience the dramatic expansion of numbers which would make Catholicism one of the most vital religious forces within the region, and in Victorian Britain generally. Catholic numbers in the northern counties from which Ushaw drew its constituency rocketed from fewer than 250,000 in 1840, to more than 1.25 million a century later. That upward trajectory continued almost precisely till the college's 150th anniversary in 1958, when it peaked at 1.75 million, by which time Ushaw had almost four hundred men training to be priests at any one time, and was on the brink of a new – and, as it turned out, final – expansive building programme.

Few Ushaw seminarians ever studied at an English university, though in the early 1840s, and then again from the 1860s, many of the men sat the external degree examinations of the University of London. Indeed, by the end of the nineteenth century the college was sending small numbers of candidates for degrees at Durham

University, five miles away. Though its founding staff-members included one major public intellectual who would achieve an international reputation – the historian and controversialist John Lingard – the college's nineteenth-century intellectual and theological traditions were deeply conservative: its only significant Victorian theologian, Vice-President John Gillow, was to distinguish himself as a virulent opponent of every shade of liberal Catholicism, from Dollinger to Newman. Yet Ushaw educated several of the major figures of the nineteenth- and twentieth-century Catholic Church, including Nicholas Wiseman, figurehead of the early Victorian Catholic revival and, at the other end of the century, Merry del Val, who, as Cardinal Secretary of State to Pope Pius X, was to be one of the instigators of the ruthless 'anti-Modernist' purge which sterilised Catholic theological, biblical and philosophical life for two generations. The college also bred scores of bishops (two thirds of the northern bishops appointed in the half-century after 1860 were Ushaw trained) and more than half of the cardinal Archbishops of Westminster so far, from Wiseman, the first and most flamboyant of them all, to Arthur Hinsley, visionary leader of England's Catholics during the Second World War. Perhaps just as significantly, Ushaw priests formed the largest single body of clergy serving the Catholics of northern England: by 1850 half of the missioners working in the region were Ushaw trained and during the 1847 outbreak of cholera in Liverpool, five of the ten priests who died attending the stricken in the city were from Ushaw.

Ushaw alumnus Cardinal Merry del Val was Secretary of State to Pope Pius X.

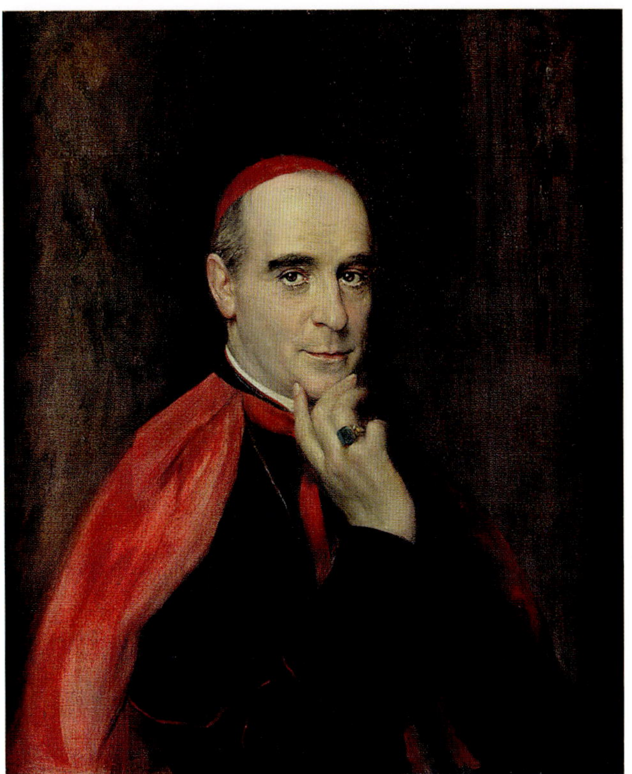

The college was more than a school or a training-centre for priests. It was a major focus of Catholic identity in the north of England, a Catholic equivalent to Durham Cathedral or York Minster, its chapels and libraries a concrete expression of the community's values and self-confidence. It was a regional rallying-point whose importance can be gauged from the more than 40,000 people who attended the open-air celebrations at Ushaw in 1951 for the thirteenth-centenary of the death of St Aidan of Lindisfarne.

Yet, although cultural accumulation was never its purpose, in the process of furthering a resurgent Catholicism, Ushaw did indeed accumulate treasure. Its own records, and the correspondence and papers of many of its staff, form part of a crucial archive for the history of Catholicism in the north and, more widely, the nation.

The mid-nineteenth century saw an astonishing transformation of the austere, even dour Georgian restraint of the original institution by a new ebullience, which manifested itself in ambitious Gothic building

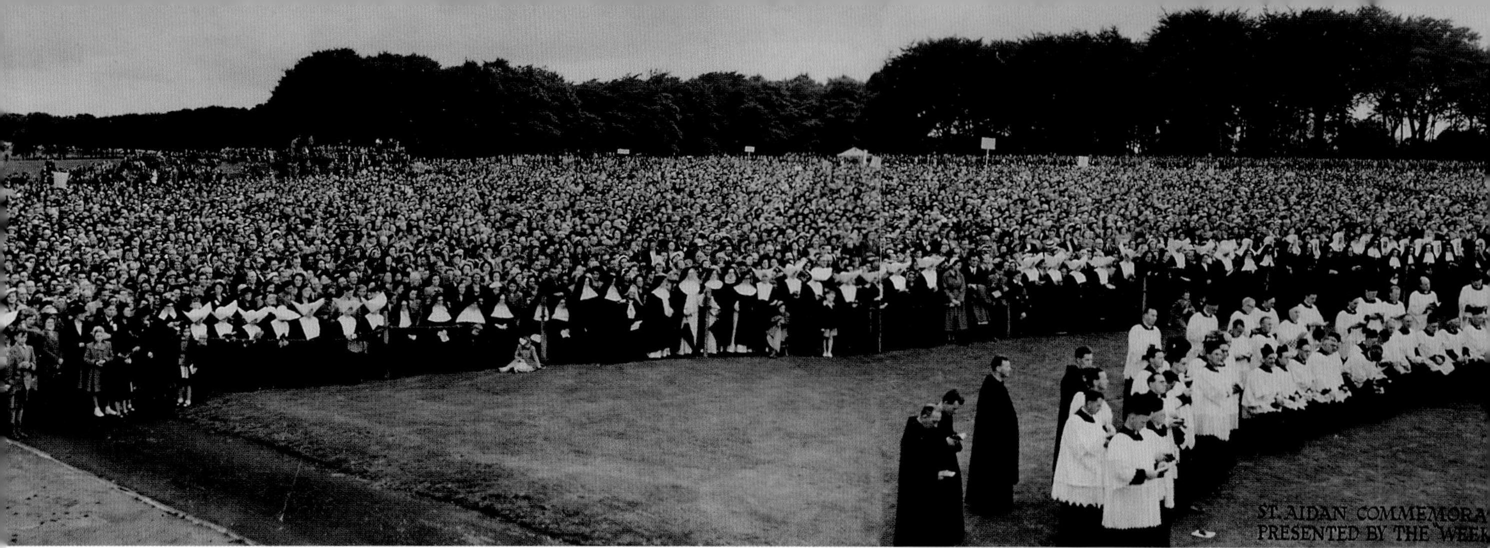

More than 40,000 people attended Ushaw's celebrations in 1951 to mark the thirteenth centenary of the death of St Aidan.

programmes and lavish commissions in the pure and applied arts. This was not, of course, a matter of art for art's sake, but was designed to service the devotional, liturgical and intellectual needs of a community consciously seeking to reassert its roots in the Northumbrian monasteries of Bede and Cuthbert and in the medieval *Ecclesia Anglicana*, as well as its continuity with the recusant tradition represented by Douai, while cultivating a vibrantly modern and assertive ultramontane Catholicism, centred on Rome. Ushaw's chapel complex, itself a cluster of gothic jewel-boxes created and expanded by, among others, successive generations of the Pugin family, would become the setting for contemporary masterpieces by the second generation German Nazarene painter Franz von Rohden and the sculptor Karl Hoffmann, and for some of A.W.N. Pugin's most sumptuous metalwork, glass and fabric designs.

In the course of the century that followed its foundation, Ushaw would acquire artefacts that concretely embody its claims to ownership of both the proximate and the more remote Catholic past – pewter chalices from penal England; the buried silver tableware from Douai College; medieval vestments, one of them allegedly from Westminster Abbey but more likely from the chapel of Richard III; another used by the last Catholic bishop of Durham, Cuthbert Tunstall; and even an episcopal ring taken from the coffin of St Cuthbert during one of the medieval translations.

Alongside that architectural, artistic and liturgical elaboration, the mid-Victorian years saw a massive expansion of the college's library, technical and scientific provision. Ushaw consciously set about accumulating an archive which embodied its links to Douai and the recusant past. The college also created a library designed to equip it to provide the kind of tertiary education denied to Catholics within the universities. That process of accumulation – begun to meet the needs of the 1840s, 1850s and 1860s – would long outlive the astonishing expansion of Catholicism which gave it its first impetus and rationale. Ushaw would go on acquiring treasures into the age of Catholic decline: the magnificent archival, book and artefact collections from Lisbon, for example, form merely the most notable of the many deposits from a Catholicism which had formed a submerged but integral part of the complexity of British religious and cultural identity, at home and abroad, since the Reformation.

The animating energy and intelligence behind the Victorian expansion of Ushaw and the originator of the educational and religious aspirations which shaped both its

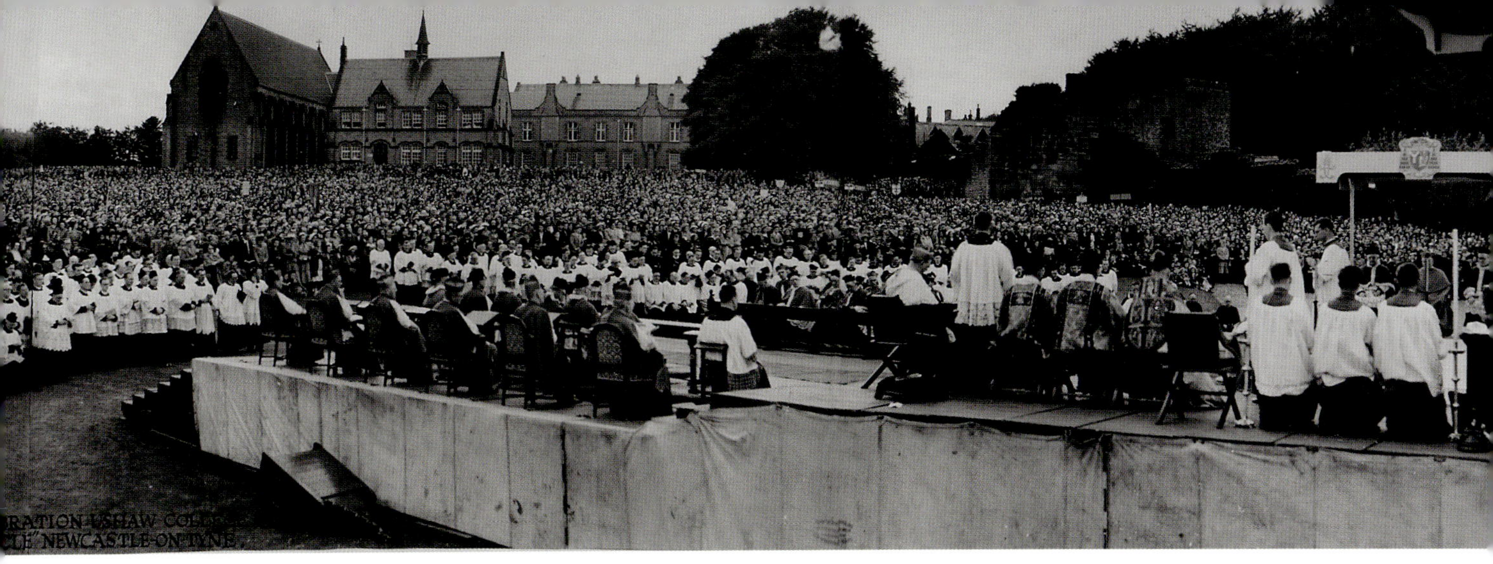

physical appearance and the superlative quality of its libraries, was Mgr Charles Newsham, vice-president from 1830 to 1837, then president till his death in 1863. Newsham was an angular and demanding personality, a dry disciplinarian who had few confidants. For almost thirty-five years he drove his staff and students mercilessly. Unsurprisingly, he aroused little affection, and his outspoken colleague and successor, Robert Tate, put it on record that 'of all the dry old codgers that ever breathed, our friend Dr. N beats all'. In 1859, reflecting on the achievements of Newsham's presidency, Tate nevertheless commented grimly that: 'Much has been done, no doubt, to extend the walls of the establishment, but nothing for years past to improve what no extent of buildings can compensate … men in mind and feeling cannot stoop to be cold shouldered, & sometimes treated as no man of right feeling would treat them'.

Robert Tate, seventh president of Ushaw College.

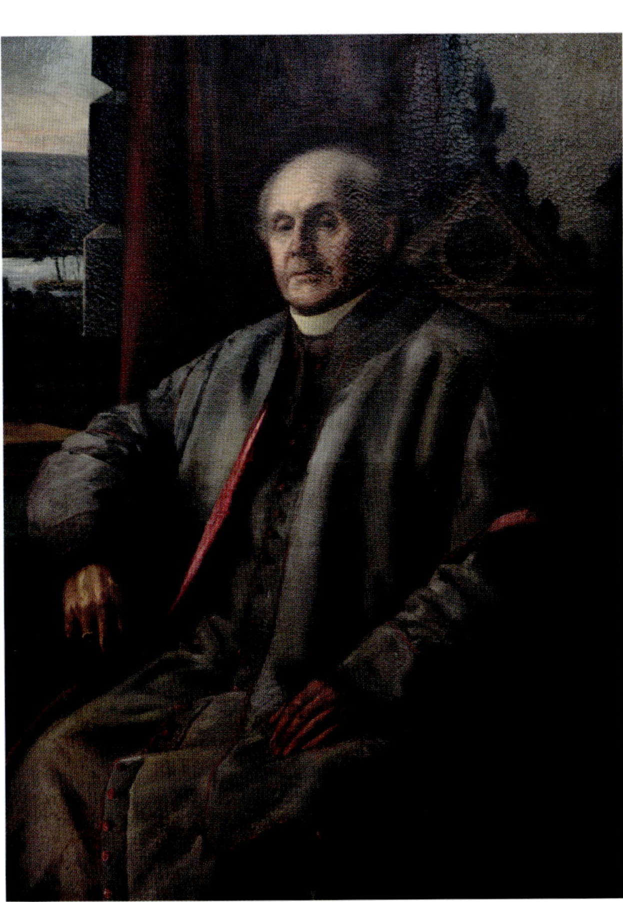

But Newsham was no mere bricks and mortar man. For all his abrasiveness, he was also a man of vision, determined to raise the educational standards of the northern clergy and laity, and to establish Ushaw as the premier Catholic college in England. With that in mind, he introduced a system of prizes and medals to encourage competitive excellence among the students, recruited academically distinguished staff like Tate himself, and drastically revised the syllabus of studies at Ushaw so as to qualify for affiliation to the new and 'godless' University of London, whose secular foundation permitted Catholics to take external degrees without subscription to religious tests. From 1840 Ushaw students began sitting for London University examinations, achieving results which far outstripped those of the other Catholic colleges, like Downside and St Edmund's, Ware.

Alongside his major building projects, Newsham pushed forward Ushaw's spiritual, cultural and educational growth. Determined to create a college equal to any in the ancient universities, he aspired to assemble a great library which would recreate the lost library at Douai, but which would outdo it in range and inclusiveness. The core of Ushaw's library had been formed round the modest collection of 750 or so religious books accumulated by an eighteenth-century vicar apostolic, Edward Dicconson. Theology would remain central to Ushaw's library collections, including rich scriptural commentary, devotional works, religious controversy and liturgy (there are more than one hundred editions of the Tridentine missal alone). But Newsham's aspirations for the library were never confined to such material. Other collections were added by mainly clerical donors, above all Thomas Wilkinson of Kendal, a voracious bibliophile who presented Ushaw with more than 12,000 books, including hundreds of rare works on architecture and art, geography and travel, science and literature. The library has more than 60 incunabula (books printed before 1501). In 1840 a benefactor presented the college with the historic Leadbitter legal library, created by a former recorder of Newcastle. The Rev Dr Henry Logan, disgruntled Victorian former president of the Midland seminary at Oscott, donated his personal collection of 8,000 rare philosophical, mathematical and scientific books and, after Lingard's death in 1851, his historical library and papers came to Ushaw.

The library is rich in theological and devotional material from the sixteenth to the eighteenth centuries, and in pamphlets and ephemera not in the British Library or other libraries. There are 20 boxes of seventeenth-century pamphlets, a similar

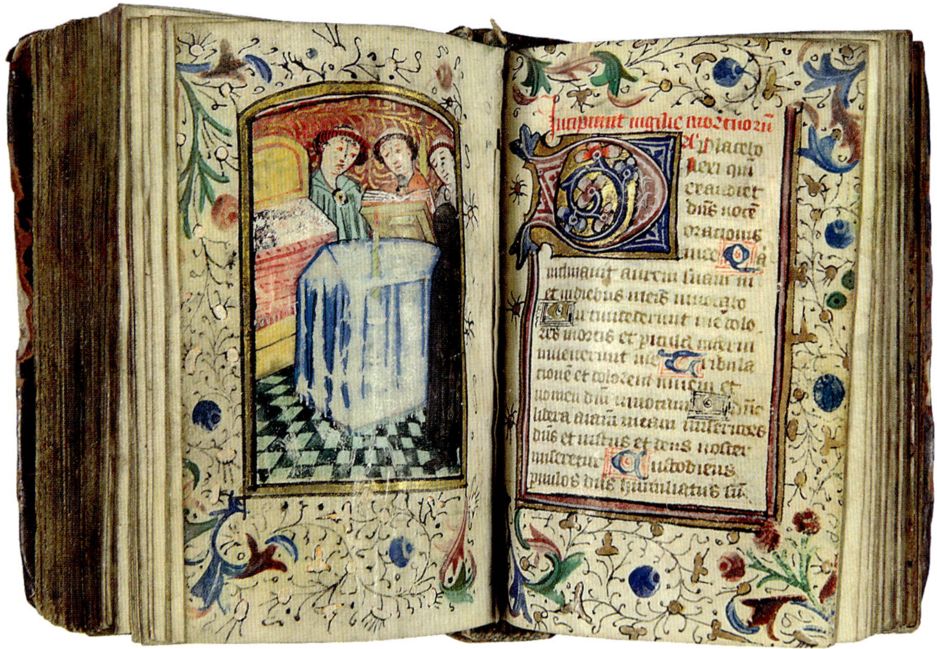

An illuminated Book of Hours, formerly owned by Richard III.

number for the eighteenth century, and over 4,500 from the nineteenth century, many of them printed by fugitive or obscure local presses. There are remarkable collections on travel, numismatics and early science. The library also houses valuable collections of books in Latin, French and Dutch. Among its most notable holdings is a collection of more than 50 early printed books from the library of Durham Priory. The library also contains a small but significant collection of medieval manuscripts, including early medieval bibles; theological, devotional and historical texts; illuminated Books of Hours, one of them formerly owned by Richard III; the cartulary of the sacrist of Durham Priory in its original binding; and a rare and precious binding-fragment from an eighth-century Northumbrian liturgical text, containing part of the office for Christmas day, the earliest known Anglo Saxon office-book. Among the medieval manuscripts is the Esh Missal, a unique survival of a York missal acquired for the parish chapel of Esh sometime before 1490 and annotated by the local curate, John Walshe. It was rescued at the Reformation by the Catholic family on whose land Ushaw was built, making it the only pre-Reformation parish liturgical book which has never left the parish for which it was first bought.

For all his dryness, Newsham was an accomplished composer. One of the most interesting collections at Ushaw is its vast holdings of printed and manuscript music, both sacred and secular. Stretching from early-medieval liturgical manuscripts to the sometimes dubious liturgical settings for the post-Vatican II liturgy, these collections include rare and important material from the early plainsong revival, eighteenth-century polyphonic settings for Mass and the office, and Newsham's own liturgical compositions, making the collection a uniquely copious resource for the study of post-reformation Catholic music and music-making.

Though Newsham denied A.W.N. Pugin the commission to build the Big Library, he did appoint him as the architect for the new college chapel. Pugin's chapel was a small-scale but sumptuous and highly decorated gothic jewel-box, which placed Ushaw at the forefront of the English Gothic Revival. Pugin's magnificent brass eagle lectern and the three-metre-high paschal candle designed for the new chapel went on display at the Great Exhibition of 1851. But if the new chapel looked back to the Catholic England of the Middle Ages, it also looked outwards to the resurgent *Romanitas* of the ultramontane movement which was re-centring Catholic Europe round the papacy and papal Rome. In this movement the rediscovery of the heroic days of the early Christian Rome of the martyrs played a central role – witness the European celebrity of Nicholas Wiseman's best-selling novel of the Roman catacombs, *Fabiola* (1855). In 1846 Newsham petitioned the new Pope for 'the body of a Holy Martyr' for the college's new chapel. The petition was promoted by Thomas Grant, rector of the English College in Rome, and an Ushaw alumnus who served as the English bishops' agent in Rome. It was Grant who chose from the Vatican relic collections the whole-body relic of an alleged Roman boy-martyr, St Septimianus, 'a youth of 18 years of age, because I thought that the thought of a martyr having died at their own age and as if he were one of their own number would move the students to

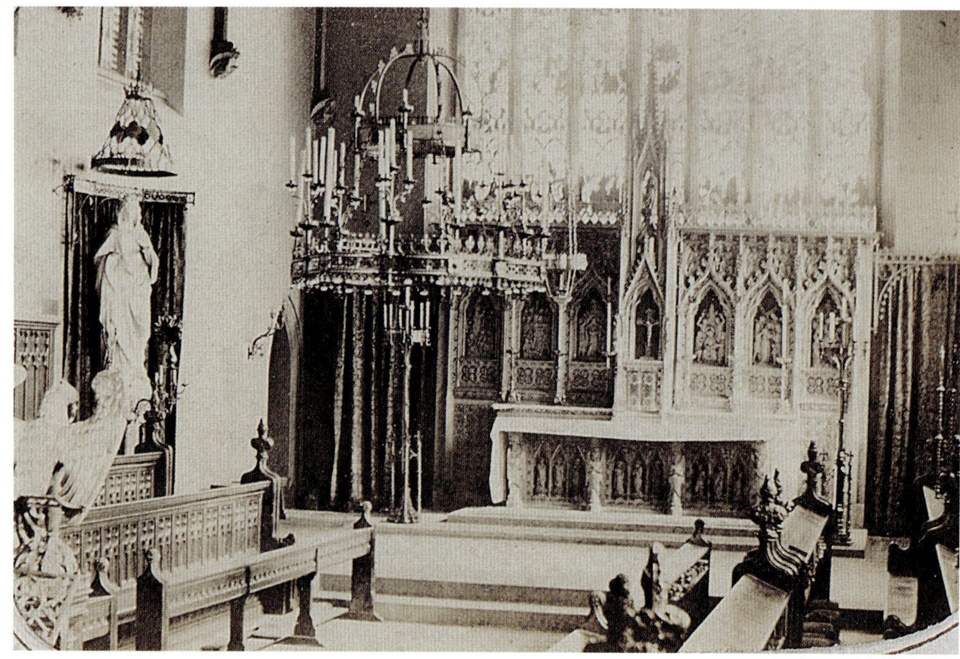

A.W.N. Pugin's original St Cuthbert's chapel, *c.*1860–80.

tender devotion towards him'. This 'precious treasure' from the cemetery of Hermes in the Via Salaria was duly despatched to England, together with a vase alleged to contain the martyr's blood, enclosed in a small wooden box with an inset glass panel, designed to allow customs officers to inspect the relics without breaking the official ecclesiastical seal.

Pugin and his son, Edward, would go on to elaborate and extend the chapel complex in the 1850s and 1860s, by the addition of a cloister and a series of exquisite side-chapels, which were to remain one of the hidden glories of Ushaw. In the 1880s, as the college's numbers continued to expand, Pugin's chapel itself was demolished and totally rebuilt on a much grander scale to seat 400 by the Newcastle firm Dunn and Hansom, though much of the detail and many of the furnishings of Pugin's masterpiece were incorporated into the new structure.

The commissioning of Pugin's chapel reflected a novel devotional intensity at Ushaw. The alleged contrast between the sober rationalism of an older recusant piety and the more emotive and extrovert devotion of Victorian Catholicism has often been exaggerated. But there is no mistaking the devotional wind of change blowing through Ushaw under Newsham. In 1842 he established a Confraternity of the Living Rosary, by rescript from Rome; in 1845 a Confraternity of the Immaculate Heart of Mary for the conversion of sinners; in 1846 May devotions to Mary began, along with the recitation of Wiseman's prayers for the conversion of England. Here again, Thomas Grant was a crucial influence, not merely advising Newsham on the niceties of applications for specific indulgenced devotions, but urging him on in the promotion of a

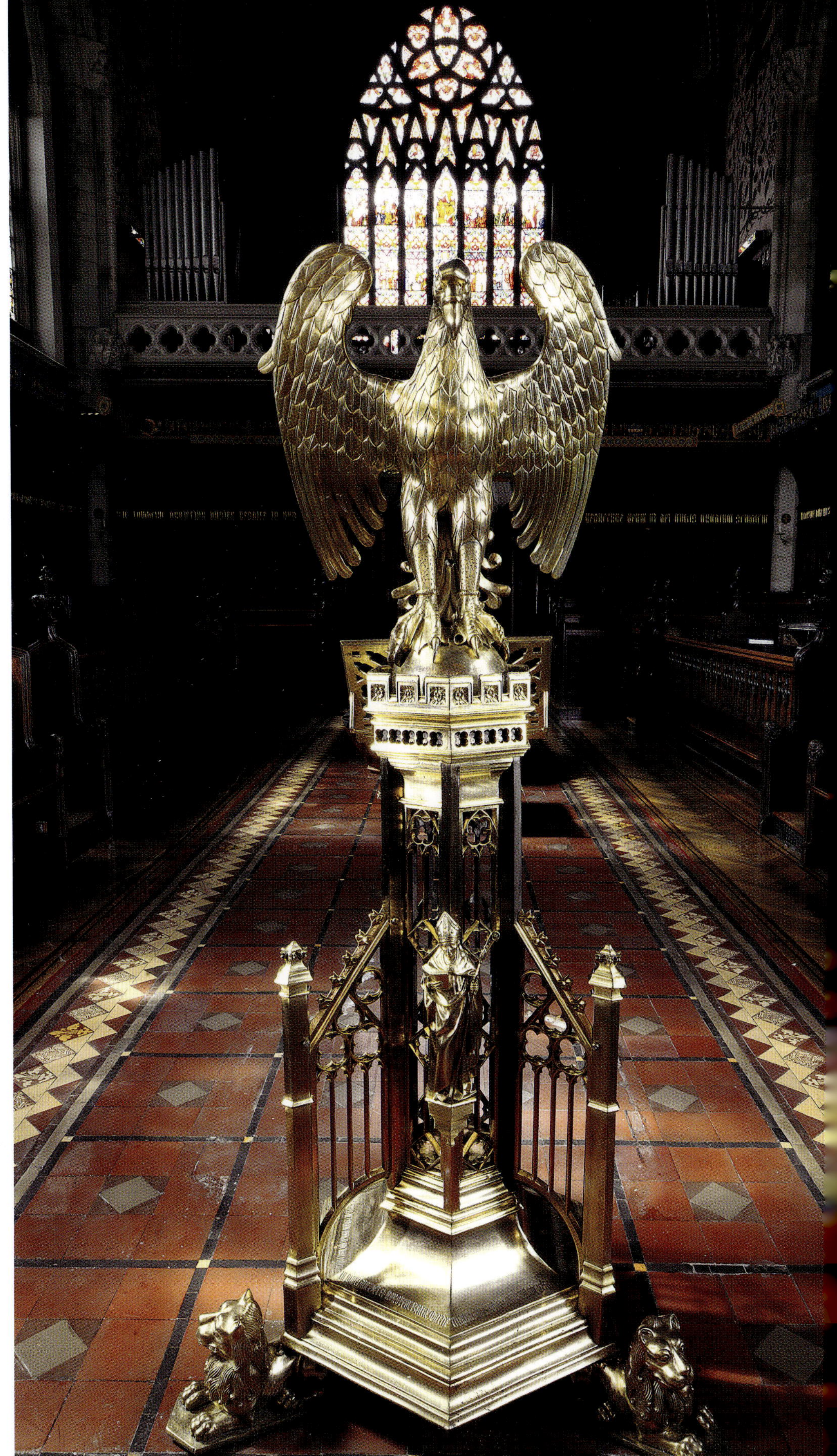

A.W.N. Pugin's brass eagle lectern, designed for the college chapel, was displayed at the Great Exhibition of 1851.

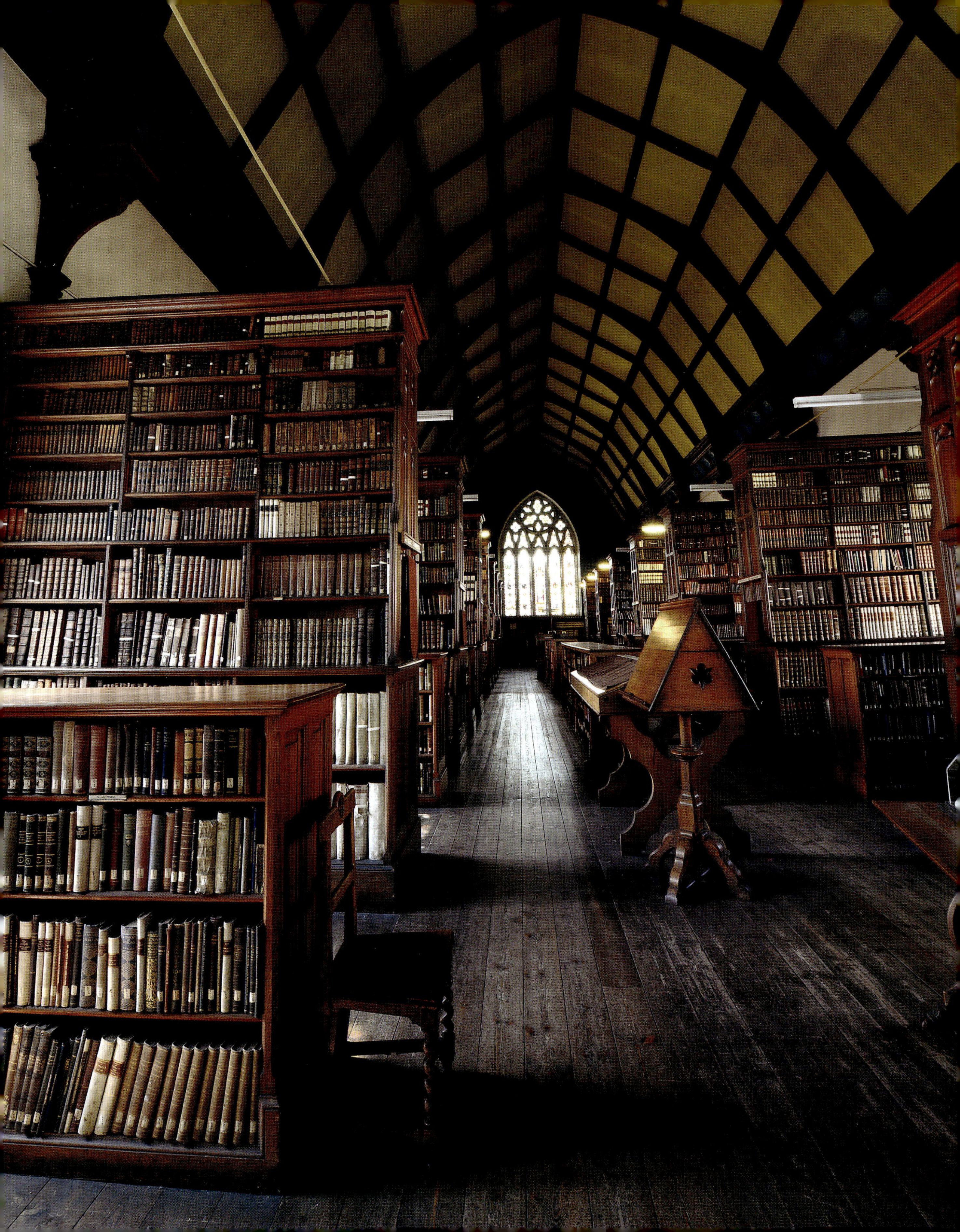

warmer kind of piety – novenas to the Virgin, St Cuthbert and the Sacred Heart; elaborate intercession for the souls in purgatory; the introduction of the stations of the cross, which, as Grant told Newsham, 'would make them love the Passion and the Blessed Sacrament, and could accustom them to wish to introduce the same holy exercise in their future congregations'. As Grant urged Newsham, 'We want more heart in all things.'

To furnish Ushaw's chapels Newsham, probably on the suggestion of Nicholas Wiseman, sent to Rome for paintings by Franz von Rohden and statues by Karl Hoffmann, both of them late exponents of the earnest Christian primitivism of the 'Nazarene' movement, Germany's equivalent of the Pre-Raphaelites. Here again Newsham's Roman connections were crucial. After Grant's departure for England and the bishopric of Southwark, Newsham's main agent in Rome was Vincent Eyre, a wealthy student for the priesthood who was also an avid bibliophile. Eyre, an amateur of the arts, kept a watching brief on the commissions to Rohden and Hoffmann, even offering Rohden tips on how to improve the landscape background and the need to add more blood to the crucifixion scene, which Eyre himself nevertheless described as 'the finest picture of the subject that ever was painted'.

But Eyre's main contribution to the treasures of Ushaw was to haunt auction rooms and bookshops in search of rarities for the Ushaw library. Eyre cascaded Newsham with booksellers' and auctioneers' catalogues, urging him to send lists of books needed or desired, begging for a catalogue of Ushaw's holdings so he could spot and fill deficiencies. Eyre was critical of the emphasis on the classics, secular literature and the profane arts in Wilkinson's benefactions, though he urged Newsham to get Wilkinson to pay for some of the more expensive items he himself located. He was equally critical of other Ushaw library benefactors like Henry Logan who, he thought, had 'filled the library with all sorts of German books about philosophy and mathematics'. Nevertheless, his own mainly theological and church-historical acquisitions on behalf of the college were copious – one consignment in a single crate quite literally weighed a ton – and he had a nose for rare editions, fine printings and sumptuous bindings.

Eyre was a fiercely competitive book-buyer, jealous of other English Catholic bargain hunters in Rome – including Henry Manning – and grumbled about predatory English bishops on the hunt for canon law, liturgical and ceremonial texts. He even complained of the Earl of Shrewsbury's pet antiquarian, Dr Daniel Rock, though, as he told Newsham dismissively, 'he only buys curious books'. Eyre warned Newsham that Oscott was spending £600 a year on its library, and observed that 'it has always seemed to me there has been a want of enthusiasm about the Ushaw Library on the part of anyone but yourself, who seem to be the sole as well as the prime mover of what goes on'. Nevertheless, he professed himself consoled by the thought that 'if our other Colleges are all going down the hill, we secular clergy have one at least that is an honour to religion'.

Eyre was not the college's only agent in the acquisition of treasures. He crossed swords in 1852 with the egregious Mgr George Talbot, Newman's great Roman

The Big Library.

detractor, who had been asked to arrange for Hoffmann's statue of Our Lady of Clemency to be blessed by Pius IX. But with characteristic high-handedness Talbot had scheduled the ceremony, without consultation, for a day when Eyre and all the staff and students of the Venerabile were on holiday in the Alban hills, and refused to alter it. Thus, to Eyre's fury, no-one connected to Ushaw attended the ceremony.

Yet it was Talbot who was responsible for the college's acquisition of a very different kind of treasure: the purchase in 1860 of a remarkable collection of relics, formed in the early eighteenth century by the Neopolitan ecclesiastical lawyer, Don Nicola Antonio de Bonis. Reputedly including 20 relics of Christ's birth and Passion, and more than 800 other relics of the saints – including a phial of the miraculously liquefying blood of the Neopolitan St Francis of Paola – the Ushaw relic collection was considered at the time to be the most extensive and spectacular of its kind in Britain. It was another of the ways in which Newsham tried to link English clerical piety with older and deeper traditions.

The Chapel of the Holy Family holds roughly a thousand relics, mostly in the wooden cabinets seen at its sides. The painting is Rohden's *The Adoration of the Magi and the Shepherds.*

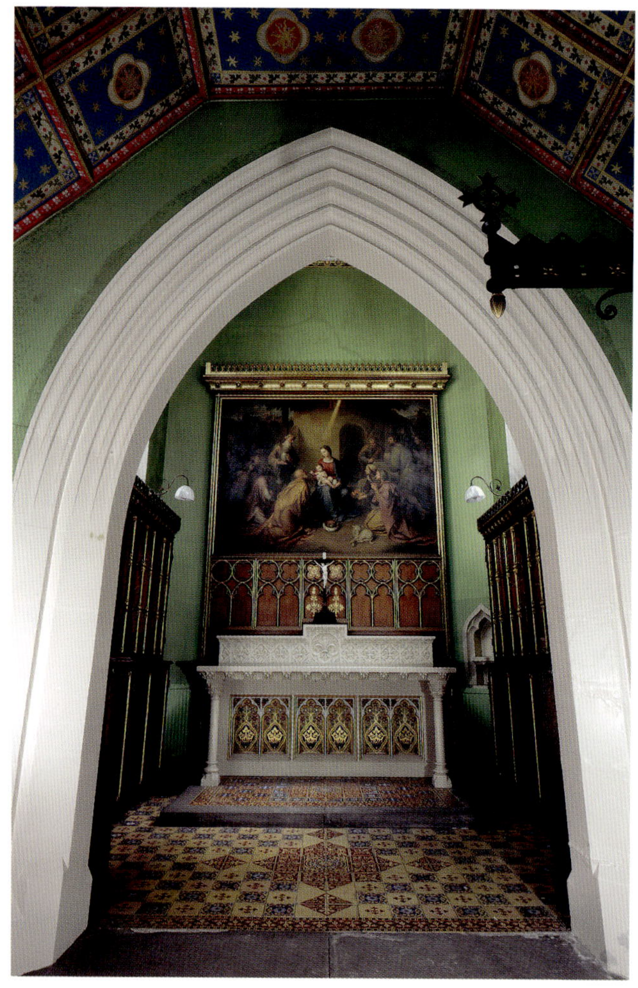

Newsham's efforts to expand and improve the college and its holdings in due course attracted other benefactors. One of the most generous of these was the wealthy lay entrepreneur and mining magnate Joseph Francis Sloane. One of the first intake of lay students in 1808, Sloane's family had fallen on hard times while he was still a pupil. The college waived his fees and Sloane remained devoted to his 'dear old Alma mater' for the rest of his life. After some years as assistant librarian and tutor to the children of the Russian count and bibliophile Dmitrij Petrovic Boutourline (1763–1829), who moved his family from St Petersburg to Florence in 1817, Sloane took over his employer's copper mining ventures in the Volterra region and became immensely rich. An ardent ultramontane, in the 1860s he acquired the Spinelli chapel in Santa Croce in Florence as a family oratory and burial place, commissioning for it notable windows in celebration of the doctrine of the Immaculate Conception. It was Sloane who paid for the controversial gothic marble façade of Santa Croce. But in the mid-1840s his generosity was directed mainly towards Ushaw, where he established a foundation to educate poor boys. He provided the metal for Pugin's great brass lectern and paschal candlestick, and he presented the college with a spectacular early seventeenth-century chalice, reputedly a gift to a clerical member of the Guicciardini family of Florence from

Pope Paul V. Cardinal Wiseman persuaded the then Pope to use the chalice at a papal Mass and attach a special blessing to its use at Ushaw.

Another of Sloane's gifts in 1847 was to prove more fraught. He acquired a magnificent set of French eighteenth-century vestments – chasuble, dalmatic, tunicle, and four copes in a blatantly secular-looking figured red silk edged with silver lace. Although the chasuble is now missing, it remains one of the most sumptuous sets of vestments at Ushaw. Unable to attend the dedication of Pugin's new college chapel, Sloane begged Newsham to allow him, in return for the vestments, to choose the day of the consecration (he suggested Holy Cross Day, 14 September), at which he hoped his vestments would be used. At this point, however, Pugin arrived in Rome and on being shown the vestments, 'instead of admiring the really magnificent silver brocade … he looked confused and immediately said "this stuff and this style of vestments will not suit the new church of Ushaw, and if sent there all my ideas will be deranged and the unity and oneness of my plans will be destroyed"'. With pointed understatement, Sloane told Newsham, 'I did not quite like this.'

There was of course far more to this than an aesthetic disagreement. Material culture matters and is often close to the heart of religion. The alarm caused to the Goths, as Sloane pointedly called them, by vestments 'of the received Latin form', represented an ideological divide about the nature of Victorian Catholicism, and Sloane was seriously offended by Newsham's support for the gothic faction. He threatened to give the vestments to the new chapel of St Barbara which he had built for his miners in Volterra, and to send Ushaw instead some lesser gift 'which shall not shock the hypercritical precision of Mr Pugin's Gothic purity'. Sloane's ruffled feelings were eventually soothed and the vestments did come to Ushaw, with a solemn injunction against their modification into gothic form. They were not, however, used at the consecration ceremony.

No subsequent president of Ushaw was to match Newsham's impact on the spirit and the appearance of the place. His successor was the scholarly Dr Robert Tate, whom Newsham had recruited. Despite deep differences between them in personality and style, in order to raise academic standards in the college Tate would restore the severed links with London University and make many improvements to Ushaw's curriculum. Subsequent presidents would extend Ushaw's buildings, with major new campaigns in 1882–85 (the enlargement of St Cuthbert's Chapel), 1912–14 (St John Boste lecture block), and 1962–64 (East Wing, now the Margaret Clitherow conference centre). But Newsham's legacy – not least the burden of debt he left, which was not to be paid off till well into the next century – gave Ushaw its visual character and much of its enduring tone.

Despite some fluctuation in numbers, especially during the First World War and the hungry 1920s and 1930s, Ushaw remained for the first half of the twentieth century one of the most flourishing Catholic institutions in England. Educational reform and economic and social changes within the college's recruitment base in the close-knit Catholic sub-culture of northern England would affect the make-up of the student

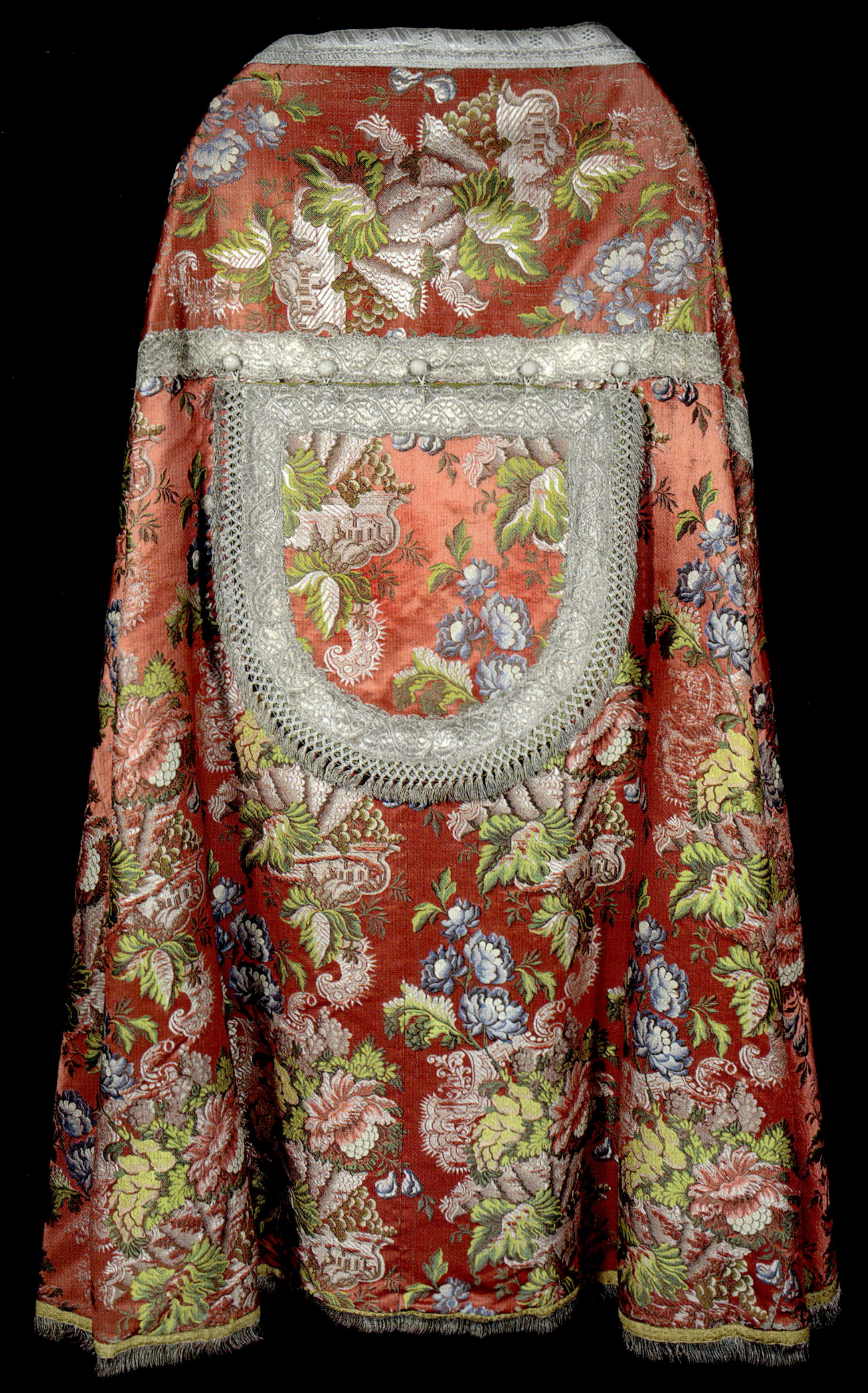

body. Numbers of lay boys peaked in the early 1920s, when they made up a quarter of the total student body. Thereafter they slowly declined and Ushaw gradually became more exclusively a seminary for priestly formation, known for the toughness of its spiritual regime and the austerity of its living conditions. The future Cardinal John Carmel Heenan, a Londoner who was a seminarian at Ushaw in the early 1920s, found the harsh, obedience-centred spirituality intimidating and attributed the poor health of his classmates to malnutrition!

The building of a new accommodation block in the early 1960s marked the peak of a century and a half of expansion at Ushaw. The era of the Second Vatican Council coincided with radical social, political and moral upheaval in the wider culture, reflected within the Catholic Church in the collapse of clerical and religious vocations, and the opening of a closed Catholic sub-culture to the forces transforming society at large. The college did what it could to adapt to the new situation and inaugurated a fruitful collaboration with Durham University, with many of the abler seminarians taking degrees in theology. But the glory days were over. No-one now thought it right to earmark boys at the age of eleven for a life of priestly celibacy and, in 1973, the Junior College closed. Though the decline in the numbers of adult seminarians was slowed by the closure of the other northern seminary at Upholland in 1975, steadily the numbers of men offering themselves for ordination dwindled. By 2011 there were just 26 men preparing for priesthood at Ushaw and the bishops' conference of England and Wales judged the college to be no longer viable. The seminarians were moved to Wiseman's financially better-endowed Midland seminary at Oscott, and Ushaw closed its doors.

EAMON DUFFY

The eighteenth-century cope given to the college by Joseph Francis Sloane.

Introduction: Architectural

William Gibson was the key figure in the establishment of Ushaw. At the outbreak of the French Revolution at the end of the eighteenth century he had been president of Douai for some years. He was subsequently created bishop with responsibility for the Northern District in 1790 in succession to his brother. The Gibsons hailed from Northumberland and the family had produced a number of priests, all of whom were educated at Douai. The question facing the vicars apostolic in England was what to do with the returning students forced to flee from Douai as conditions in revolutionary France worsened, particularly after the execution of Louis XVI in 1793. The last remaining 26 students along with six Benedictine monks (the *trente-deux* as they were known) finally made it back to England after imprisonment – and sometimes terrible conditions – in 1795.

While the Catholic Relief Act of 1791 had made the saying of Mass legal and provided a much greater measure of freedom for Catholics, the act had a clause prohibiting the establishment of 'any School, Academy or College by persons professing the Roman Catholic Religion'. There was thus a feeling among many Catholics that the refugees from Douai would only have temporary shelter in England, similar to that granted by the government to the thousands of French émigrés after 1792. There was talk of them going back to the continent, to Brabant or the Austrian Netherlands. Bishop William Gibson and Bishop John Douglass of the London District had been particularly concerned about the future of the students.

In the event, Bishop Douglass alighted upon Old Hall Green at Ware in Hertfordshire (now the school of St Edmund's College) which had been operating in a low-key way as a school since 1769 but which had Catholic roots going back to the time of James I. However, it quickly proved too small and as more and more students found their way back from France it was clear something had to be done.

Five of the students belonged to the Northern District. Bishop Gibson, concerned that he might lose their vocations, brought them north to a lay school at Tudhoe some five miles from Durham. However, this could only be a temporary arrangement due to lack of space. Energetic discussions continued between north and south and Bishop Gibson travelled extensively to look at various possible locations. Whilst there was a strong feeling in the south that a single college could suffice, there was an equally strong feeling among the northern clergy – not least Bishop Gibson – that there needed to be a separate college in the north of England.

Eventually, the decision was made by Gibson to take on Crook Hall, near Durham. The early eighteenth-century house was in poor condition but an appeal to the laity quickly raised over £600 to prepare the building. Seven students moved in with the Rev Thomas Eyre, the missioner at Pontop, County Durham, in October 1794. Eyre would later become the first president of Ushaw. Soon others followed, including professors and students from Old Hall Green. The northerners had not felt at home at Old Hall, being regarded as outsiders. This prompted one student to remark on arrival at Crook, 'After escaping Egyptian slavery, we arrived safe at the land of promise; at the same time, I wish I could say it flowed with milk and honey.'

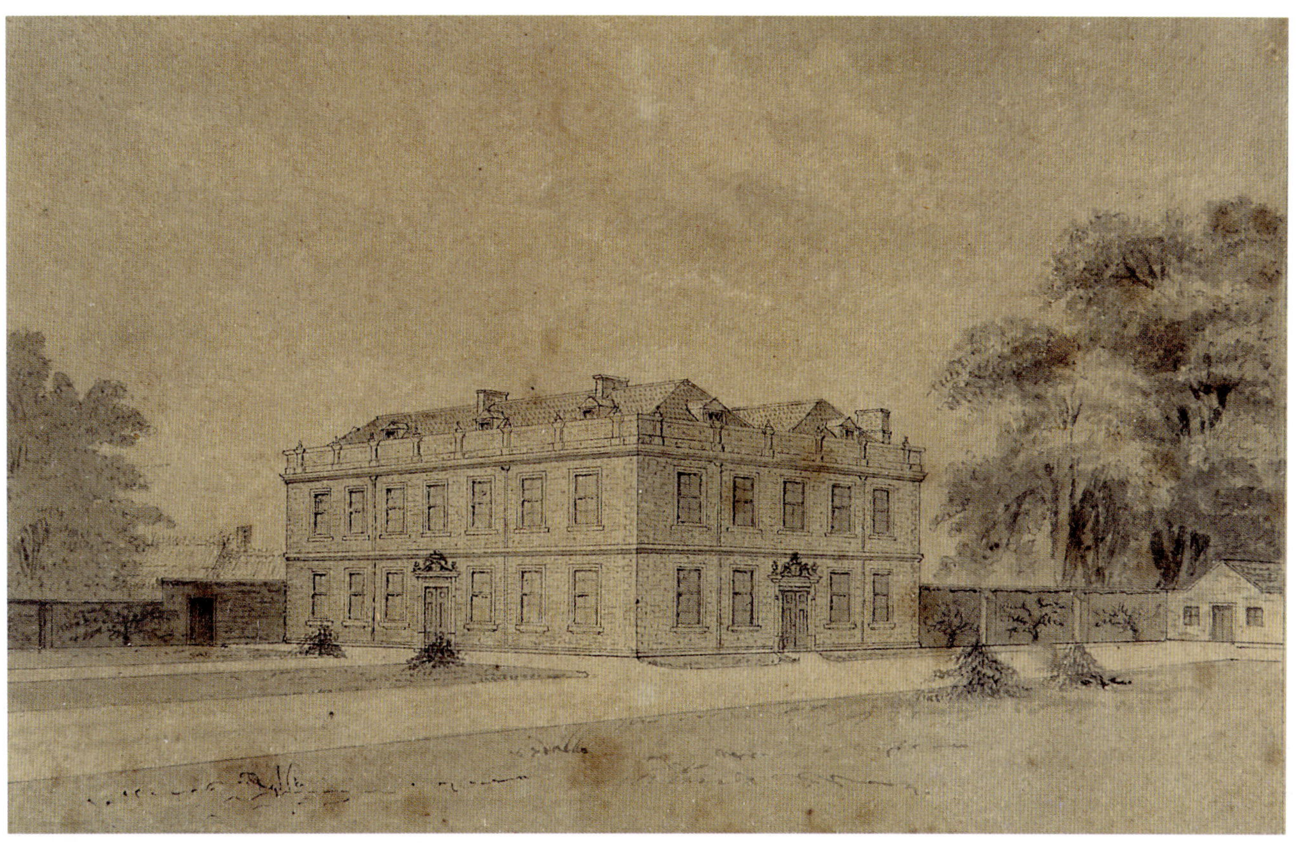

Crook Hall, temporary home to Douai's northern students from 1794 to 1808 while the site for a permanent college was being sought.

It was still thought highly risky to try to establish a permanent ecclesiastical Catholic college in England. Indeed, in June 1795 Bishop Douglass, increasingly concerned at the overcrowding at Old Hall, went to see William Pitt, then First Lord of the Treasury, and the Duke of Portland, Home Secretary. Pitt's advice was firm: no new building should be undertaken as it could cause unrest. After all, the anti-Catholic Gordon Riots had taken place only 15 years earlier, in 1780. Thus, he advised the quiet extension of Old Hall Green. This meeting coincided with a windfall legacy of £10,000 to Bishop Douglass and, encouraged by Pitt's advice, he immediately had plans drawn up to extend Old Hall Green. James Taylor of Islington, himself a former pupil of Old Hall Academy, was engaged as architect. Little is known about James Taylor but he devised a simple classical plan much as he was later to do at Ushaw.

The debate about a single college continued and became quite heated before being settled pragmatically in 1797 when it was decided to split the papal pension of £1,000 (which long ago had been granted to Douai) between Crook Hall and Old Hall Green. This was an unexpected windfall for Crook Hall, even though the grant only lasted for two years before being finally suspended. Psychologically it was important because it implied papal recognition to the concept of a northern college.

For all his vision, Bishop Gibson was renowned for being difficult and hopelessly indecisive. The clergy in Lancashire, who held very strong views about the desirability of a proper northern college, became increasingly impatient with him as Crook Hall was always regarded as temporary. Ushaw had already been identified as a potential site and its owner, Sir Edward Smythe, had agreed to a possible sale. Not all the northern clergy were convinced, particularly those in Lancashire, but Gibson finally made the decision to acquire the estate at Ushaw in 1799. It cost £4,626 5*s*. Funds for the purchase were loaned predominantly – perhaps unsurprisingly given the rivalry between north-west and north-east – by the clergy of Northumberland and Durham.

Disputes and delays continued, however, with Gibson and Eyre famously not getting on while murmurings from the Lancashire clergy continued. But Gibson wanted to get building and for a model he looked to the new buildings at Old Hall and to James Taylor of Islington who subsequently produced a very similar design to his previous work. William Bell of Newcastle oversaw the building work over a three-year period. Work began on the foundations in the spring of 1804 when the first stones of the east wing were laid. It was roofed by October of the following year. Funds were raised across the Northern District – although some Lancashire clergy remained unconvinced. However, conditions at Crook Hall were deteriorating as it was grossly overcrowded with numbers growing every year. In 1804 there were more

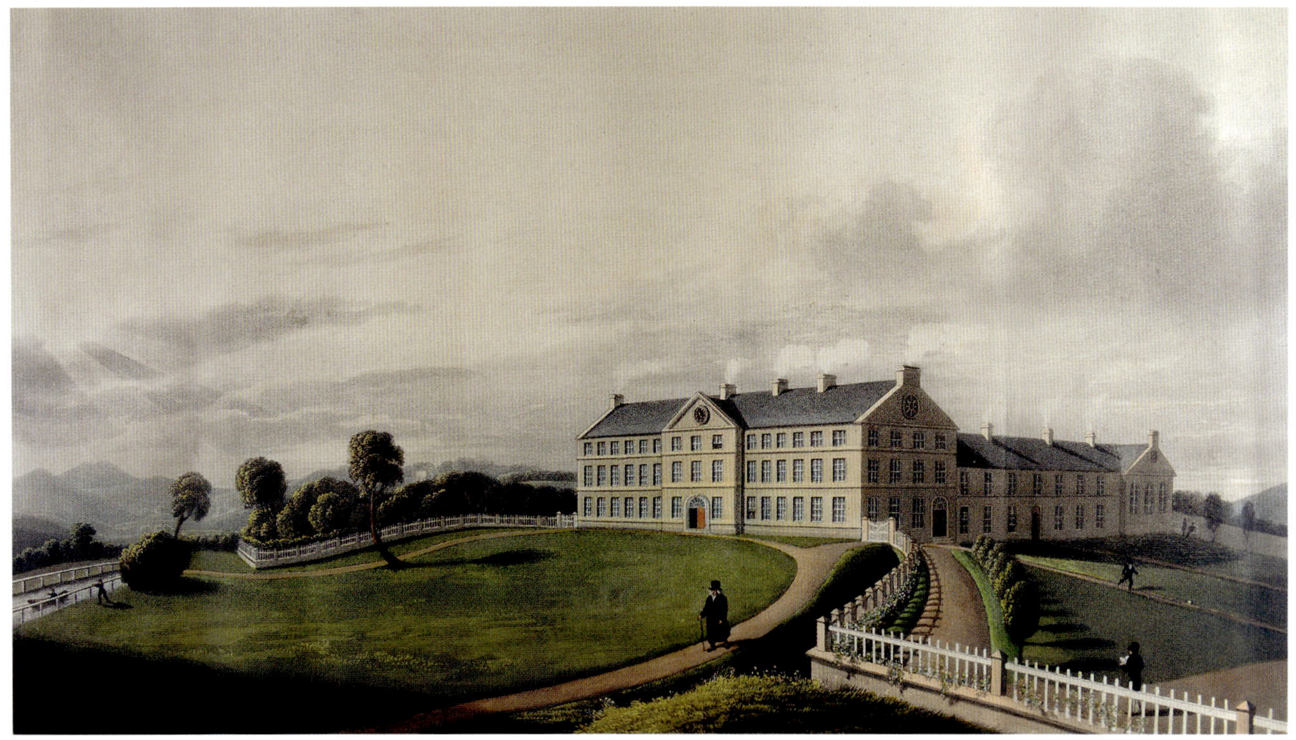

Print made by C. Turner in Newcastle upon Tyne, showing Ushaw 1821–22. The location of the original chapel can be seen to the right, at the rear.

than 40 men crammed into the old house with more to arrive before the final move to Ushaw in 1808.

By August 1805 the north wing of Ushaw was nearly ready to receive its roof but money was running short and work at Ushaw slowed. According to John Lingard, by 1806 three wings had been covered and some of the rooms plastered. When the move took place, the building was still not finished, with floors unflagged and many of the windows unglazed and boarded up to keep out the wind and rain. Ushaw was a windswept spot with, as yet, no trees. The style of the building was distinctly old-fashioned for its date.

Fifty-two men moved in, but numbers rapidly increased and by July 1809 there were 80 in the new college. Not helped by poor sanitary conditions, an outbreak of typhus during the winter of 1808–9 caused havoc. Some 57 people at Ushaw caught the fever; five students died and were buried alongside each other in a new cemetery that had to be hastily created in the woods near the college. Thomas Eyre, the first president, died the following year and is buried there.

A further fundraising effort was launched by Gibson in 1814 which enabled the building of the west wing. This was not finished until 1819. The chapel, on the north-east corner of the substantial quadrangular block of Taylor's Georgian building, was plain, classical with an unpretentious flat plaster ceiling; the kitchen and refectory were located along the north wing where they remain today. On the first floor, the president's gallery and the library occupied the south front with student accommodation above, a mix of lay and seminarian. At this date there were large numbers of lay boys at Ushaw, very much as there had been at Douai. Gibson died in June 1821 at the age of 82, by then almost completely paralysed and senile, but he had lived to see the creation of a worthy successor to the college at Douai over which he had once presided. He too lies buried in the Ushaw cemetery.

The next phase of building transformed Ushaw into the vast complex it is today. Catholics were given full rights as citizens with the Catholic Emancipation Act of 1829 and it is from this time that the great expansion of Catholicism in England began, aided, particularly in the north of England, by the vast numbers of Irish coming over to the industrial cities in search of work. In May 1837 Mgr Charles Newsham became president of Ushaw. His two immediate predecessors had often been absent and, as vice-president since 1830, Newsham had effectively been running Ushaw for some time. Now properly in charge, he first made changes to the senior staff, surrounding himself with people who, like him, wished to see Ushaw pre-eminent as a place of learning, discipline and piety. Newsham had clearly developed his thinking before he took office because within the first few months of becoming president he was writing to Bishop Briggs outlining the need for gas lighting, new kitchens, reorganising studies and building a preparatory school. As a first step he invited the architect Ignatius Bonomi to prepare a plan for a new kitchen block and to design a gas works. Ushaw was thus fully lit by gas from a very early date. A Mr Green of Newcastle carried out the work.

During the summer of 1837 the washing facilities for the students were improved, the front parlour refitted and the chapel redecorated. When the boys came back that autumn they found the old pewterware in the refectory had been replaced with earthenware crockery. Then Newsham began a fundraising initiative to provide for proper offices and storerooms, sleeping quarters for the servants, new outbuildings for the kitchens, a separate infirmary (clearly remembering the horrors of the typhus epidemic), expansion of the refectory and the chapel, and the fitting out of a public room which would have a teaching museum attached to it.

Newsham's major building campaign started with the new chapel. The old one was far too small by Newsham's time and its classical style unappealing. Despite the views of Lingard, who thought the design should be classical, Newsham was very clear that the new chapel should be gothic and the obvious choice of architect was Augustus Welby Northmore Pugin. By 1843 a design had been agreed upon and an appeal launched for £4,500. A large tower and spire were part of Pugin's original plan but were never built as Newsham considered them too extravagant. Christmas Mass was celebrated in the chapel in 1847 and it was formally opened the following year with a Pontifical Mass. Nicholas Wiseman, then coadjutor of the London District and a former student of Ushaw, preached the sermon. St Cuthbert's chapel was considered a masterpiece by those who saw it.

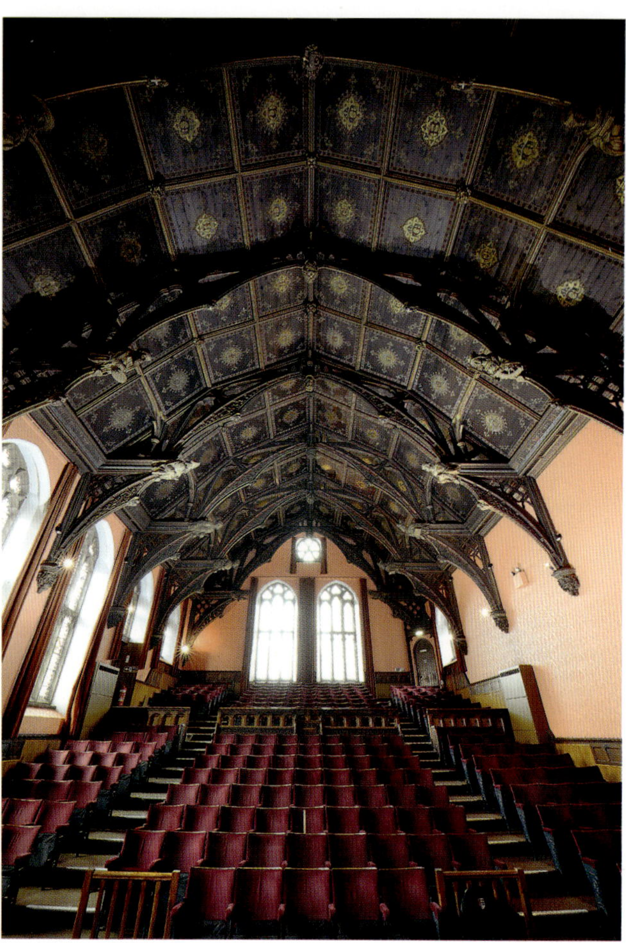

On the site of Ushaw's first chapel, the Exhibition Hall's ceiling was designed by Joseph Hansom.

The decade between 1848 and 1858 saw astonishing expansion at Ushaw. Despite debilitating deafness, Newsham must have been a persuasive communicator. He was clearly able to raise significant funds from sources that remain somewhat obscure. There was no single patron like the Earl of Shrewsbury was to Pugin. Instead there were benefactors like Francis Joseph Sloane who had been educated alongside Newsham at Ushaw in the early days and gone to live in Florence where he made a fortune, most of which he gave away, running the Grand Duke of Tuscany's copper mines at Montecatini (Val di Cecina).

After the completion of the chapel in 1848, Charles Newsham decided that the next undertaking should be the provision of what he called a 'public room' on the site of the old chapel, which now is the Exhibition Hall. Joseph Hansom, designer of the Hansom cab, founder of *The Builder* magazine and architect of many important Catholic churches, was commissioned. The new hammer-beam roof carries images of

The high altar from A.W.N. Pugin's original chapel, now situated in the Sacred Heart chapel.

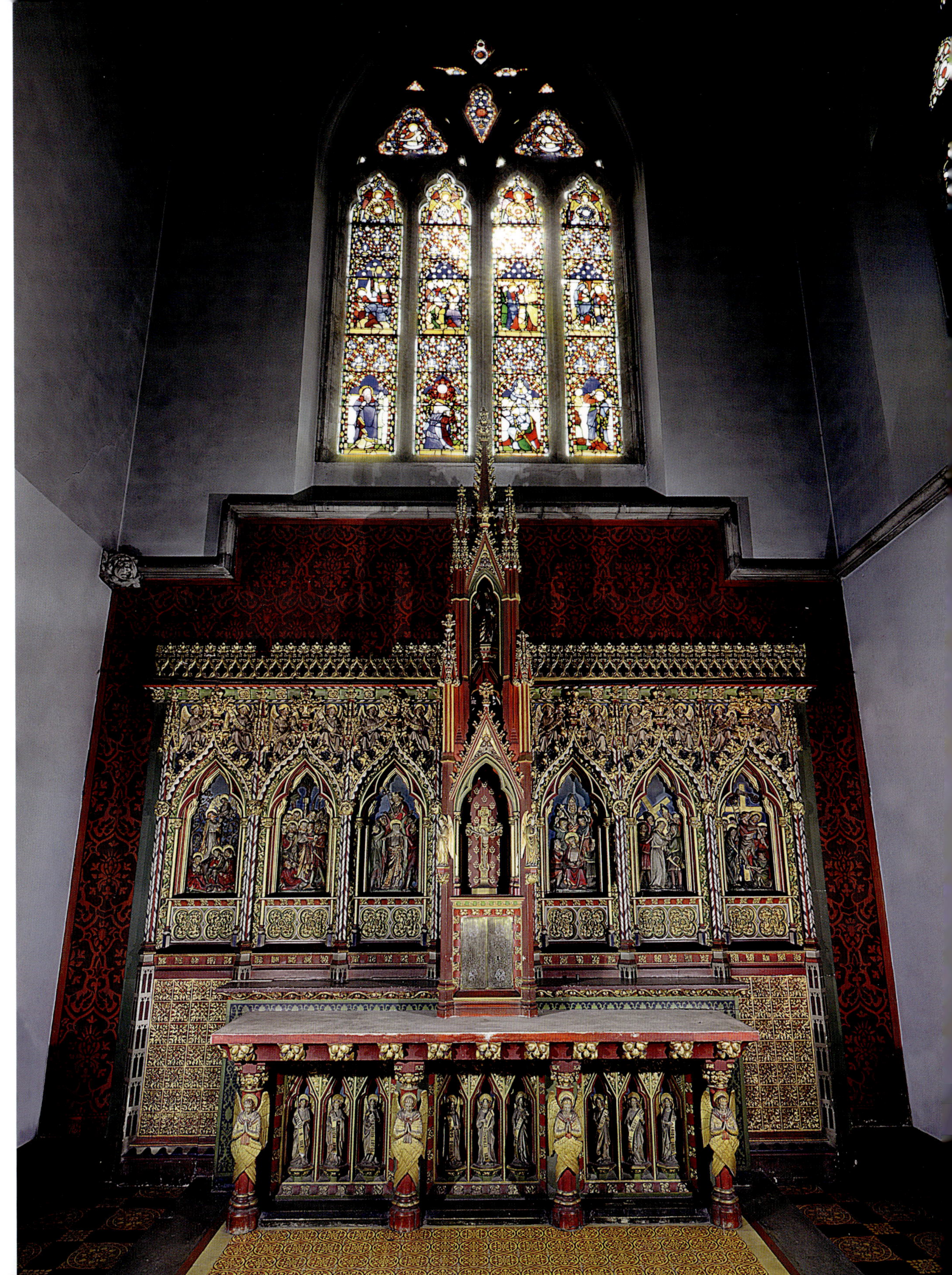

the patron saints of the arts and sciences. The windows of the old chapel were 'gothicised' with armorial glass bearing the arms of all the presidents of Ushaw from Cardinal Allen to Mgr Newsham himself.

The next major work was the creation of the library. Joseph and his brother Charles Hansom were commissioned to carry out this imposing work after A.W.N. Pugin's design was rejected as being too small. It was built between 1849 and 1851. The oak bookcases were provided by Fr Thomas Wilkinson, a key benefactor to the college. Wilkinson was by this time one of the few surviving priests ordained at Douai and it was he who had set about recreating a major library at Ushaw, to replace that lost at Douai during the French Revolution. Wilkinson personally supervised the move of books from the old library on the first floor of the south front to the new building a few years before he died. The exterior of the library was designed by the Hansom brothers to balance the Pugin chapel at the other end of the south façade.

The building of the library was accompanied by the creation of new bounds walls for the special ball games derived from those played at Douai, including the unique

Joseph and Charles Hansom designed the exterior of the library *(right)* to balance the Pugin chapel *(left)* on the other side of the main building.

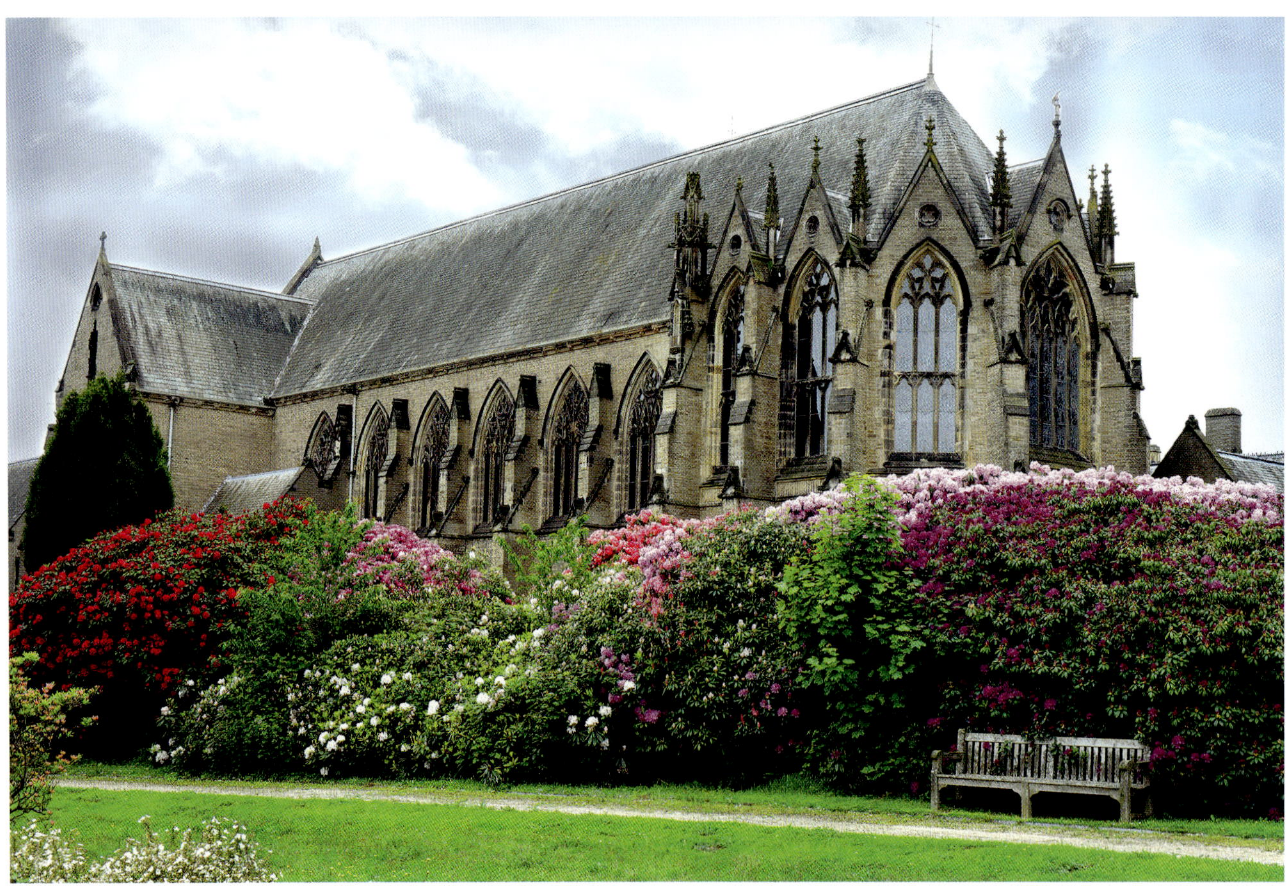

game of 'Cat'. Charles and Joseph Hansom completed the construction of these at the same time as the library. Rather like medieval fortifications, they are one of the unique architectural features of Ushaw. The grounds in front of the south façade were laid out with a shallow lake (now sadly silted up and overgrown). Skating had been popular at Douai and the tradition was continued at Ushaw.

There followed the building of the Home Farm between 1851 and 1852, also by Joseph Hansom. This was a remarkably advanced design for its time. It was built into the bank so that the ground level at the back is much higher. This enabled animal feed to be wheeled into the building from the back and then dropped down chutes to the mangers of stock housed below. The building also contained state-of-the-art farm machinery driven by steam with a complicated system of belts running between different floor levels.

Whilst the Hansom brothers were occupied designing the library, Home Farm, Exhibition Hall and the cemetery cloister, Pugin was designing the refectory and the complex of small chapels which adjoin the main chapel. Pugin's fireplace stands at the

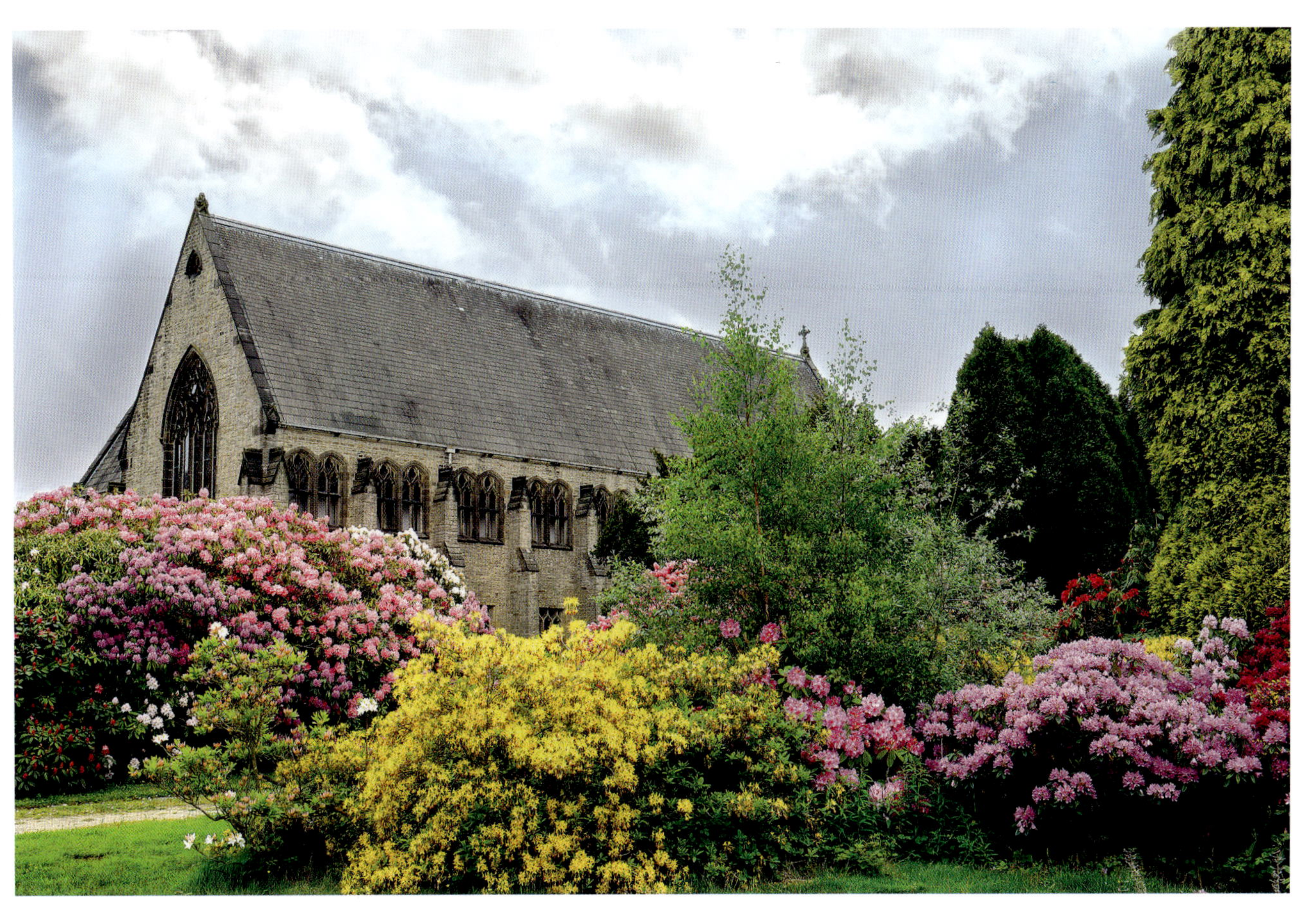

east end of the Refectory below the portrait of Cardinal Allen, and portraits of Ushaw presidents and Cardinal Wiseman adorn the walls. A drawing by Pugin for the frame of Charles Newsham's portrait survives in the archives.

A.W.N. Pugin created the corridor to his new chapel and the cloister connecting the main chapel to that of St Joseph with the Oratory of the Holy Family. The altar-piece is by Franz von Rohden and the tiles are by Minton. Either side are cabinets filled with relics. Ushaw has one of the largest and most important collections of relics in England.

A.W.N. Pugin's early and tragic death at the age of 40 in 1852 left his work at Ushaw unfinished. Edward Welby Pugin, his son, was only 17 when his father died. He completed St Joseph's chapel in 1854, designing the reredos, the tabernacle and the decorative surround for Karl Hoffmann's fine statue of St Joseph. A smaller version of Hoffmann's *Our Lady of Help* also stands in St Joseph's. This chapel was originally designed as a chapel for the servants, St Joseph being the patron saint of workers.

E.W. Pugin went on to build the laundry, the laboratory and the offices in the north-east corner. He rebuilt the kitchens and built the convent building behind. He

The refectory, originally designed by A.W.N. Pugin.

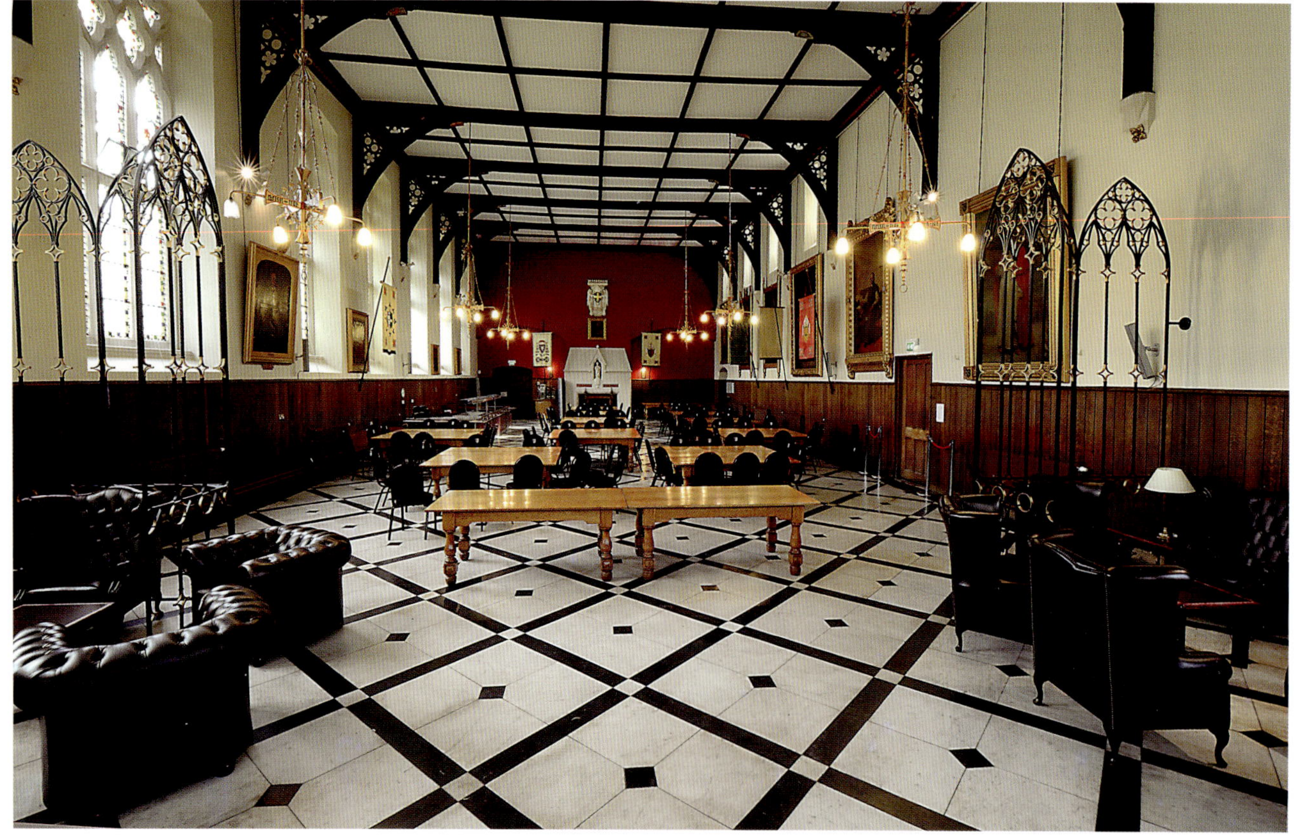

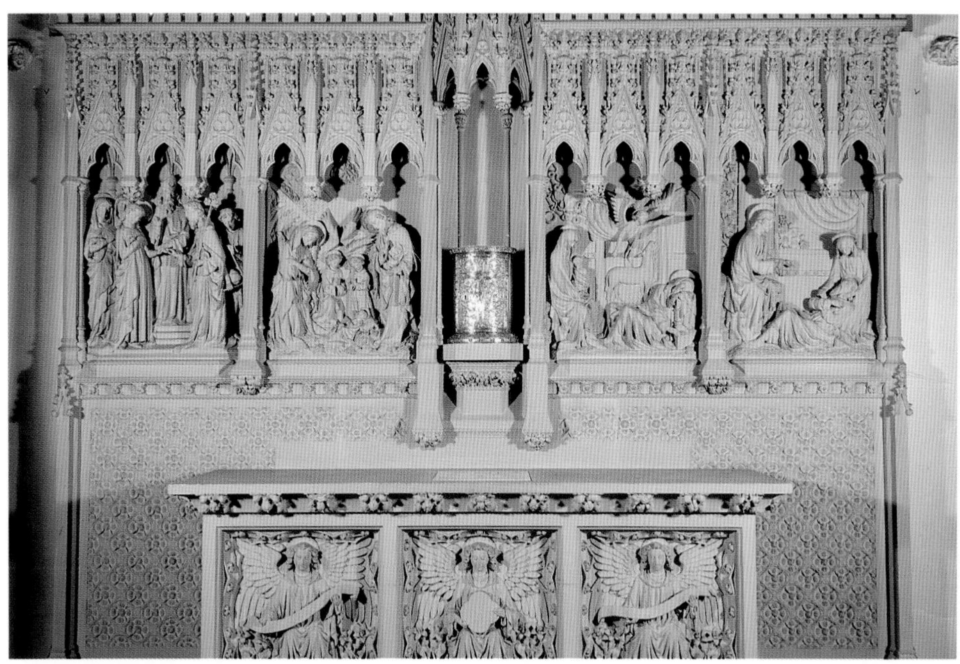

The reredos of St Joseph's chapel, designed by E.W. Pugin.

also transformed the professors' dining room by gothicising it. This room was enlarged in 1937 in keeping with E.W. Pugin's original design. Next came the construction of the separate infirmary, which Newsham had long wanted, together with its own chapel. Prior to this, the infirmary had been located above the kitchens in the main block. Then, south of the infirmary, E.W. Pugin built the new museum wing, a beloved project of Newsham's who considered a museum of natural history an essential part of the educational establishment at Ushaw. The stuffed animals and birds which once filled this long room were disposed of in the 1960s.

However, the largest building project that Newsham initiated, and which E.W. Pugin designed after winning the competition against the Hansom brothers and another well-known Catholic architect, George Goldie, was the building of Junior House as the preparatory school for Ushaw. Designed to be independent of Ushaw, it had its own chapel dedicated to St Aloysius, refectory and ball places; E.W. Pugin completed the building in 1859. As well as designing Junior House, he also completed his father's chapel cloister by adding the superbly detailed chapel of St Charles Borromeo – paid for by Charles Newsham himself – and the chapel of St Michael and St Joseph, known also as the mortuary chapel. The chapel of St Charles Borromeo is a very intimate and highly decorated space with both sculpture and stained glass depicting scenes from the life of the great Counter-Reformation saint. The little chapel of St Michael and the Holy Souls is tucked away down steps off the cloister. It was paid for by the parents of the Rev Michael Gibson who had been vice-president of Ushaw under Charles Newsham and had died in 1856. The reredos depicts the Last

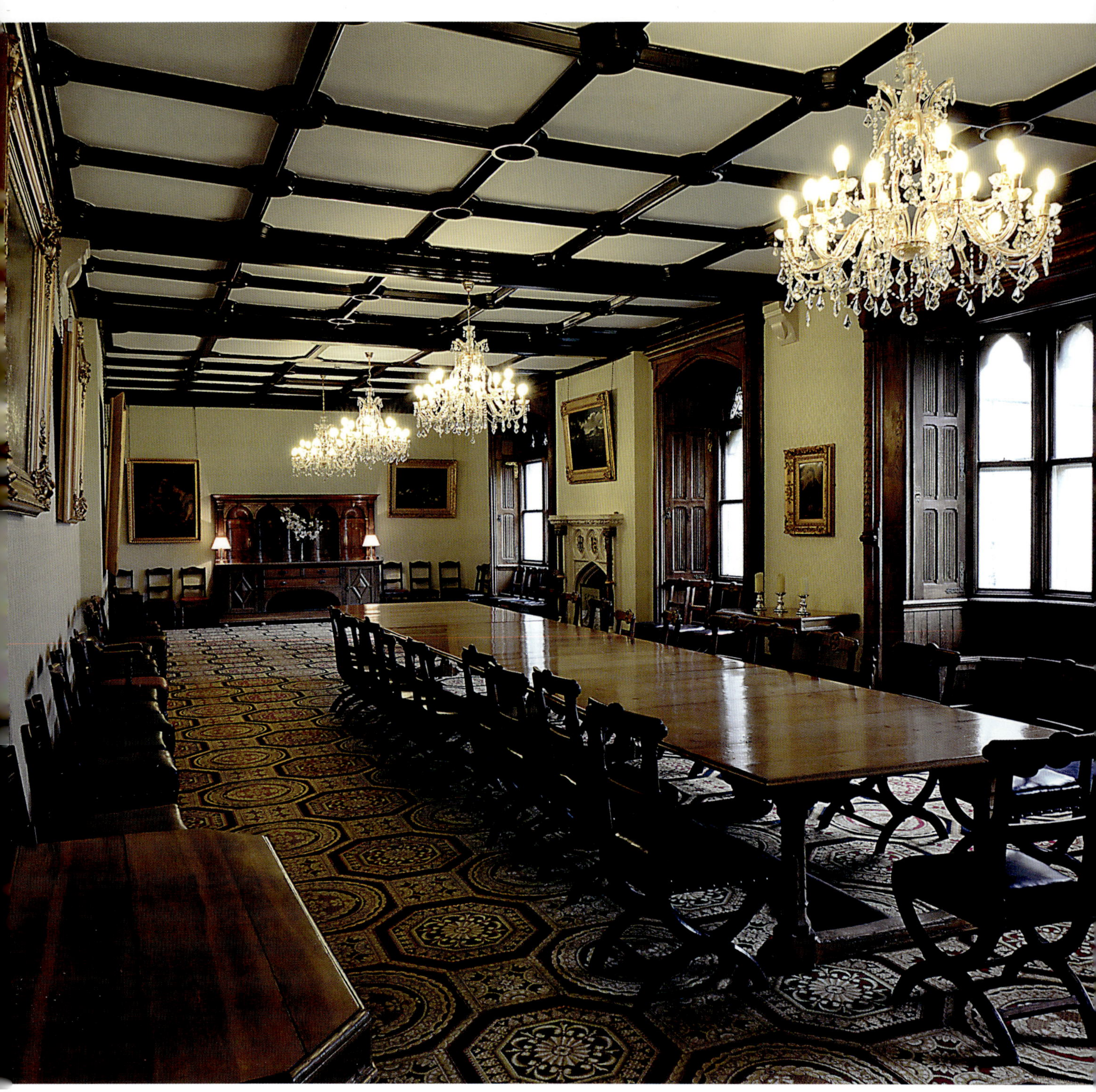

The professors' dining room, designed by E.W. Pugin.

The natural history museum, designed by E.W. Pugin.

Judgement. Both Gibson and Newsham are now buried in this highly evocative chapel.

The golden jubilee of the college was celebrated with great pomp in July 1858; all of the buildings described above were by then either complete or nearly complete. To mark this very special occasion, Cardinal Wiseman came and gave the college its treasured relic, the ring of St Cuthbert. Sadly, things did not go so well for Ushaw financially in the next few years with the college in serious debt. Worn down with worry and by then totally deaf, Charles Newsham died in February 1863 aged 71.

Dr Robert Tate succeeded Charles Newsham as Ushaw's seventh president and during his presidency the question of the governance of the college, about which there had been much argument over the years, was finally resolved. From being independent under its president as Douai had been – a position that Newsham had fought for to the end – Ushaw finally came under the control of the northern bishops. Tate was realistic; he recognised the growing power of the newly restored hierarchy and he was also well aware, following the intense building programme of the previous 20 years, that Ushaw was on the verge of bankruptcy. By ceding control to the bishops, the financial crisis would become the problem for the new board of governors: the Bishops

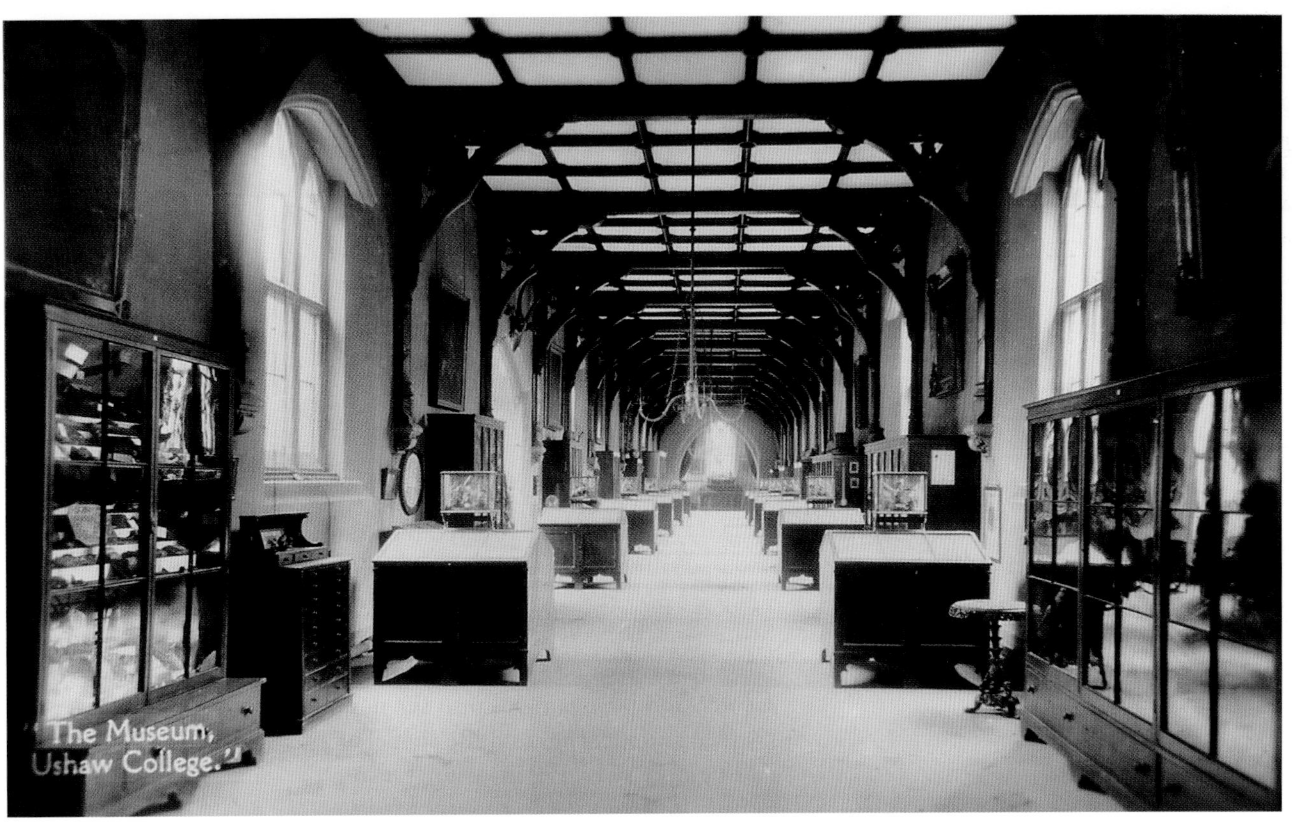

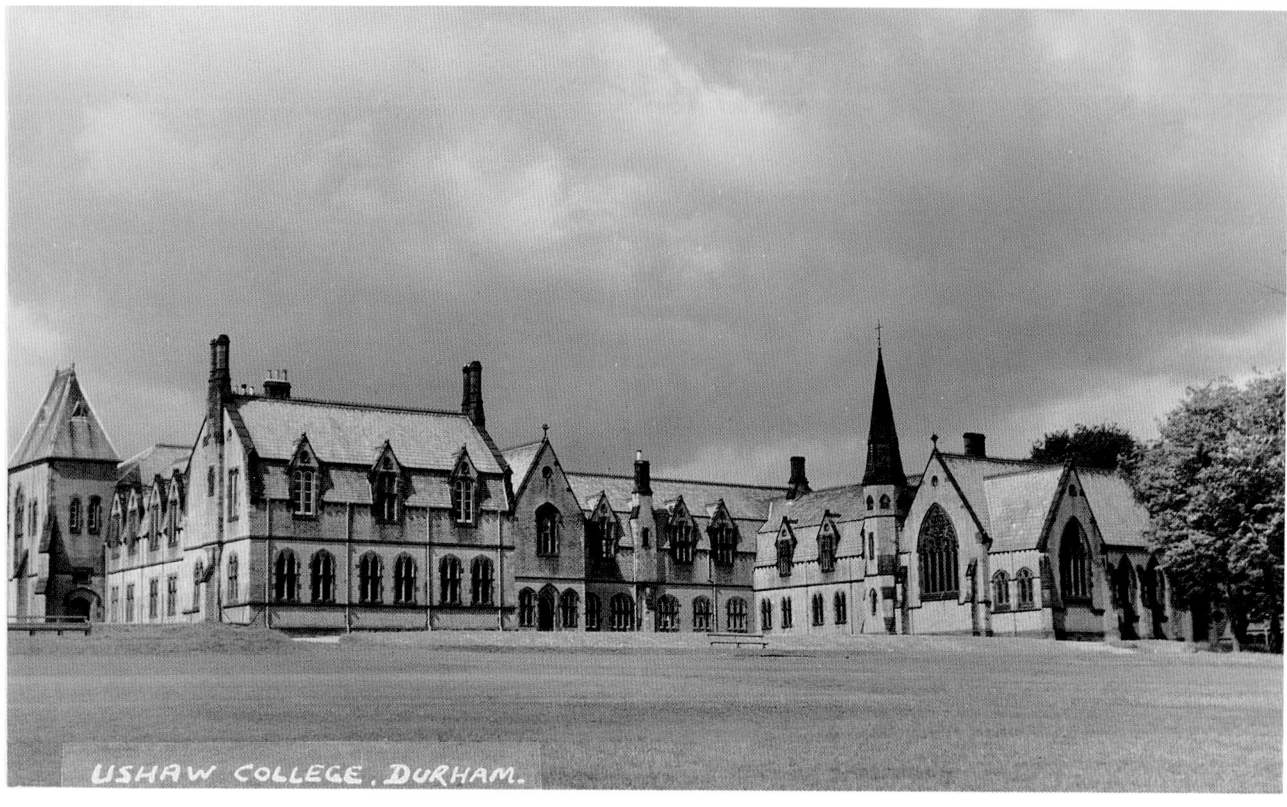

The Junior College c.1900.

of Hexham and Newcastle, Salford, Shrewsbury, Liverpool and Beverley. Happily, however, coal was plentiful under the Ushaw farms and from 1868 royalties from the sale of the mineral rights not only paid off the debts but helped create a new reserve of capital which would fund later building projects. Tate quietly got on with planting more trees around Ushaw, improving the grounds and enlarging the refectory in 1873 to designs that E.W. Pugin had drawn up some years before.

By the late 1870s it was becoming clear that there were issues with the structural stability of the east end of A.W.N. Pugin's chapel. The chapel was also by this time far too small. The architectural practice of Dunn and Hansom of Newcastle (successors to Joseph and Charles) was consulted and their advice was to dismantle, rebuild and enlarge. Work began in 1882. While the main body of the new chapel has echoes of Pugin's design, the east end is much more elaborate and the careful architectural balance between chapel and library has been lost. Instead, the chapel dominates the approach to the south front. Internally, Pugin's work was treated with great respect. Fittings and stained glass were carefully taken down and incorporated into the new, larger chapel. G.F. Bentley redecorated Pugin's screen and incorporated the chapel of St Bede which now forms a part of it. Peter Paul Pugin, A.W.N. Pugin's youngest son by his third wife, designed the matching chapel of St Gregory. On the right is the beautiful and much venerated Karl Hoffmann statue of *Our Lady of Help*. Pugin's original high altar and reredos were relocated to the back of the chapel on the south wall, now the Sacred Heart chapel, which is entered through a screen designed by Basil Champneys in 1883. Pugin's Lady chapel was redecorated by G.F. Bentley, who also designed the screen that fronts it. Pugin's panelling and stalls were carefully dismantled and extended. The chapel thus pays due homage to A.W.N. Pugin but develops the gothic tradition in new ways. The high altar, designed by Peter Paul Pugin in 1891, is highly decorative and forms the striking focus of the chapel.

Even with the completion of the new chapel, building work at Ushaw was not finished. Neither was the connection with the Pugin dynasty. In the mid-1920s two further chapels were added to the west end of St Cuthbert's chapel. That to the north was designed as a war memorial to the 79 Ushaw men killed in the First World War. It is dedicated to the English martyrs, with paintings by Elphege Pippet. The architect was Sebastian Pugin Powell, nephew of Peter Paul Pugin (who had died in 1904) and A.W.N. Pugin's grandson. The chapel to the south, again a collaboration between Sebastian Pugin Powell and Pippet, is dedicated to St Thomas of Canterbury, in memory of Bishop Thomas Wilkinson, who became both Bishop of Hexham and

Left: The chapel of St Charles Borromeo, designed by E.W. Pugin.

Right: The Lady chapel.

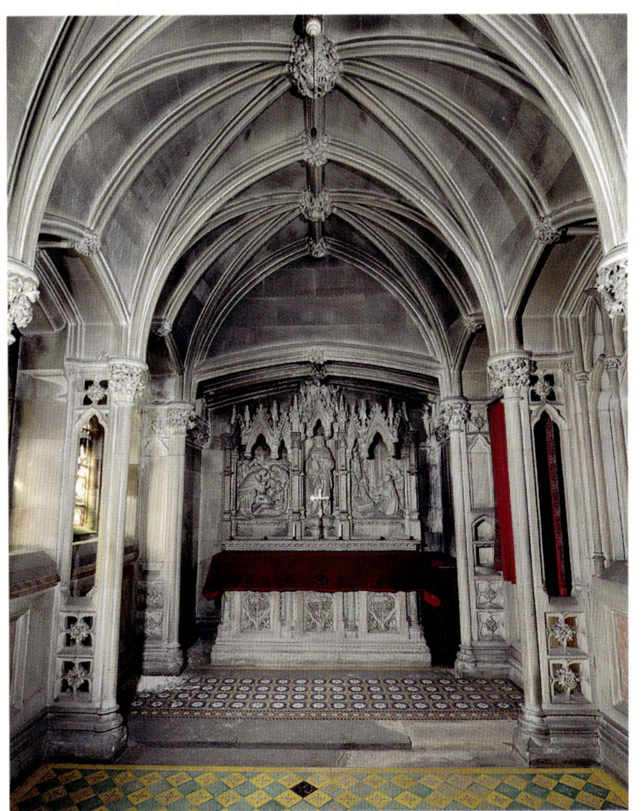

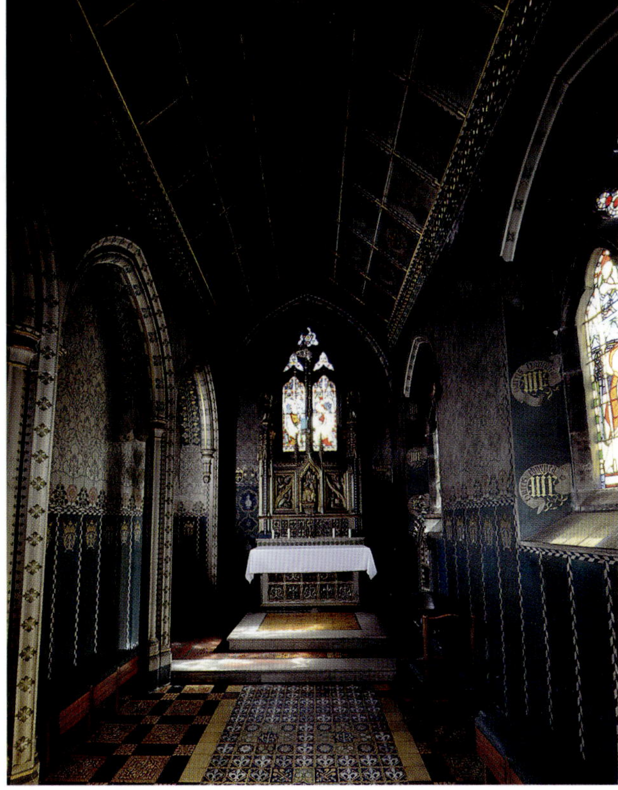

twelfth president of Ushaw in 1889 and oversaw the rebuilding of St Cuthbert's chapel through to completion. In 1935 the limewood stations of the cross were added to the cloister outside the chapels of the Holy Family and St Charles Borromeo to celebrate the 400th anniversary of the birth of Cardinal Allen.

The high altar of St Cuthbert's chapel, designed by Peter Paul Pugin.

Under Bishop Wilkinson the college was still expanding. Like Charles Newsham he also 'thought big'. New dormitories were built above the west wing and above the refectory, the latter by Peter Paul Pugin who also built the indoor swimming pool. The extra storey – known as 'Tip Top' – was added to the main front in 1906 by Sebastian Pugin Powell, who was called upon again to design the St John Boste classroom wing in 1912–14 and in 1931 to design the St Bede's wing to provide more living accommodation. A substantial new accommodation block was then added in the 1964 to the designs of Robert Burke.

In 1958 the college celebrated its 150th anniversary. The Mass, celebrated outside, was attended by 40,000 Catholics from all over the north of England. From the 1970s, however, numbers of students declined. The Junior House closed in 1975 and Ushaw College itself closed as a seminary in June 2011. Since then, and through the good offices of Durham University, there has been a burgeoning interest in Ushaw and its remarkable buildings and associated collections which previously were so little known beyond a small number of experts. The vision of Cardinal Allen, of Charles Newsham and of Thomas Wilkinson to create the new Douai in the north-east of England continues.

SOPHIE ANDREAE

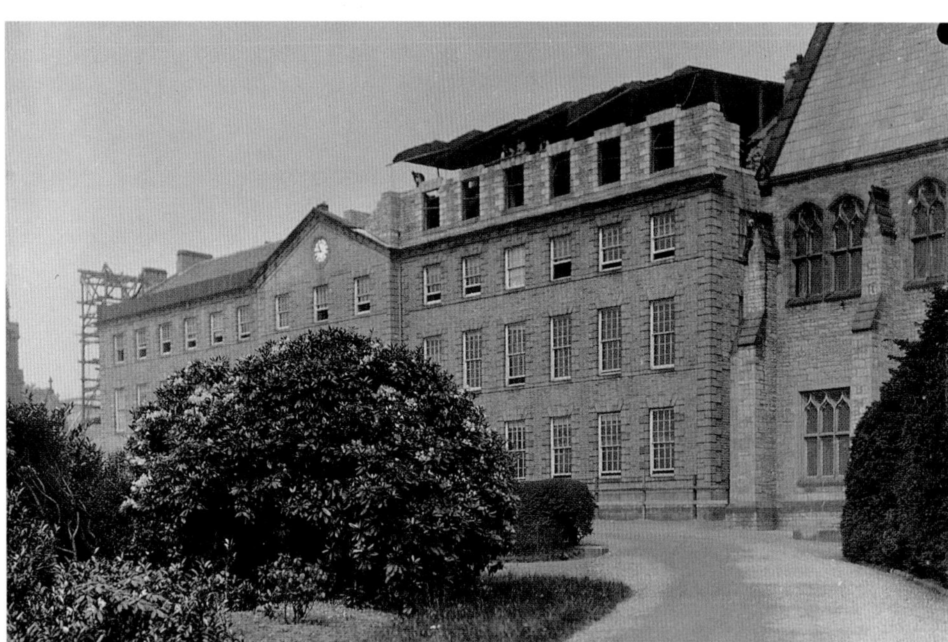

Left: The storey known as 'Tip Top' being added in 1906.

Overleaf: Aerial view of Ushaw, taken in 2008 by Dennis Briggs. The Junior College is to the left of the photo, the Cat rings to the right.

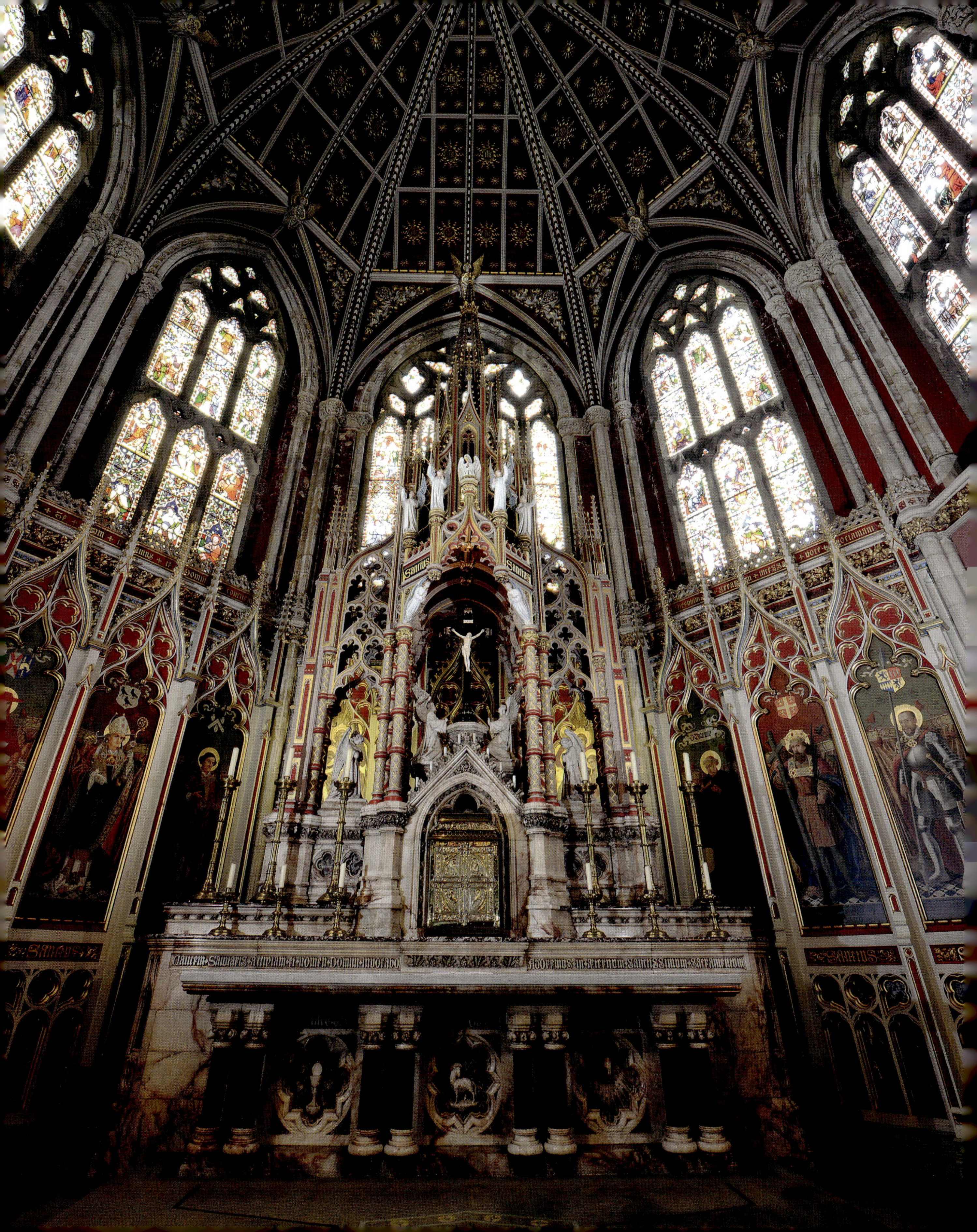
Sanctus Sanctus
Panem Salutaris accipiam et nomen Domini invocabo
Adoremus in aeternum Sanctissimum Sacramentum

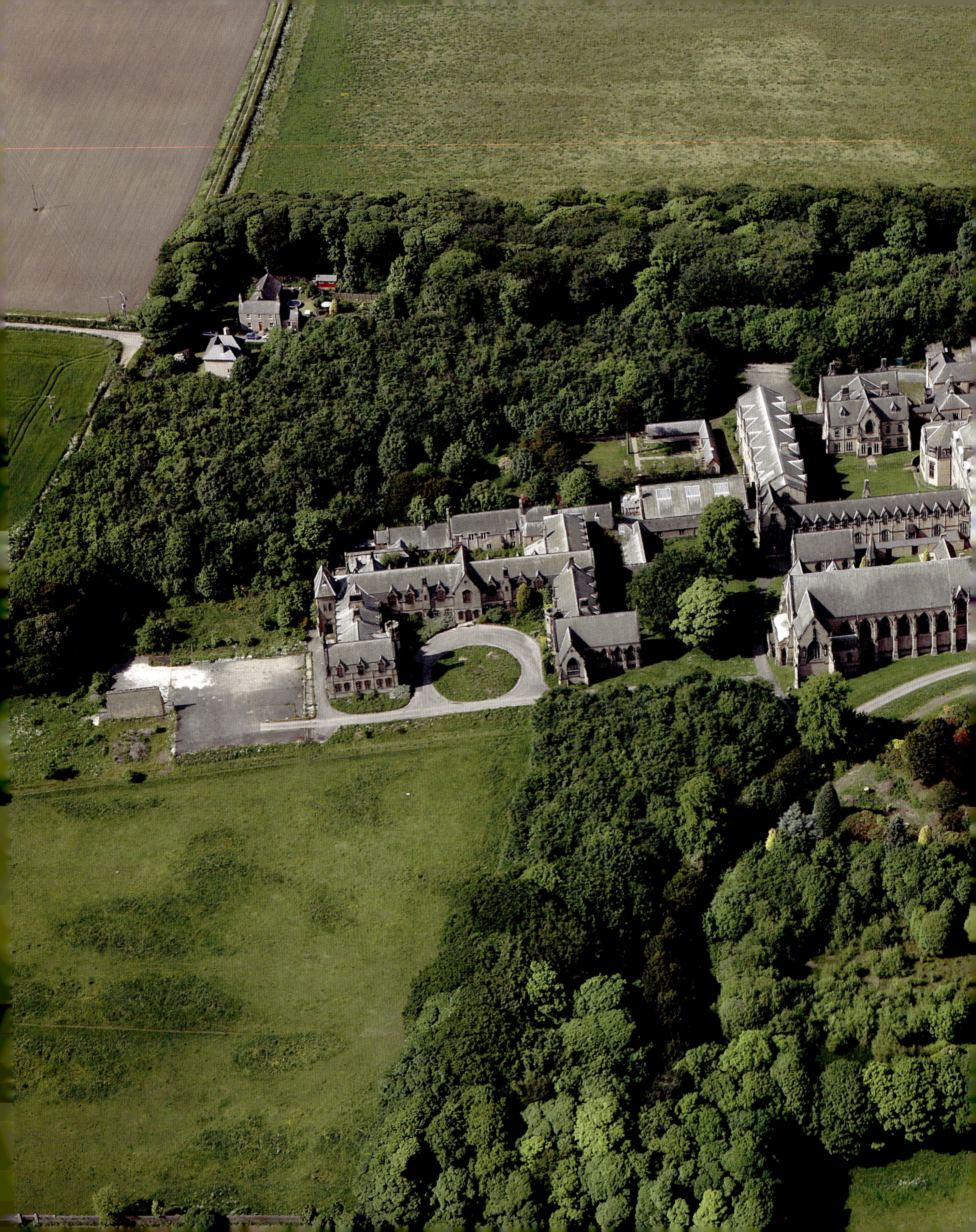

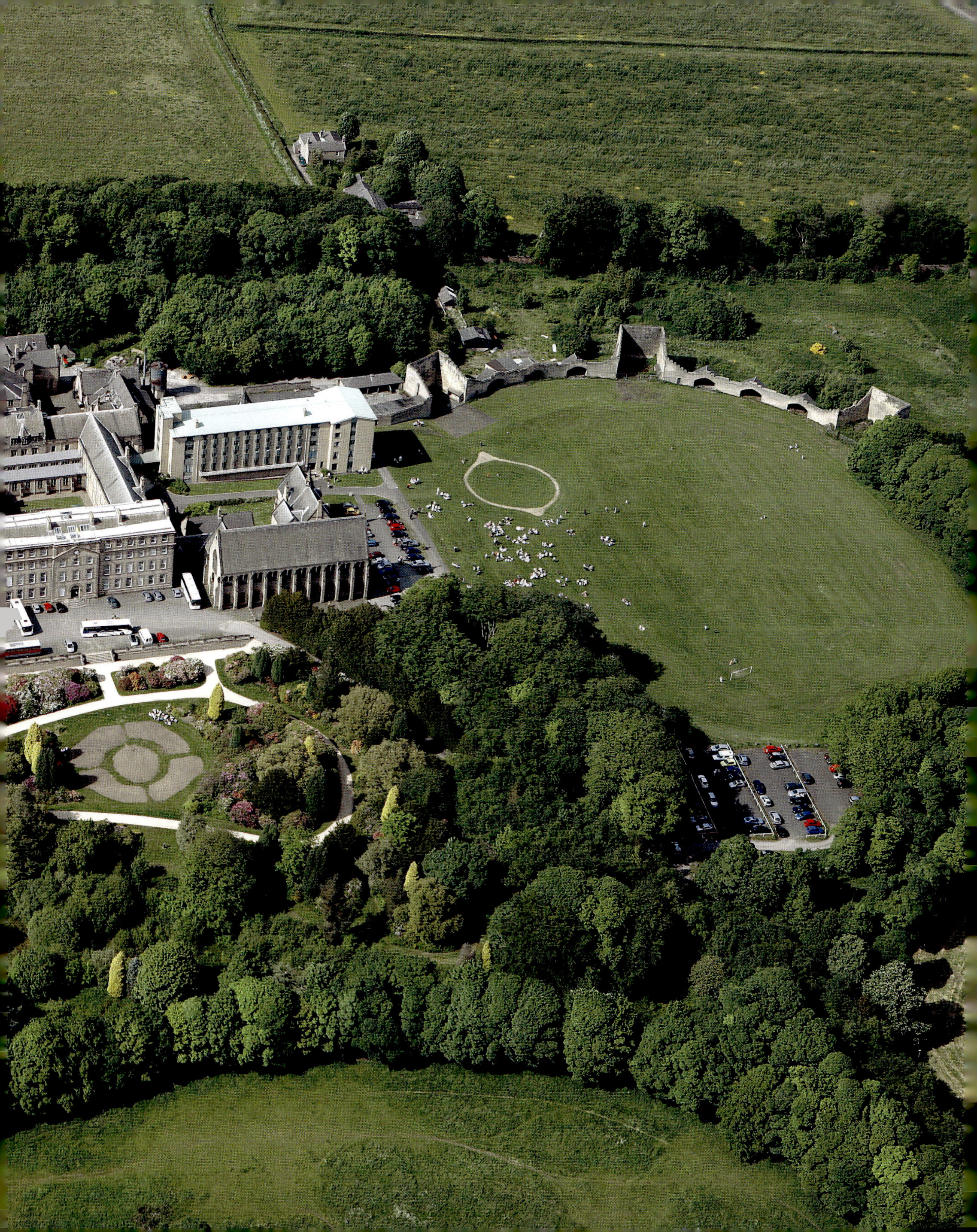

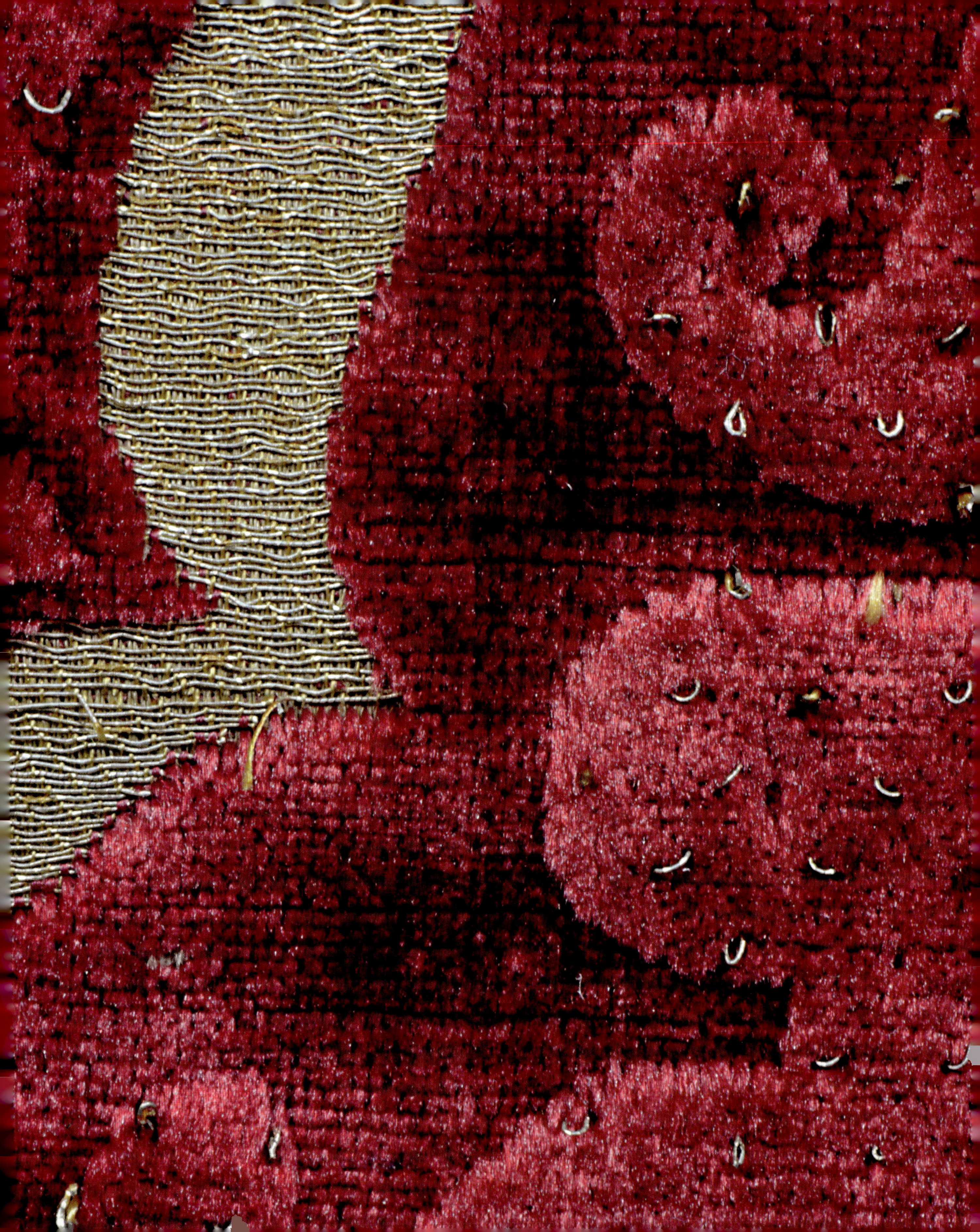

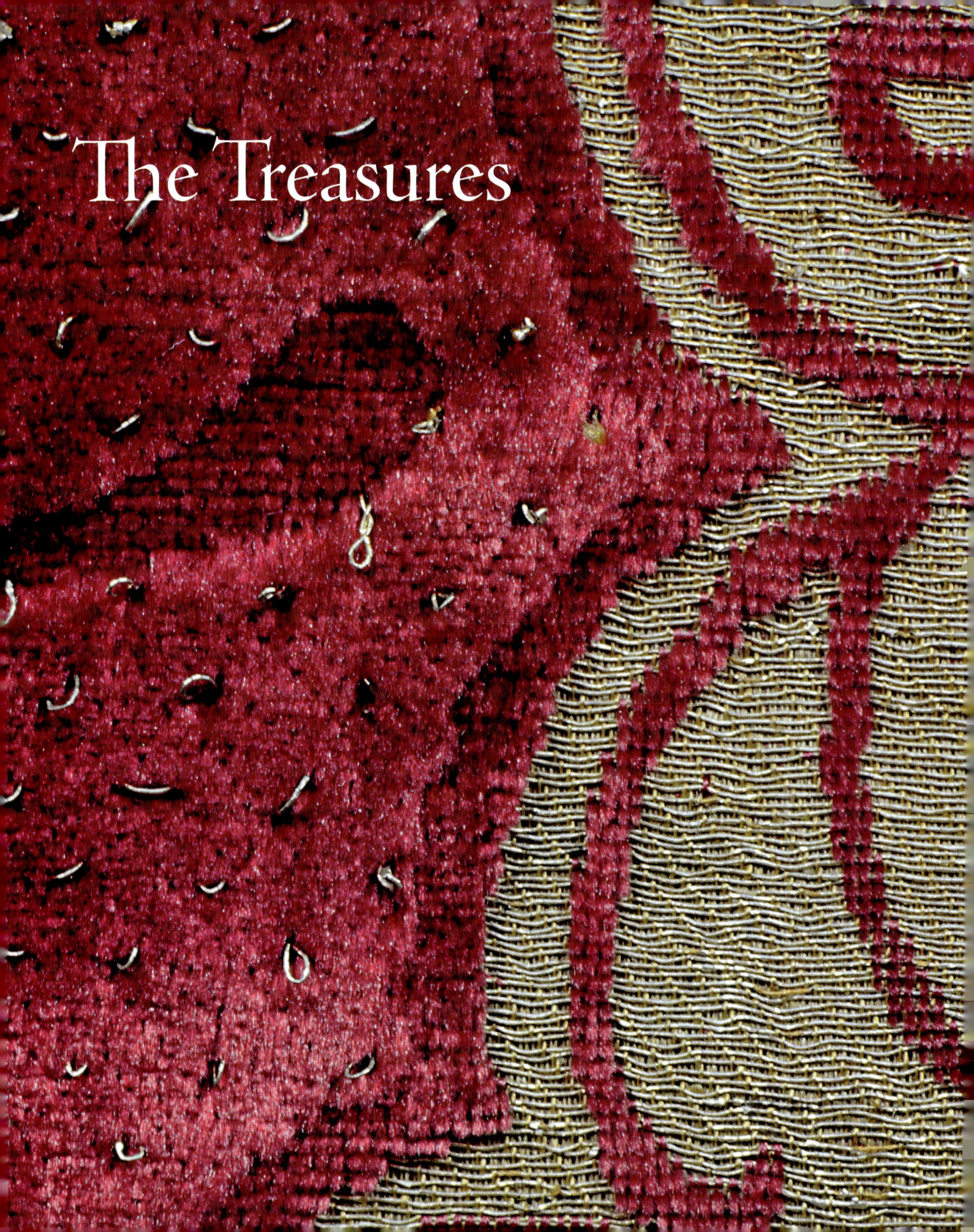

The Treasures

Local Survivors from before the Reformation

Durham Cathedral Priory books and bindings, eighth century onwards

Among the most remarkable features of Ushaw's Big Library is the number of books that belonged to the monks of Durham Cathedral Priory. Totalling more than 50, this is a higher figure than survive from any one medieval community in Britain in any other modern library.

Almost all of them came to Ushaw via a local gentry family of County Durham, the Tempests. It would seem that they came into possession of the books through two former monks who belonged to the family. Following the dissolution of their monastery in 1539, these two had become canons of the cathedral chapter, which had been established by Henry VIII in place of the officially dissolved religious community. However, the two monks were among those who refused to take the Oath of Supremacy after 1559, which recognised Elizabeth I as head of the Church in England. It therefore appears to be through these two recalcitrant churchmen that the books entered the family's collection.

A possible example in the Ushaw collections that may have come from Durham Priory is one fourteenth-century Bible, which boasts the ownership inscription of Sir Thomas Tempest, fourth baronet (1642–91). Other manuscripts he owned had similar inscriptions, as highlighted by some of the items now held in the Harleian collection at the British Library. Interestingly, in light of the fact that a portion of his library ended up at Ushaw, Sir Thomas had been educated at its continental predecessor at Douai.

Many of the fifteenth- and sixteenth-century printed books at Ushaw also bear the names and annotations of monks of that period. Furthermore, a number are in decorated bindings manufactured largely in Oxford, where the most promising monks studied. An exception is one book encased in a binding which must have

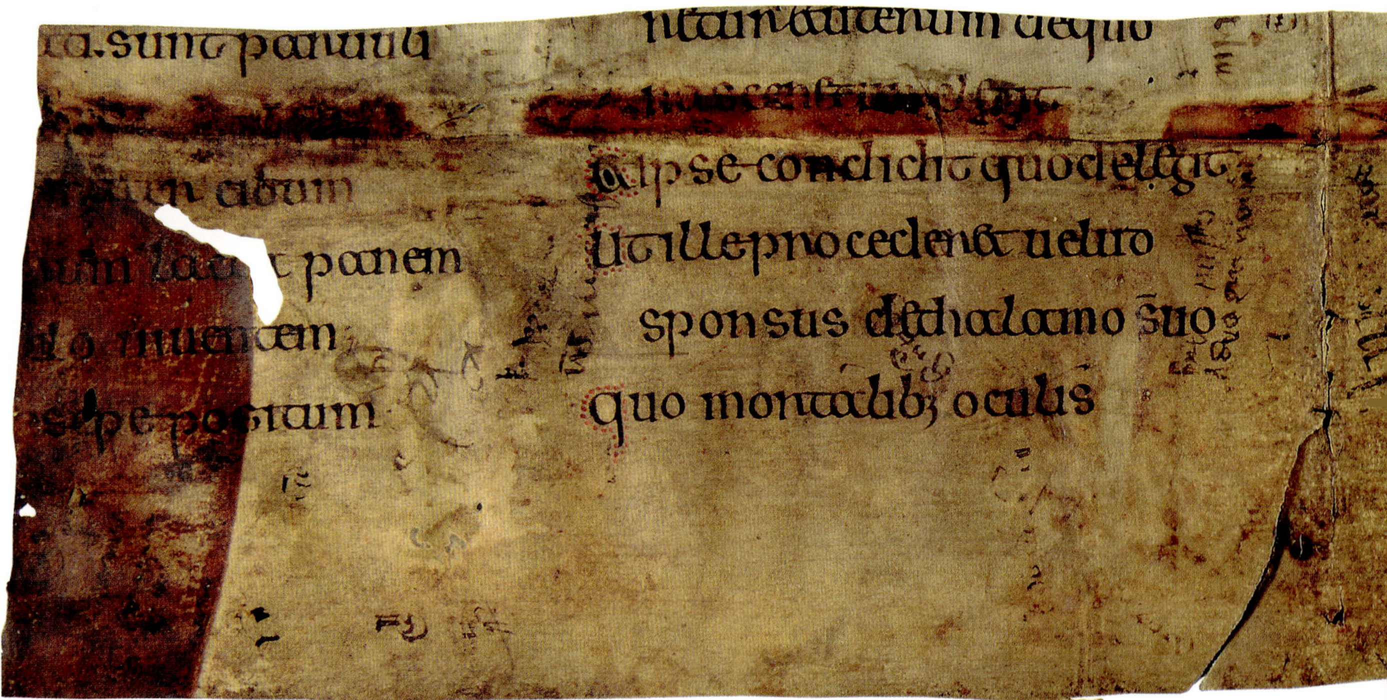

been made in Durham itself, for it is actually made from a fragment of the Christmas liturgy, otherwise unparalleled, written in Northumbria in the eighth century.

Two of the books at Ushaw contained original loose letters from several monks. They date from the 1520s and are written in Latin and English. One is to William Wylom, who used it for his notes. He was the last keeper of the shrine of St Cuthbert before its destruction on the orders of Henry VIII, so he may have been involved in the saving of St Cuthbert's ring, which subsequently passed through Catholic hands (see following pages).

The translation of Ranulph Higden's *Polycronicon* (1495) is the only one of the earliest printed books held at Ushaw to be written in English. All the others are in Latin, the latest being an edition of Erasmus's *Liber de praeparatione ad mortem …* (1534). The book's inscription uses the form of address given to a monk rather than a canon: 'dean Nicholas Marley'. Considering the already highlighted role of the Tempests in the books' survival, it is unsurprising that he was related to the family; it was with them that he took refuge before escaping to the University of Louvain situated in the Low Countries.

A.I. DOYLE

Several books from Durham Cathedral Priory are held at Ushaw. One was bound in a fragment of the Christmas liturgy, here pictured, which was written in Northumbria in the eighth century.

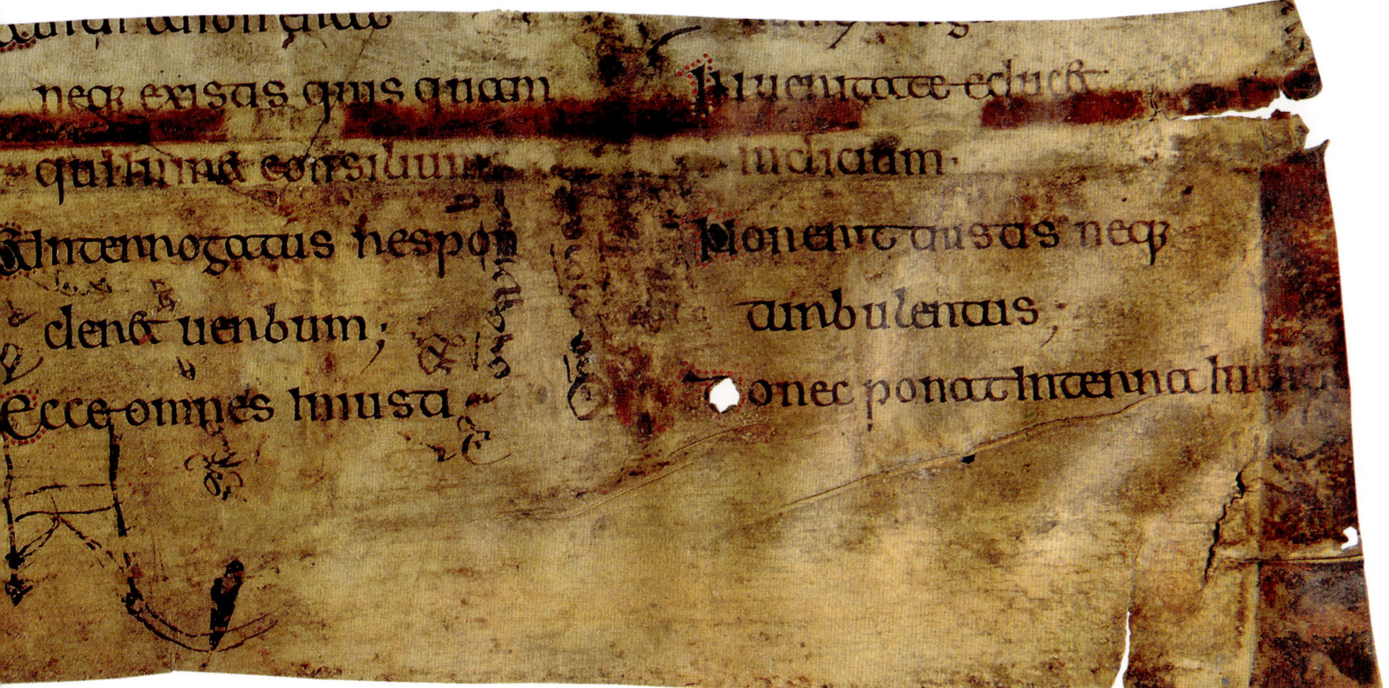

St Cuthbert's Ring

Gold and sapphire ring, thirteenth century

Surviving from pre-Reformation times, the story of St Cuthbert's ring is one tied inextricably to that of proscribed Catholicism.

The shrine of St Cuthbert (d.687), located behind Durham Cathedral's high altar, was a major site of pilgrimage in the medieval period, with people travelling long distances to venerate the tomb of the seventh-century bishop of Lindisfarne. St Cuthbert's ring – made of solid gold with a large uncut hexagonal sapphire in an irregular mount – dates from the thirteenth century and this medieval period of veneration. It was most likely a gift left by a wealthy pilgrim, perhaps for some favour done by the saint.

Along with most other shrines, that of St Cuthbert was destroyed in 1542 during Henry VIII's dissolution of the monasteries. Thomas Watson (1515–84), a pupil at Durham Priory school, later dean of Durham and then bishop of Lincoln under Mary I, came into possession of the ring; Nicholas Harpsfield, archdeacon of Canterbury under Mary I, alleged in his *Historia Anglicana Ecclesiastica* that it was taken from the finger of St Cuthbert in 1537, when it was evident which way the religious winds were blowing in Henrician England. Whether it was Watson or one of the monks who did the rescuing is not known. Nevertheless, Watson would spend the last 25 years of his life in jail for refusing to recognise Elizabeth I as head of the Church in England.

At some point, Watson passed the ring to the recusant antiquarian, Robert Hare (*c.*1530–1611), who in turn gave it to Anthony Maria Browne, second Viscount Montague (1574–1629). Montague's chaplain was a priest called Richard Smith (1568–1655), who would subsequently be named Bishop of Chalcedon, in what was effectively the first attempt to create a vicar apostolic to oversee the Catholic community in England since the Reformation. The move was highly controversial amongst the persecuted Catholic community, many believing such an appointment would further provoke the authorities, and Smith was, in the end, forced to retreat to France, the nation of his patron, Cardinal Richelieu.

Here he helped found an English community of Augustinian Canonesses in Paris. He spent the remaining 13 years of his life living with them in the grounds of the convent and was buried in the convent church in March 1655. To their protection he left St Cuthbert's ring and it remained with the community for the next 200 years.

According to the canonesses, it was kept in an 'oval, wood gilt reliquary' of 'dark coloured gold, with a layer [of] sapphire in it'. The original reliquary is not held at Ushaw and its whereabouts are unknown.

The sisters recorded that all visitors to their convent viewed the ring as a genuine relic and it was held in high esteem by the community. Every year they displayed it for public veneration in their church on the feast of St Cuthbert.

Unusually amongst English exile communities, the Paris Augustinian house remained in its adoptive homeland after the French Revolution. Travelling back and forth between the Continent, Nicholas Wiseman – the future Cardinal Archbishop of Westminster following Catholic Emancipation in 1829 and the restoration of the Catholic hierarchy in 1850 – regularly visited the convent to venerate the relic.

In the mid-1850s he wrote to the community about 'the College of St Cuthbert at Ushaw,' which is 'without exception the noblest establishment in England,' boasting a splendid chapel dedicated to St Cuthbert but lacking 'a particle of his relics' or even 'an object that belonged to him'. Indeed, England's Catholic community possessed no relics of the medieval bishop and he asked the community if they would be willing to send the ring. This the community did, expressing their delight that their custodianship of the Catholic past had resulted in the ring's reinstatement to its former geographical home.

From that point on, the Bishop of Hexham and

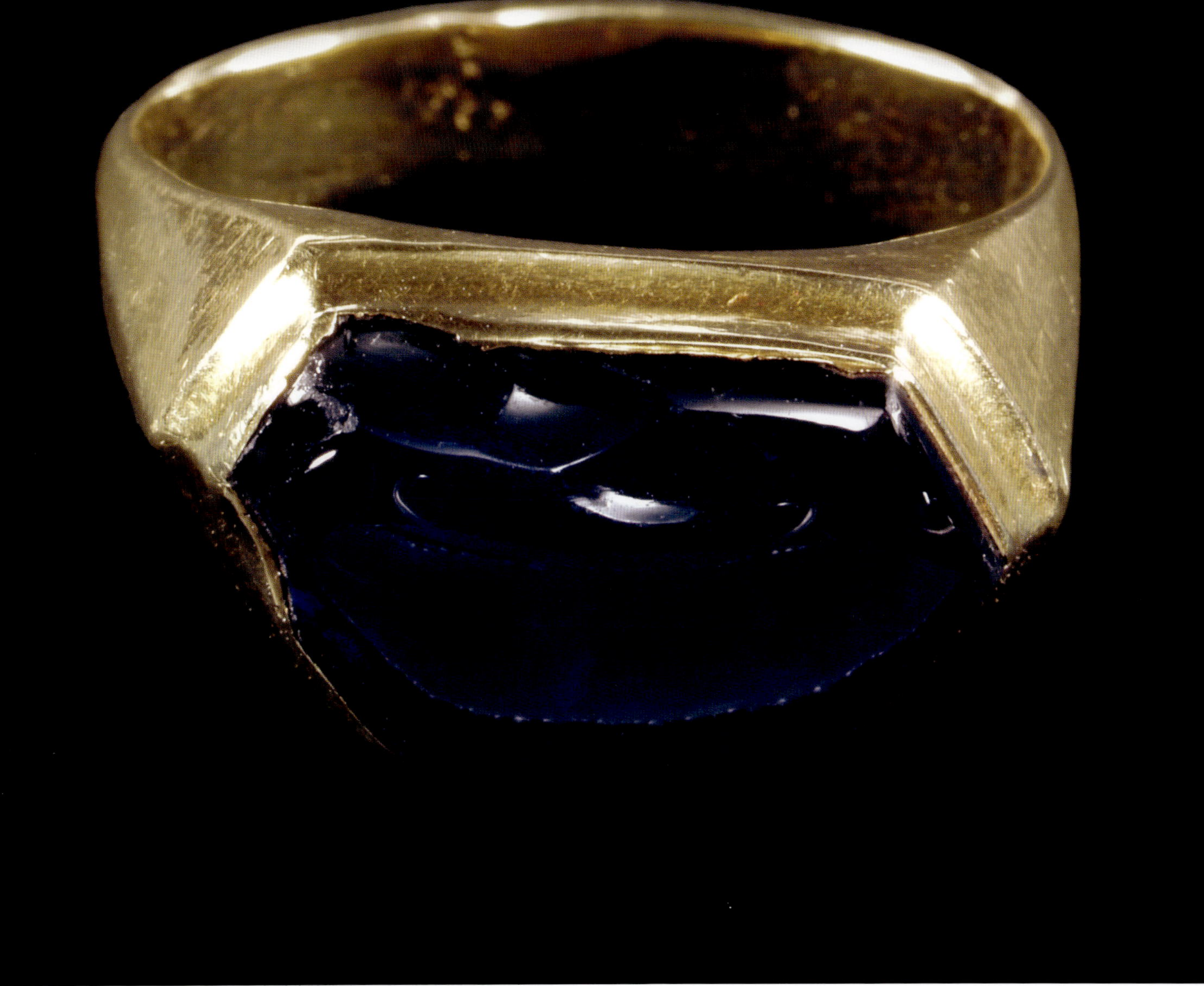

Newcastle – and, in later years, every bishop – arriving at St Cuthbert's College, Ushaw, to perform an ordination would wear the ring of St Cuthbert during the ceremony, establishing a material link to his medieval forbears.

JAMES E. KELLY

The story of St Cuthbert's ring and how it came to be at Ushaw is closely linked to that of proscribed Catholicsim in England.

A Rare Fourteenth-Century Survival

Esh stole and maniple panels, 1330–50

This stole and maniple belong to an era when English embroidery had reached its artistic peak and was eagerly sought-after by rulers and leading clerics throughout Western Europe. Documentary evidence indicates that sets of vestments, copes and, occasionally, just orphreys were given as diplomatic gifts by a succession of English monarchs between the mid-thirteenth and mid-fourteenth centuries. As a consequence, more examples of thirteenth- and fourteenth-century English embroidery are preserved in continental treasuries than in England. A Vatican inventory of 1295 lists over a hundred embroideries as English work and such was the demand that two popes in the third quarter of the thirteenth century employed a gold embroiderer, Gregory of London, to undertake work for the papal household for which he was paid an annual salary of 15 marks. Workshops established in London also often spent years producing a single item. For example, four needlewomen took three years and nine months to embroider a frontal for the high altar of Westminster Abbey, which was completed in 1271.

The Esh panels, although modest in scale, are, therefore, rare examples of a special style of English embroidery known as *opus anglicanum* to be preserved in their country of origin. Given to the college by Canon Harris of nearby Esh Hall, nothing further is known of their history. They are worked in silver-gilt thread, which is spun round a core of white silk, and coloured silks in underside couching and split stitch on a linen ground. The colours are limited to a delicate palette of blue, green, yellow, pink, brown and off-white with touches of crimson silk in a trefoil on the stole. The outlining in black silk is part of the restoration work performed by the Poor Clare community then resident at Darlington. Although it attempts to copy that on the original vestments, the stem-stitching by the nuns looks crude in comparison and demonstrates how skilful the embroiderers were in the fourteenth century when extremely fine thread and fine needles would have been used. Fortunately, the subtle background patterns worked in metal thread – and now extremely worn – remain untouched.

The three bearded apostles and crowned female saints portrayed on the panels are representative types rather than identifiable individuals bearing specific attributes. Each is enveloped in a cloak wrapped around a full-length robe stitched in a contrasting colour. The women's cloaks are fur lined whereas the men are shown with bare feet. The combination of alternating male and female figures is unusual for a stole and maniple where male figures, whether apostles, saints or prophets, appear to have been more typical, based both on the evidence of surviving examples and written sources.

FRANCES PRITCHARD

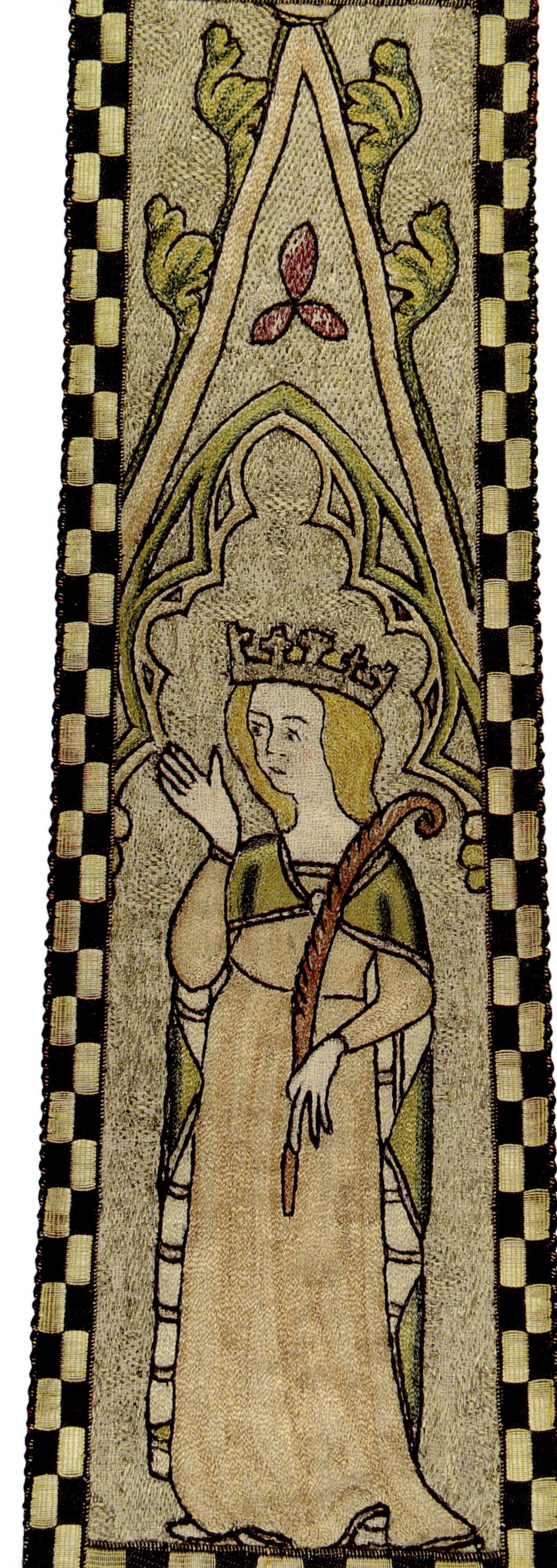

Esh stole and maniple panels, 1330–50. Dimensions of stole panels: height 27.5 to 33.5 cm, width 6 to 7.8 cm. Dimensions of maniple panels: height 35 cm, maximum width 7.5 cm.

Exporting Private Prayer

Horae (Sarum rites), Bruges, *c.*1408–9. Ushaw, MS 10

On 21 January 1409, in Bruges, a scribe called John Heineman finished writing the text of a Book of Hours – the private prayer-book of late medieval and Renaissance laity – appending to the final item these very details plus a request for the reader's prayers. The start of subdivisions within his volume were marked with a decorated initial plus border bars, sometimes enhanced with stock drolleries that range from the diverting (birds, hybrids, an amorous couple, a virgin with a unicorn) to the bawdy (a defecating monk). In addition, 24 full-page miniatures – some inserted on separate sheets of parchment, others an integral part of the structure of the book – depict: saints who are the subject of suffrages; the events of the Passion (for the Hours of the Virgin); plus Virgin and Child, Pieta, Last Judgement, Saved Souls, Christ as man of sorrows, and St Jerome for appropriate texts.

If the generous use of gold and lapis lazuli confirms that this was a costly albeit not extravagant volume, its 'production-line' nature reflects its origin in the commercial book trade: its scribe and artists were busy professionals whose hands reappear both together and separately in other manuscripts, and they were adept at expediting their work. The crucial importance of this book in particular is that, thanks to John's note, it is precisely dated and localised, meaning that other manuscripts linked to it by shared hands and styles provide a critical mass of evidence for the book-trade in Bruges at the beginning of the fifteenth century. The oeuvre in question not only reveals the ready flow of scribal and artistic styles around north-west Europe *c.*1400 (parallels can be found in northern Germany and southern England as well as the Netherlands), it also shows how international was the book-trade itself, for booksellers in Bruges deliberately targeted overseas as well as home markets. In fact, the great majority of the manuscripts associable with our scribe and artists are *Horae* of Sarum rites – thus exclusively appropriate and evidently destined for England.

That this work rapidly passed into English ownership is proven by the series of prayers and other notes in English (including a poem in honour of King Henry VI, who died in 1471) that were added by various fifteenth- and early sixteenth-century hands. Equally, its current binding is probably English work of the early sixteenth century. Happily, the owners in question are identifiable: a couplet added to the calendar is signed by a sketch of a chess-rook plus 'clyff' – the rebus of Brian Roucliffe, a baron of the exchequer who died in 1495. Bequeathing the book to his son, John, Sir Brian further revealed that he had himself received it from a Margaret Burgh (probably his grandmother) who had in turn acquired it from a certain Elizabeth Elyngham, and she was demonstrably of the right age to have procured it fresh from the pen of John Heineman in 1409.

In sum, this charming volume is a vital document for book production and decoration in the southern Netherlands in the early fifteenth century; it provides an early glimpse of the export trade in books from the Low Countries to England that flourished then and thereafter; and it offers vivid insight into the central role that Books of Hours – a potent mix of piety, *objet d'art*, status symbol and heirloom – played in the spiritual life of the laity prior to the Reformation.

RICHARD GAMESON

A couplet and signature added to the calendar show that the book was once owned by Brian Roucliffe, a baron of the exchequer who died in 1495.

Aprilis.

Kl Denus et undenus est mortis vulnere plenus.

xv		g	Kl. Walerici abbatis
iiii	xi	A	
		b	Ricardi episcopi
xii		c	Ambrosii episcopi
i		d	N.
	xviii	e	Sixti pape et martyris
ix	v	f	
		g	Id.
xvii	xiii	A	Marie egypciace
vi	ii	b	Leonis pape et conf.
		c	Guthlaci conf.
xiiii	x	d	Id.
iii		e	Id.
	xviii	f	Tyburcii et Valeriani
xi	vii	g	
		A	
xix	xv	b	
viii	iiii	c	
		d	Alphegi archiepiscopi et martyris
	xii	e	Victoris martyris
	i	f	
		g	
	ix	A	Georgii martyris
		b	
	xvii	c	Marci euangeliste
	vi	d	
		e	
	xiiii	f	Vitalis martyris
	iii	g	Petri martyris
		A	

The next sonday after the blak pryme
shall be pasche day. hold so it tyme

· M Rclyff ·

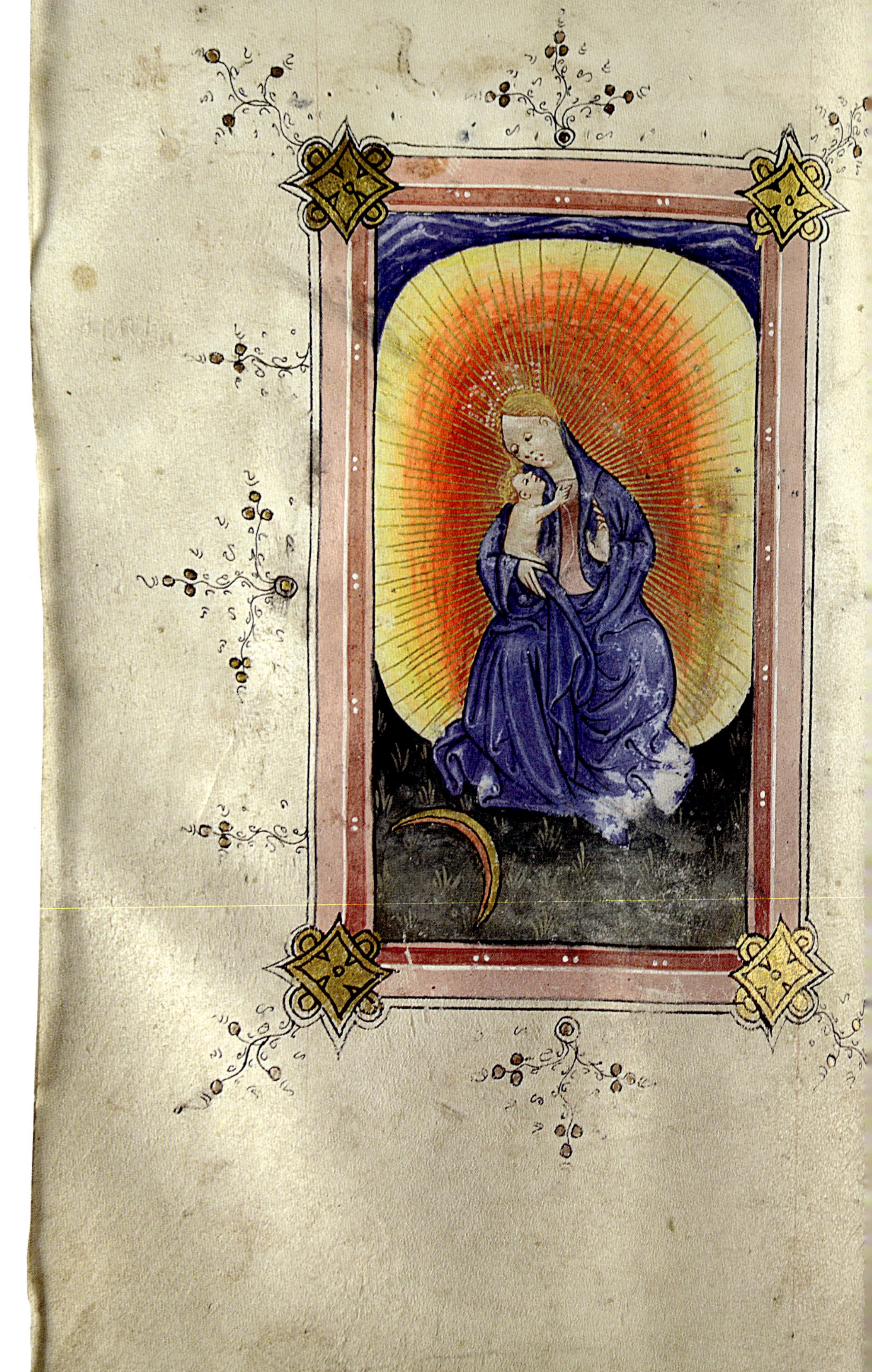

This fifteenth-century Book of Hours was produced in Bruges for the English market.

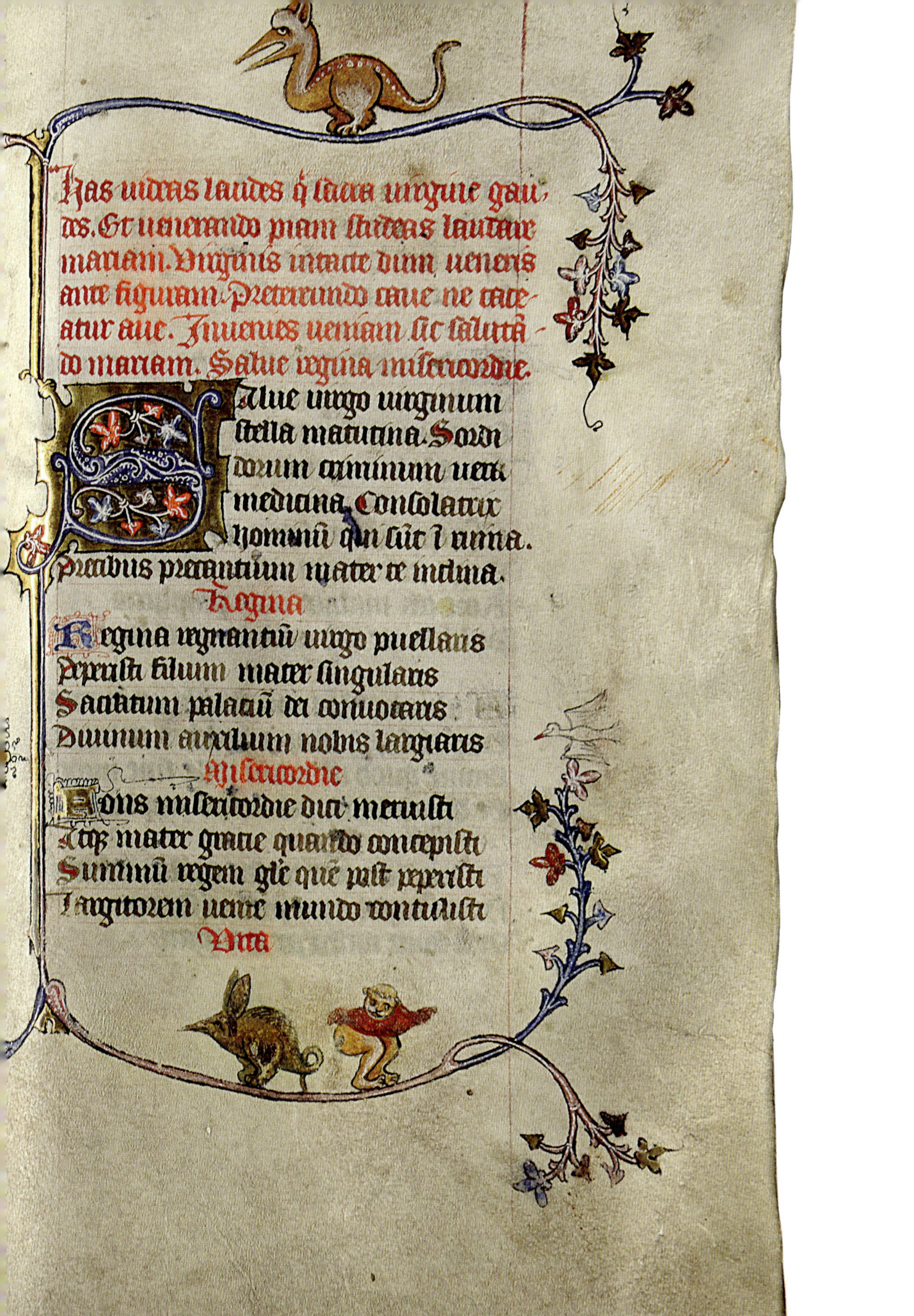

Has uideas laudes q sacra uirgine gau-
des. Et uenerando piam studeas laudare
mariam. Virginis intacte dum ueneris
ante figuram. Pretereundo caue ne tace-
atur aue. Inuenies ueniam sic salutã-
do mariam. Salue regina misericordie.

Salue uirgo uirginum
stella matutina. Sordi-
dorum criminum uera
medicina. Consolatrix
hominũ qui sunt i ruina.
Precibus precantium mater et medina.

Regina

Regina regnantiũ uirgo puellaris
Peperisti filium mater singularis
Sanctitatum palaciũ dei conuocaris
Diuinum auxilium nobis largiaris

Misericordie

Fons misericordie dici meruisti
Cũ mater gratie quando concepisti
Summũ regem glie quẽ post peperisti
Largitorem uenie mundo contulisti

Vita

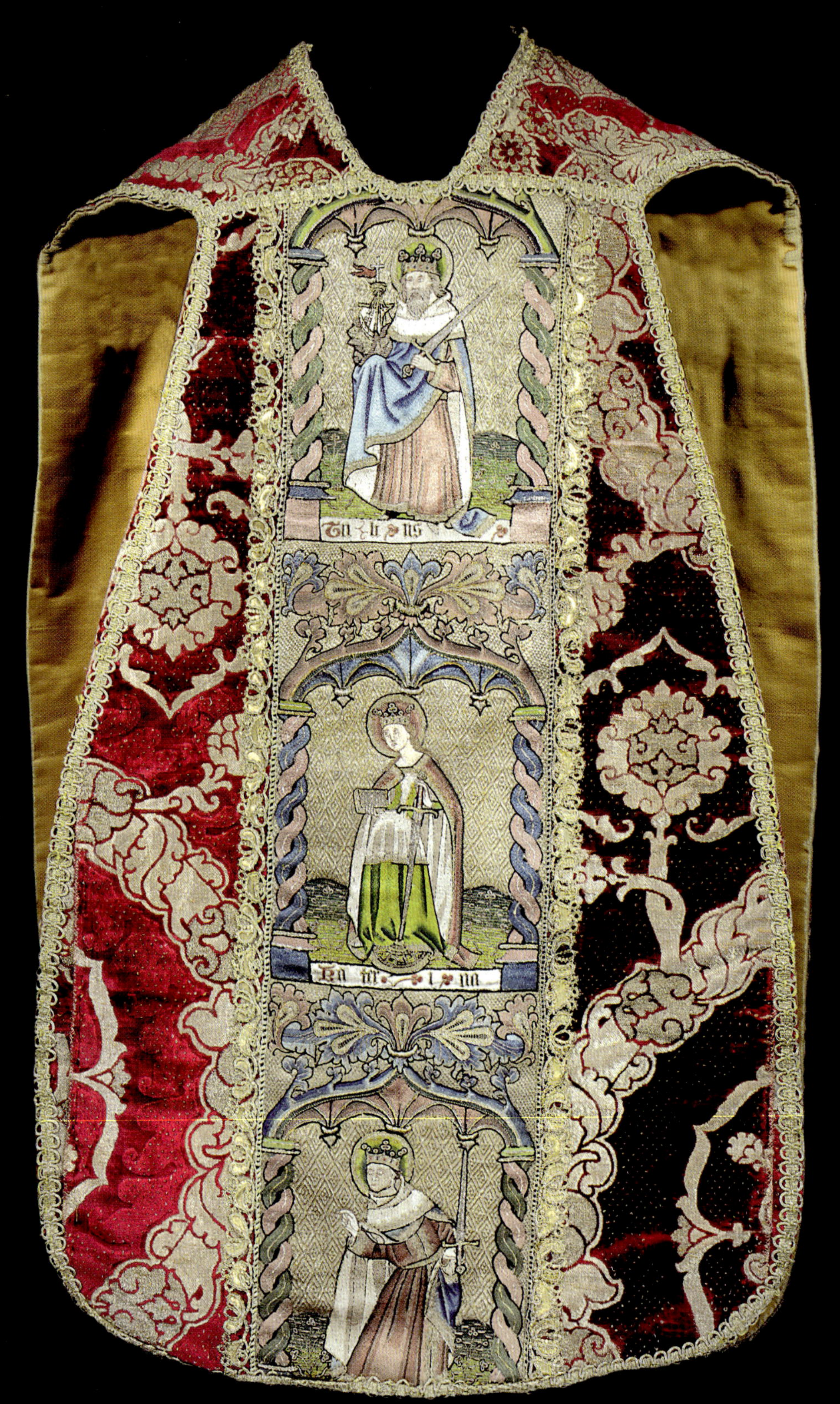

A Royal Link

Westminster vestment, 1460–90

Presented to Ushaw College in 1867 by Fr R. Gibson, this chasuble's history can be traced back to the preceding century when it was bequeathed by Bishop William Walton, Vicar Apostolic of the Northern District and Titular Bishop of Trachonitis, to his nephew, also William Walton, in 1780. According to a family tradition the vestment was used at Westminster Abbey before the Reformation but there is no surviving evidence to corroborate this. Nevertheless, the catalogue of the Richard III Centenary Exhibition in 1973 suggests that the chasuble belonged to the royal wardrobe of Richard III.

The chasuble is notable for the sumptuous velvet cloths of tissue used in its construction and for the superb quality of its embroidered orphreys. The shape of the vestment suggests that it was cut down during the seventeenth century and it is probable that the two different velvets were combined at this period. The velvet forming the back – a crimson velvet cloth of tissue with two heights of cut pile with details in uncut pile and loops of silver-gilt brocading thread – dates to the third quarter of the fifteenth century. By contrast, the velvet forming the front panel, and the 23 scraps which were made into a matching maniple and stole, dates to the early sixteenth century.

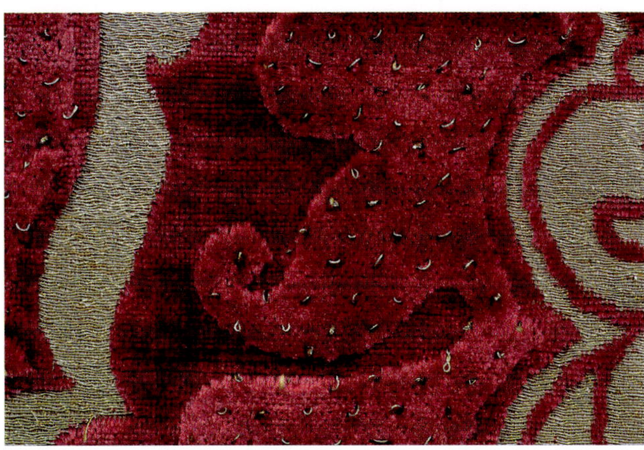

Left: The Westminster vestment, 1460–90, height 114.5 cm, maximum width 75 cm.

Above: The superb quality of the vestment's embroidered orphreys.

The embroidery is executed in what was then a modern Flemish style. It employs an *or nué* (shaded gold) technique and the figures are subtly modelled using a variety of coloured silks on gold backgrounds worked with raised diaper patterns. The skilful shading is very apparent in the portrayal of the crucifixion. Below stands the centurion Longinus holding a scroll inscribed with the words from St Mark's Gospel, *Vere filius Dei erat iste* (Truly that [man] was the Son of God). Longinus is dressed in fashionable, figure-hugging plate armour, a fur-lined cloak and voluminous hat. In addition to a sword and dagger, he holds a lance, the weapon with which he pierced Christ's side. Remarkably, a cross-orphrey of almost identical design is preserved on a chasuble now in the Victoria and Albert Museum in London, indicating that both were based on the same cartoon, although differences in the choice of threads and degree of expertise suggests that they are not the products of the same hand.

The pillar orphrey on the front is embroidered in matching style with three saints, each of whom is named in an inscription positioned below the figure. At the top, a crowned saint holds a ship in his right hand and a sword in his left. The name has been read as 'Tulius' but it may be an abbreviation for St Nicholas, the patron saint of merchants and sailors. Next is St Catherine standing on a wheel. At the bottom is St Pancras, whose name is now concealed by the lining. A teenage martyr, who was beheaded in 304, he is depicted in an elegant S-shaped pose. The choice of this saint is unique in English embroidery and provides a clue as to the commission of the work. Perhaps the wealthy donor worshipped at the parish church of St Pancras situated in Soper Lane, London, close to where many embroiderers and silkwomen lived and worked at this time.

FRANCES PRITCHARD

A Reminder of the Last Catholic Bishop of Durham

Tunstall vestment, *c.*1470

According to tradition, this chasuble belonged to the Prince-Bishop of Durham Cuthbert Tunstall (1474–1559), commonly referred to as the last Catholic bishop of Durham. He was deprived of his bishopric and died under house arrest in Lambeth Palace for refusing to take the Oath of Supremacy recognising Elizabeth I as head of the Church in England. The vestment later passed by marriage to the Trappes family and in 1866 the Rev M. Trappes presented it to Ushaw College. Following a dispute over ownership, the chasuble was transferred for a short time to Jesuit-run Stonyhurst College, Lancashire, but in 1903 it returned to Ushaw.

The chasuble underwent extensive restoration in the 1930s by the Poor Clares of Darlington when fragments of the ground fabric were pieced together to give it a 'gothic' shape with a wider shoulder line. This resulted in all the original mid-fifteenth-century crimson velvet cloth of tissue being used to form the back of the vestment and a contrasting modern red and yellow floral-patterned velvet was chosen for the front. At the same time the orphreys were applied in a far from authentic arrangement and there remains minimal evidence of their original layout. There is also very little of the original embroidery stitching preserved apart from the diaper and chevron-patterned backgrounds worked in silver-gilt *filé* thread.

On a cross orphrey the usual convention was to depict the crucifixion as the centrepiece. As each figure is shown here in an architectural framework with an acanthus-leaf canopy, it is probable that this orphrey is made from panels that have been rearranged and that the original centrepiece is missing. The central scene appears to show St Stephen in the act of being stoned. He wears the dress of a deacon with an open-sided dalmatic over an alb, but his headwear argues against this identification. On the left is St Thomas holding a book and a spear, the emblem of his martyrdom in India, and on the right is St Andrew with a saltire cross. Below, holding a tower with three windows symbolising the Trinity, is St Barbara, a female saint who featured in the *Golden Legend*, a book about the lives of saints that was popular in the fifteenth century and printed in an English translation by William Caxton in 1483. Two figures are portrayed on the front pillar orphrey, both enclosed within similar canopies, but neither can be easily identified either from their dress or attributes.

The vestment, therefore, does not in itself provide any evidence to link it to Cuthbert Tunstall. The iconographic programme of the orphreys is elusive and the costly velvet cloth of tissue was produced before Tunstall was born. Valuable old textiles were often given to churches to be recycled. For example, Sir William Estfeld (d.1463), a mercer and alderman of the city of London, bequeathed his personal apparel of silk and gold to be converted into vestments. Thus, it is probable that the Tunstall vestment too has undergone various phases of recycling.

FRANCES PRITCHARD

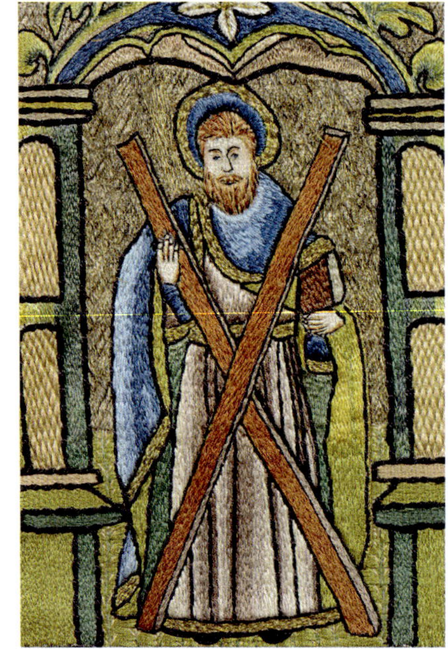

St Andrew holding the saltire cross upon which he was martyred.

Right: The Tunstall vestment, *c.*1470 with later alterations, height 120 cm, maximum width 100 cm.

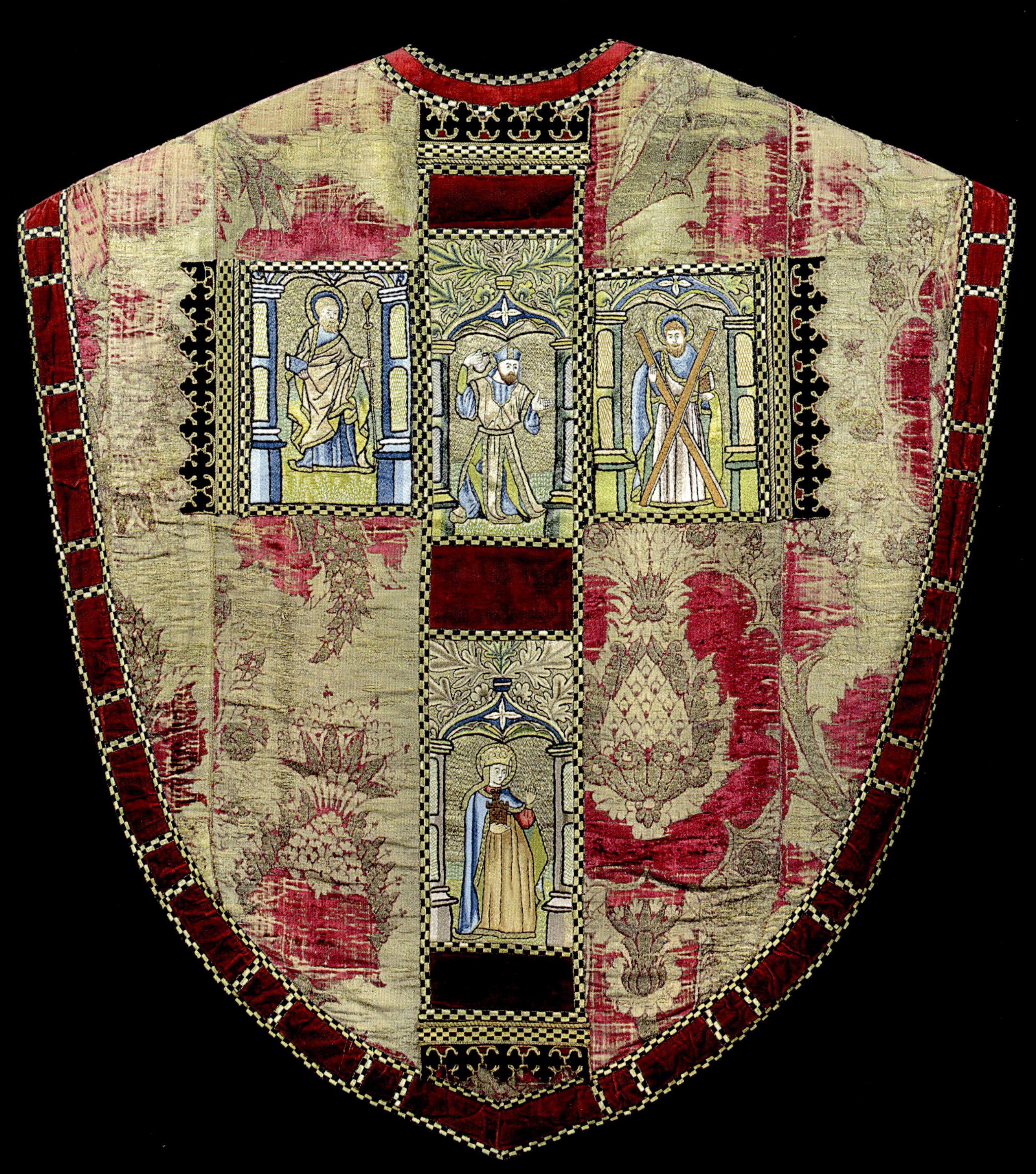

The Esh Missal

Missal combining the Sarum and York rites, late fifteenth century. Ushaw MS 5

This beautiful missal was given to the parochial chapel of Esh in County Durham by Master John Rudd, Bachelor of Laws, who died in November 1490. His gift is commemorated in a note at the end of its canon, asking for prayers for his soul, presumably added after his death. The date of his gift is unknown.

John was the son of Thomas Rudd of Allertonshire and had been given a scholarship to Durham College, Oxford, by Durham Priory in 1446. His candidature was backed by two well-known lawyers who worked for the bishop and prior: Sir James Strangeways and Robert Danby. In 1459 he became Bachelor of Laws and can later be found as a lawyer acting for both the bishop and the priory of Durham. He became dean of Lanchester collegiate church with Esh as part of his prebend. In 1490 he was buried in Lanchester church with a memorial plaque.

The missal is of good quality with gold lettering and fine pen flourishing. It now lacks a few pages and is in a modern binding (from Andrews of Durham). It has several corrections and some marginal additions, including some music. The liturgy envisaged is odd, combining Sarum rite with a canon of the York use. Lanchester College, set up by Anthony Bec in 1284, allowed either Sarum or York to be used, so Rudd may have had the missal specially produced. It has many signs of use, including a note that four pieces of land have been given to the chapel to sustain a light, with the signature of John Walche, curate of Esh. His date, alas, has been lost with a page of the text but the hand is early sixteenth century.

The effects of the Reformation under Henry VIII can be seen here, though the erasures are patchy. Where on Good Friday the people would have prayed for 'papa N', 'papa' has been erased, though the rest of the prayer is still totally visible. Likewise, where in the Canon people, pope and king are to be prayed for, 'papa' is erased and 'henrico' has been added in the margin and 'Rex Henricus' added at the foot of the page, presumably to remind the priest what he must say. 'Papa' has been erased also from the attribution of an indulgenced prayer to 'Johannes papa'. In a similar way the whole of one prayer for the Translation of St Thomas à Becket has been scored through, though it is still legible, but the feast of St Peter's Chair remains untouched, as does an indulgenced prayer by Pope Clement VI.

In 1622 Esh Hall came into the hands of the recusant Smythe family whose descendant in 1808 sold the land upon which Ushaw College was to be built. The missal presumably came at this time as part of the deal, travelling the two miles to the new college, leaving for the first time the chapel to which it had been given in the fifteenth century. The parish at Esh no longer exists. This book is a rare example of an ordinary, non-luxury Mass book, made with the needs of a priest primarily in mind.

MARGARET HARVEY

This fifteenth-century missal was rescued at the Reformation by the Catholic family on whose land Ushaw was built, making it the only pre-Reformation parish liturgical book which has never left the parish for which it was first bought. During the Reformation, the word for the Pope was scrubbed out and Henry VIII's name inserted in its place.

Te igitur cle
mentissi
me pater
per ihesum christum
filium tuum dominum nostrum supplices
rogamus ac petimus ·
Hic erigens se sacerdos
osculetur altare et dex
tris sacrificii dicens uti
accepta habeas et benedi
cas hec + dona hec
+ munera · hec sancta
+ sacrificia illibata
Factis signaculis super ca
licem eleuet sacerdos
manus suas et dicens
In primis que tibi offeri
mus pro ecclesia tua sancta ca
tholica quam pacifica
re · custodire · adunare
et regere digneris
toto orbe terrarum una
cum famulo tuo papa nostro
N. et antistite nostro N.
Et rege nostro N.
Et hic nominetur [illegible]
et omnibus orthodoxis at
que catholice et apostolice fi
dei cultoribus Hic oret
sacerdos cogitando pro vi
Memento domine
domine famulorum fa
mularumque tuarum N. et N.
et omnium circumstantium
atque omnium fidelium christia
norum quorum tibi fides cog

nita est et nota deuotio
pro quibus tibi offerimus
vel qui tibi offerunt hoc
sacrificium laudis pro
se suisque omnibus pro redemp
tione animarum suarum pro spe
salutis et incolumitatis
sue tibique reddunt vo
ta sua eterno deo viuo
et vero Sequatur
Communicantes et
memoriam venerantes
In primis gloriose semper
virginis marie parum
inclinando dicat genitri
cis dei et domini nostri ihesu christi
Sed et beatorum apostolorum
ac martirum tuorum Petri
Pauli Andree Ia
cobi Iohannis Thome
Iacobi Philippi
Bartholomei Ma
thei Symonis et Ta
ddei Lini Cleti
Clementis Sixti
Cornelii Cypriani
Laurencii Griso
goni Iohannis et Pau
li Cosme et Dami
ani Et omnium sanctorum tuorum quorum
meritis precibusque
concedas ut in omnibus
protectionis tue muniamur
auxilio Per christum dominum ./. eundem
nostrum amen Hic respiciat
sacerdos hostiam dum

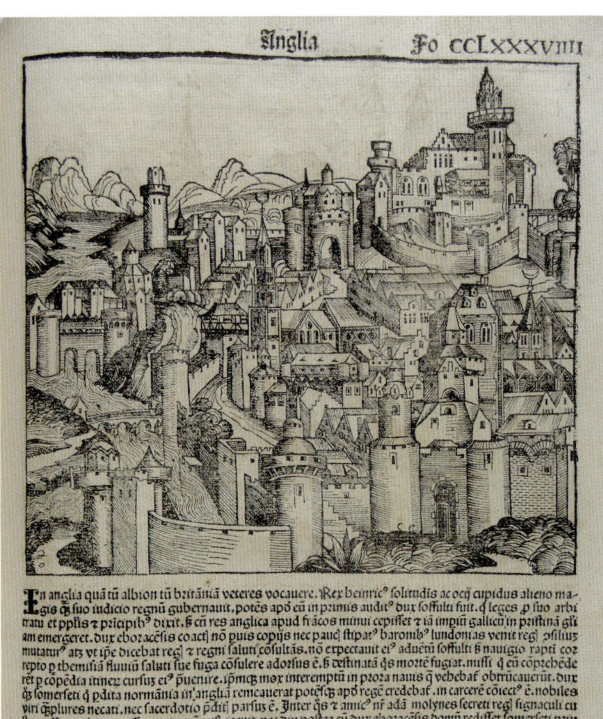

Anglia Fo CCLXXXVIII

De Scocia

De Hibernia

The original *World Chronicle*, printed in Nuremberg in 1493.

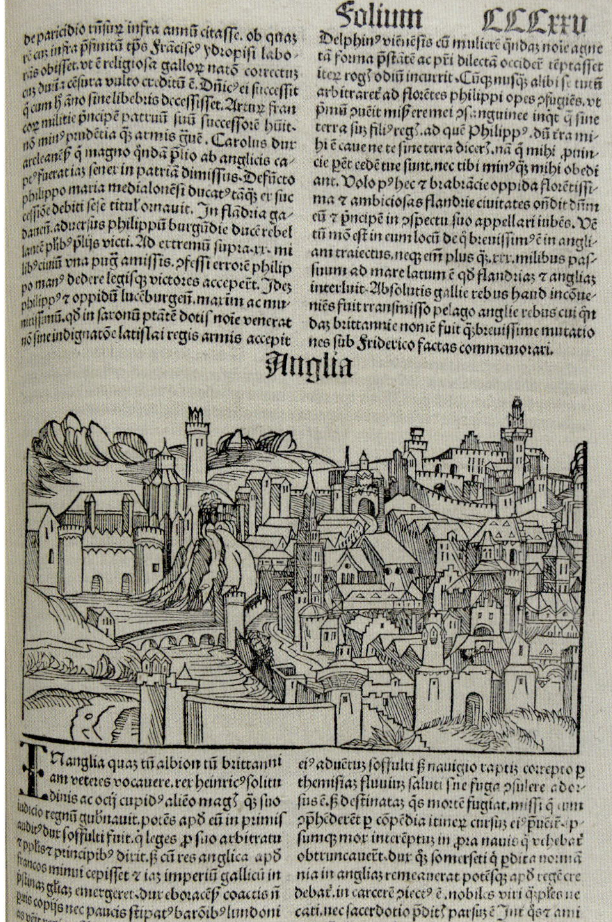

Folium CCCxxv

Anglia

The same, less detailed, image from the pirated copy published in Augsburg in 1497.

An Act of Piracy

Hartmann Schedel, *Liber chronicarum*, Nuremberg, 1493; Augsburg, 1497.
Ushaw, XVIII.G.3.16, XVIII.B.3.4

The *Liber chronicarum* of 1493, also known as the *World Chronicle*, *Nuremberg Chronicle* or *Schedel's Chronicle*, stood in a tradition of world chronicles – one-volume surveys of world history – that stretched back several centuries. Hartmann Schedel (1440–1514, physician) drew on previous chronicles and the Bible to compile his version, recording the six ages of the world.

The *World Chronicle* was printed by Anton Koberger (1440/1445–1513) as part of a venture financed by Sebald Schreyer and Sebastian Kamermaister, with the cooperation of the artistic house of Michael Wolgemut and Wilhelm Pleydenwurff. Printers often instigated a project, but the *World Chronicle* was the brainchild of Schreyer and Kamermaister. Printing projects were incredibly expensive to undertake; at minimum, a venture would require outlay for the paper or parchment, the type for the letters and the woodcuts for illustrations, plus wages. The *World Chronicle*, with over 1,800 woodcut images, and issued in both Latin and German editions, was the most complex book printed in the fifteenth century. Based on the contracts in the Nuremberg City Archive, Koberger's financial involvement was limited to purchasing the paper, for which he was reimbursed by the financial backers, Schreyer and Kamermaister, who themselves underwrote the venture as a whole.

As printing schemes were expensive and were slow to produce financial returns, elaborate plans could quickly ruin a printer or financier. The *World Chronicle* was no exception: Schreyer and Kammermaister could only recoup their outlay once the books sold. Since so much money and time was invested (according to the contracts, the project was in planning stages up to two years before copies were available), secrecy was essential to prevent competition from rivals: the contract with Koberger stipulated that he keep all proofs in a designated room and return all spoiled sheets to the financiers. But once the book had been published, it was vulnerable to plagiarism and indeed it was copied only a few years later by Johann Schensperger in Augsburg. His version of 1497 used exactly the same text as, and similar but smaller illustrations than, Koberger's Latin edition. Clearly Schensperger believed that the production of a pirated edition was worth the outlay. Whether or not he made much profit, his more economical version seems to have affected sales of Koberger's editions: the 1509 accounts of the Nuremberg venture reveal that many copies remained unsold, attributed to the undercutting by Schensperger's pirated edition.

Ushaw College has the rare privilege of owning both the original *World Chronicle* in Latin and the pirated edition. Both editions may have belonged to the Durham Cathedral Priory library and were dispersed at the priory's dissolution in 1539. The original edition was owned by the Morisot family from the fifteenth to seventeenth centuries. The pirated edition spent time in the personal library of Thomas Horsley in the late sixteenth and early seventeenth centuries, then in that of Thomas Eyre, who became the first president of what would become Ushaw College in the late eighteenth century. It has been housed at Ushaw ever since.

KATHERINE KRICK

Opus Anglicanum Chasuble

Powdered velvet chasuble, *c.*1500

Made from imported red silk velvet with plain cut pile, the surface is powdered with applied motifs. On the back there are staggered rows of seraphim, fleurs de lis and lilies, which are sometimes referred to as 'water flowers' in contemporary inventories, and on the front pomegranates, which are more sparsely spaced. They are worked in silver-gilt *filé* thread and coloured silks on a linen or silk ground and tiny spangles add to the embellishment.

The shape of the vestment has been cut down as shown by the truncated powdered motifs on the back and the front. The blue, woad-dyed linen lining is probably original but the orphreys superimposed on the powdered ground do not match one another and are probably later additions. The same applies to the seventeenth-century bobbin lace worked in metal thread that trims the outer edge.

The cross orphrey and a pillar orphrey are similar in their general style but differences can be detected: for example, in the architectural details of the canopies, column capitals and the golden-patterned backgrounds. On the cross orphrey, the central scene shows Christ crucified. Below is St Peter holding a large key and at the bottom is a Church Father or prophet with a forked beard, who wears a hood, hat and wide-sleeved gown. The figures on the pillar orphrey are, reading from the bottom upwards, St Paul, who holds a sword in his right hand and a thick book in the crook of his left arm; a figure in a blue gown wearing a small pointed hat, which some have suggested is St Jerome; and a saint, identified as St Matthias, the disciple who replaced Judas Iscariot as an apostle. This identification is aided by a similar representation of the apostle with a halberd on the mid-fourteenth-century Butler Bowden cope, which is held at the Victoria and Albert Museum in London.

After the Reformation many church vestments embroidered with sacred subjects were destroyed or converted for other uses. This vestment is therefore a beautiful survivor and is in remarkable condition for its age. However, nothing is known of the history of this chasuble and there is little in its iconography to provide a clue as to its original ownership. Ushaw did receive numerous gifts during the nineteenth century, largely from Catholic families who had concealed pre-reformation vestments and church plate throughout the penal era and were then eager for them to be openly used again in a Catholic setting.

Like many English vestments of the late fifteenth and early sixteenth centuries it was made in a workshop, probably located in London, to a standard formula. Ordinances of the Brouderers drawn up in 1495 stipulated that any manner of embroidered work such as flowers, images or orphreys set upon velvet, satin and damask must be carried out in 'fyne gold, fyne silver and right silke'. The different powdered motifs were cut using templates so that they could be mass-produced. However, finding exact matches on different vestments is not easy, suggesting that there may have been more workshops operating than is sometimes supposed. The seraphim here stand on four-spoked wheels with their uppermost pair of feathered wings crossed behind their heads. Radiating from the wheels are 15 surface-couched gold rays with rows of spangles in between. A comparative example of a vestment decorated in this manner is the cope of Cardinal Morton, Archbishop of Canterbury (d.1500), indicating that the style was popular even among the most powerful prelates in the land at the time.

FRANCES PRITCHARD

Opus anglicanum chasuble, *c.*1500, height 118 cm, maximum width 82 cm.

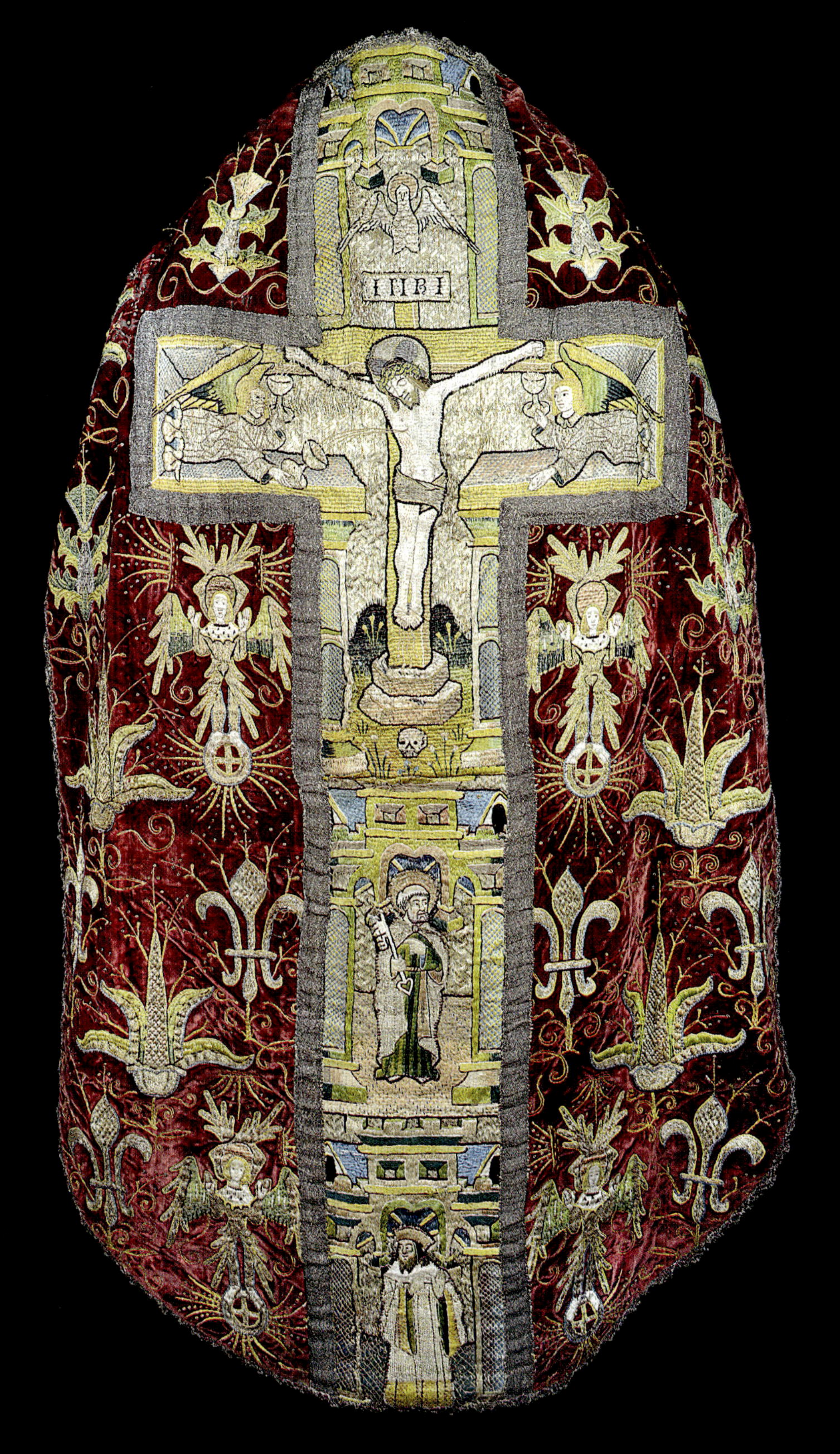

Thomas Cranmer's Lutheran Books on Romans

Andreas Knopken, *In epistolam ad Romanos … interpretatio*. 1525.
Ushaw, XVIII.C.9.4

Paul's epistle to the Romans was one of the most critical works of the Bible for Protestants of the sixteenth century. Emphasising notions of justification by faith alone and the centrality of God's grace, early Lutheran readings of Romans broke sharply with others holding that works and human agency contribute to the salvation process. This volume perfectly represents these Reformation debates, including not only a revised text of the epistle itself, but also the interpretations of Andreas Knopken (d.1539) and Martin Luther (1483–1546).

By the early 1520s, Knopken ('the reformer of Riga') was one of Luther's followers and had established connections with Johannes Bugenhagen (1485–1558), Desiderius Erasmus (1466–1536) and Philipp Melanchthon (1497–1560). After his education at Frankfurt an der Oder, he taught in Pomerania and became the leading voice of moderate Lutheran reform in the Baltic after he settled in Riga in 1521. One of the many early editions of his *In epistolam ad Romanos*, the first item in this volume was printed in 1525 and included Erasmus's Latin translation of the original Greek along with Melanchthon's marginal annotations. These texts were published as one work and complement the second item in the volume, Luther's own preface to Romans translated into Latin in 1524. The preface was originally published in his German bible of 1522 and quickly became a fundamental work for later Protestants.

Combining these four authorities into one volume on so central a text to the Lutheran movement, the binding is equally suggestive. The front and back panels allude to Revelation 4:7 by depicting Paul in the centre, surrounded by the Gospel writers Matthew, Mark, Luke and John. These panels are known to have been used on English books from the 1520s and 1530s, so it is highly likely that the works by Knopken and Luther were bound together after they had been brought to England about that time; indeed, tempting is the notion that they were bound near St Paul's churchyard, the centre of the London book trade.

Making this volume unique is that the name of Thomas Cranmer (1489–1556), Archbishop of Canterbury and principal architect of the Church of England, is written on the first title page. In the rush to inventory Cranmer's goods after his arrest in 1553, one of the archbishop's secretaries wrote 'Thomas Cantuarien[sis]' in his books, thereby offering posterity the possibility to recreate his library. Although we cannot assert with absolute certainty that Cranmer owned the Luther text (his name does not appear on its title page), the likelihood that the volume was bound decades before 1553 leads one to conclude that the book as it exists today was alongside other Lutheran works known to have been owned by Cranmer. This volume is all the more significant because so few Protestant works remain from Cranmer's library (likely one of the more impressive private collections in sixteenth-century Europe), presumably because they were confiscated, burnt or collected by others.

The dispersal of his books makes tracking this volume's history particularly difficult, but a couple of things are clear. Around 1600 a later owner, a certain Simon, crossed out Cranmer's name and wrote his own above it; and it came to Ushaw in 1943 from the parish of Dodding Green near Kendal, Cumbria. Among the predominantly later items from Dodding Green, this early Reformation volume is an outlier, but its survival sheds light on the international and pan-Protestant tastes of the Church of England's most significant early theologian, Thomas Cranmer.

DAVID GEHRING

IN EPISTO-
LAM AD ROMANOS ANDREAE
KNOPKEN COSTERINEN-
ſis interpretatio, Rigæ apud Liuo-
nios prælecta, ubi is paſtorē
agit Eccleſiæ.

ADIECTA EST IPSA PAV-
li Epiſtola, à PHILIPpo Melanchtho-
ne, paßim notis quibuſdam illuſtrata, quibus & diſputationis ordo, & ſermonis cō-
poſitio indicatur.

ARGENTORATI KNOBLO-
CHVS EXCVDEBAT.
M. D. XXV.

Andreas Knopken, *In epistolam ad Romanos … interpretatio*, printed in 1525. Thomas Cranmer's crossed-out name can be seen at the top of the image.

EXERCITIA

SPIRITVALIA.

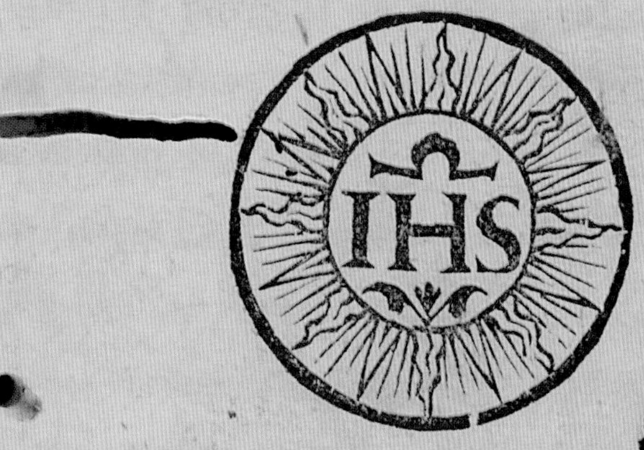

M. D. XLVIII.

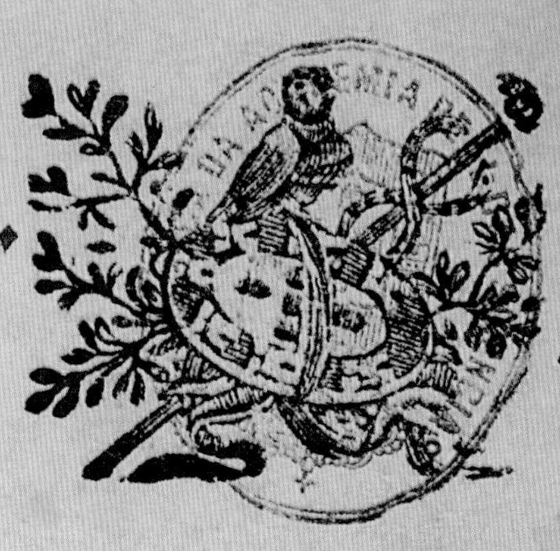

Rare First Edition of the 'Spiritual Exercises'

Ignatius Loyola, *Exercitia Spiritualia*, 1548

One of the most influential spiritual works in the history of Christianity, this small volume was written by a former Spanish soldier, Ignatius Loyola (*c*.1491–1556). Wounded in a battle at Pamplona in 1521, Ignatius underwent a protracted recovery at home in the family castle at nearby Loyola (Azpeitia), during which he had a conversion experience, a consequence of his reflections on the different texts that he was reading. These included Jacobo de Voragine's lives of the saints *Aurea Legenda*, Ludolph of Saxony's *Vita Christi*, and chivalric romances. Consequently he set off as a poor pilgrim towards Jerusalem; on the way he delayed at Manresa, near Barcelona, for nearly a year of intense prayer, fasting and mortification. Frustrated in his desire to remain in Jerusalem, he undertook studies in Spain and Paris 'in order to help souls' and eventually gathered around himself companions who would in 1540 become the Society of Jesus.

Exercitia Spiritualia ('Spiritual Exercises') is traditionally held to have originated in notes taken at Manresa, even though it never refers to Ignatius's own experiences. Ignatius, helped in many ways by other Jesuits, developed the text before it was published in this formal Latin version in 1548. The book presents a loosely structured programme of pater and asceticism, written in a potpourri of literary styles and genres. For Ignatius, a spiritual exercise is any means of 'preparing and disposing the soul in order to rid oneself of all its disordered affections', and then to 'seek and find the divine will in the disposition of one's life towards the salvation of the soul'. John O'Malley, SJ, rightly considers *Exercitia Spiritualia* 'more like a teacher's manual than a student's textbook', because it is intended to assist the director of the retreat and not the retreatant.

Ignatius encountered some opposition to his teachings. On several occasions, religious authorities examined him and his writings for suspected affinity to so-called *alumbrados*, figures who promoted direct communication with God in ways perceived as subversive and threatening. However, Ignatius and his work were always exonerated. This 1548 edition was in fact approved by Pope Paul III.

The book that originated as an aid for serious Christian commitment in general came to serve as a foundational document specific to the Society of Jesus, its function comparable to that of the Rule of St Benedict in Western monasticism. As such, the text is often thought to be central for understanding the global missions, ministries and history of the Jesuits.

Copies of the first edition are rare and valuable: Ushaw College possesses one of the few examples in the United Kingdom. This copy came to Ushaw from the English College, Lisbon, an institution not known for pro-Jesuit fervour. Two inscriptions suggest that the volume originally belonged to a Portuguese Jesuit community. The first '*Aplicado ao 6.o cobicolo vindo do do Pe. Reitor*' means that the volume belonged in the sixth cubicle or cell down the hall from the room of the rector. The second '*non p~hibetur - Do Recolhim.to*' translates literally as 'Not Prohibited, From the retreat'. *Recolhimento* may refer to a specific retreat house or indeed a Jesuit novitiate.

THOMAS M. MCCOOG, SJ

A rare first edition of one of the most influential spiritual works in the history of Christianity, Ignatius Loyola's *Exercitia Spiritualia*.

The Reading of Elizabeth I's Torturer-General

William Allen, *A True, sincere and modest defence of English Catholics ....* Rouen, 1584. Ushaw, XVIII.F.2.20

William Allen, founder of the English College at Douai – the institution from which Ushaw College is descended – penned this defence of English Catholics in response to William Cecil's *Execution of Justice in England* (1583). Following the international news story created by the torture and execution of the Jesuit Edmund Campion (d.1581), Cecil, Elizabeth I's lord treasurer, felt it necessary to go into print to defend his government from the charge of religious persecution. His case, essentially, was that Campion and others had been executed as political, not religious, dissidents and that the Elizabethan regime did not use torture in cases of religion.

Allen's *Defence* was a passionate and audacious vindication of the English Catholic movement, and of the men he trained and sent to England as missionaries. He insisted, with colourful examples, on the cruelty perpetrated by English officials and equally stressed that the English Mission had nothing to do with treason or rebellion. That the mission was not a covert military operation may be true, but Allen was no political neutral. He believed that Elizabeth I had no right to outlaw Catholicism and promote what he viewed as heresy. To save England from this fate, he attested that the Pope had the right to decide when a prince's conduct had nullified their subjects' duty of allegiance. Allen outlined these arguments in his *Defence*, although he carefully kept the discussion of the Pope's deposing power theoretical, not giving an explicit opinion on the deposition of Elizabeth in particular.

Ushaw's copy of Allen's *Defence* is especially interesting for its ownership: the title page is signed and annotated by Richard Topcliffe. Topcliffe, a royal servant, was notorious among Catholics as a persecutor and indeed the evidence suggests that he was thoroughly ruthless and capable of terrifying cruelty to prisoners, including the liberal use of torture. He was also, clearly, a man who liked to know his enemy: hence the personalised copy of Allen's apologia. Beneath the main title, Topcliffe has clarified the authorship: 'compiled by that monsterous trator Doctor Allen'. Where the subtitle reads 'how unjustly the Protestants do charge the Catholics with treason; how untruly they deny their persecution for religion', Topcliffe has erased the 'un' in both instances. 'Woe betide to him, who calleth good, evil, and evil, [good]' is his comment on Allen's thesis. Topcliffe seems to apologise for allowing the book to spread further: he notes that it has been 'lent' (presumably why he signed it), but 'Lent for the service of God, Queen Elizabeth and England, xi June 1599, by me Ryc. Topclyff.'

The quarrel between William Cecil and William Allen was a recurring one between English Catholics and their Protestant adversaries: religious persecution or national defence? Martyrs or traitors? As modern editors have pointed out, neither man was entirely transparent in his polemic. But the issue at stake was more profound than that: Allen did not see himself as a traitor because he did not measure treason by disloyalty to Elizabeth I. What divided Cecil and Topcliffe from Allen were conflicting ideas of what treason and patriotism were; divergent visions not only of the 'service of God', but of the 'service of England'.

LUCY UNDERWOOD

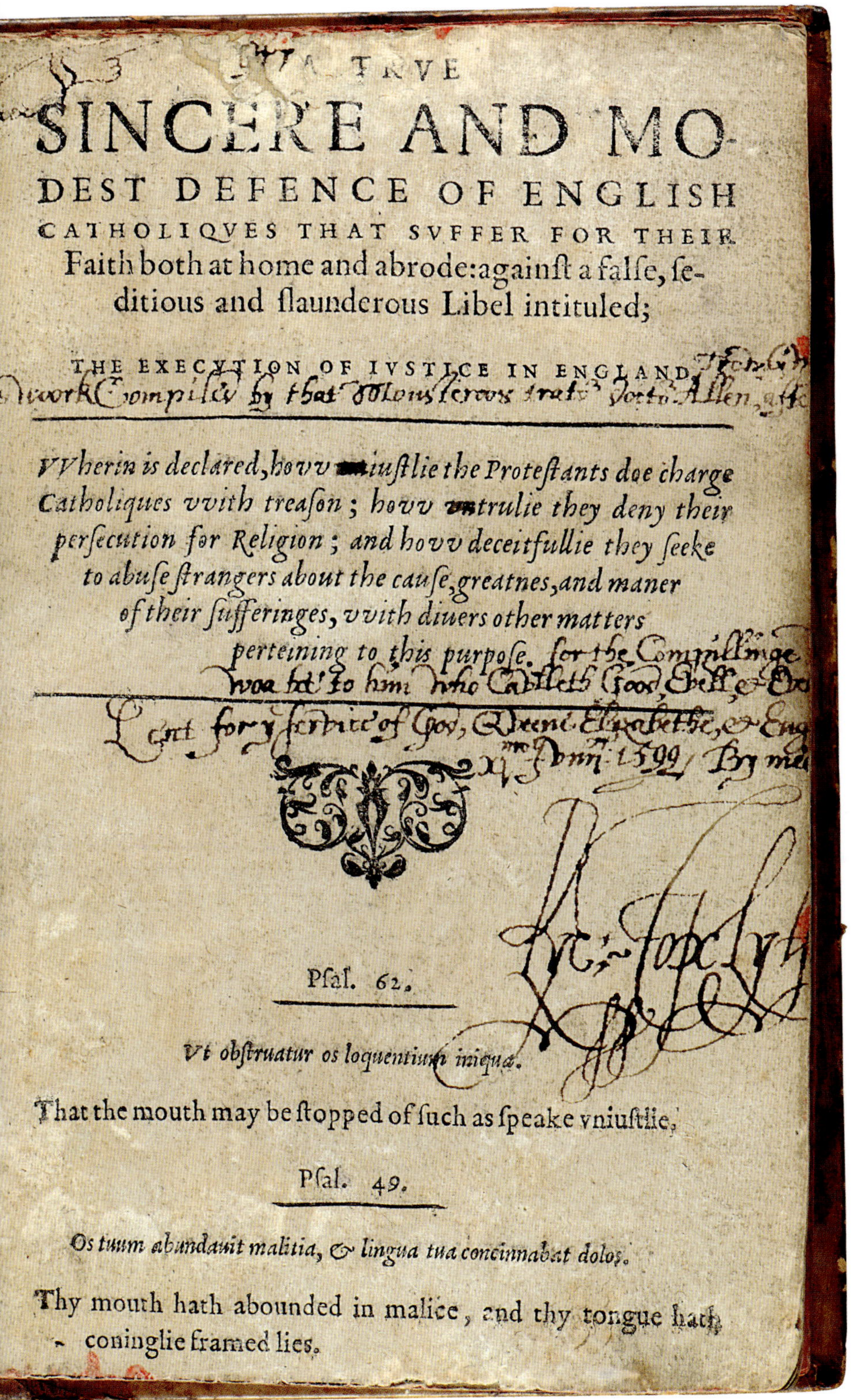

A TRVE
SINCERE AND MODEST DEFENCE OF ENGLISH CATHOLIQVES THAT SVFFER FOR THEIR Faith both at home and abrode: against a false, seditious and slaunderous Libel intituled;

THE EXECVTION OF IVSTICE IN ENGLAND.

VVherin is declared, hovv vniustlie the Protestants doe charge Catholiques vvith treason; hovv vntrulie they deny their persecution for Religion; and hovv deceitfullie they seeke to abuse strangers about the cause, greatnes, and maner of their sufferinges, vvith diuers other matters perteining to this purpose.

Psal. 62.

Vt obstruatur os loquentium iniqua.

That the mouth may be stopped of such as speake vniustlie.

Psal. 49.

Os tuum abundauit malitia, & lingua tua concinnabat dolos.

Thy mouth hath abounded in malice, and thy tongue hath coninglie framed lies.

Title page of William Allen, *A True, sincere and modest defence of English Catholics …*, displaying the signature of Richard Topcliffe and annotations made by him. Topcliffe was notorious for his brutal treatment and torture of Catholic prisoners.

Catholic Controversy from Charles II's Library

Nicholas Sander, *De origine ac progressu schismatis Anglicani*. Cologne [false imprint], 1585. Ushaw, XVIII.G.7.16

This is the first edition of a work of Elizabethan Catholic religious controversy popular in mainland Europe in an era rife with the genre. It was printed anonymously in 1585 with a false Cologne imprint. In reality, it was produced at Rheims by Jean Foigny, who produced several other works by Catholic writers in the 1580s, the best known of which is *Briefe historie of the glorious martyrdom of xii reuerend priests* (1582) by Douai College founder William Allen.

The repaired binding of this copy bears on its front and rear covers the backward- and forward-facing double 'C' of King Charles II, indicating that it once belonged to his collection. It was part of the royal library at the Court of St James, the 'Old Royal Library' (in contrast to George III's later 'King's Library'), from which this volume likely was separated between Charles's death in 1685 and the presentation of the library to the British Museum in 1757. Other materials at Ushaw associated with Charles II include the papers of Bishop Richard Russell, who acted as chaplain to his queen, Catherine of Braganza, and was a witness at the couple's private Catholic wedding ceremony.

The principal author of *De origine ac progressu schismatis Anglicani*, Nicholas Sander (1530–81), was educated at New College, Oxford. He left for Rome in 1560 and there was ordained a priest before teaching theology at Louvain for nine years. Sander became actively involved in the quickly suppressed Spanish invasion of Ireland in 1579, before which he had been appointed papal nuncio to Ireland. He wrote several important theological works, including *De visibili monarchia Ecclesiae*, printed by John Fowler in Louvain in 1571.

The manuscript of *De origine ac progressu schismatis Anglicani* was left incomplete when Sander died in Ireland in 1581. It was edited and its fourth and final book written by Edward Rishton (1550–85), a seminary priest who studied at Douai, was ordained at Cambrai in 1577 and travelled to Rome. He departed for England in April 1580 in the company of several other priests, including the Jesuits Edmund Campion and Robert Persons. After arrival, arrest and four years of imprisonment in England, Rishton was banished to France in early 1585 and facilitated the publication of the completed manuscript later the same year.

Sander's work was the first sustained Catholic narrative of the dramatic changes in church and state in sixteenth-century England, from the time of the 'most impious and sacrilegious tyrant Henry VIII' to the mid-reign of Elizabeth, 'who set herself up as the highest authority in matters pertaining to God, above even popes and priests'. Strongly polemical in tone, the work is arranged in four reign-by-reign parts of unequal length, the longest covering the reigns of Henry and Elizabeth. The 1586 Rome edition contained substantial additions by Robert Persons; the 1610 Cologne edition included supplements by another famous Jesuit, Pedro de Ribadeneira. Translated quickly into French and German, Sander's book inspired numerous derivative works in Latin, Italian, German, French and Spanish between 1585 and 1640. It did not appear in English until the nineteenth century.

BRAD S. GREGORY

DOCTISSIMI
VIRI NICOLAI SANDERI,
DE ORIGINE AC PROgressu Schismatis Anglicani,
Liber.

Continens historiam maximè Ecclesiasticam, annorum circiter sexaginta, lectu dignissimam: nimirum, ab anno 21. regni HENRICI 8, *quo primum cogitare cæpit de repudianda legitima vxore serenissima* CATHERINA, *vsque ad hunc vigesimum septimum* ELIZABETHÆ, *quæ vltima est eiusdem* Henrici *soboles.*

Editus & auctus per Edouardum Rishtonum.

Præcipua capita totius operis post præfationem authoris continentur.

Coloniæ Agrippinæ, Anno Domini
1585.

Nicholas Sander, *De origine ac progressu schismatis Anglicani*, actually published in Rheims in 1585.

The backward- and forward-facing double 'C' of King Charles II, indicating that the book once belonged to his collection.

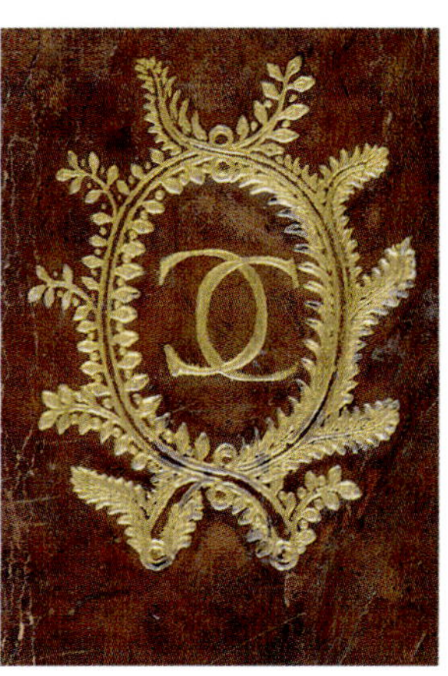

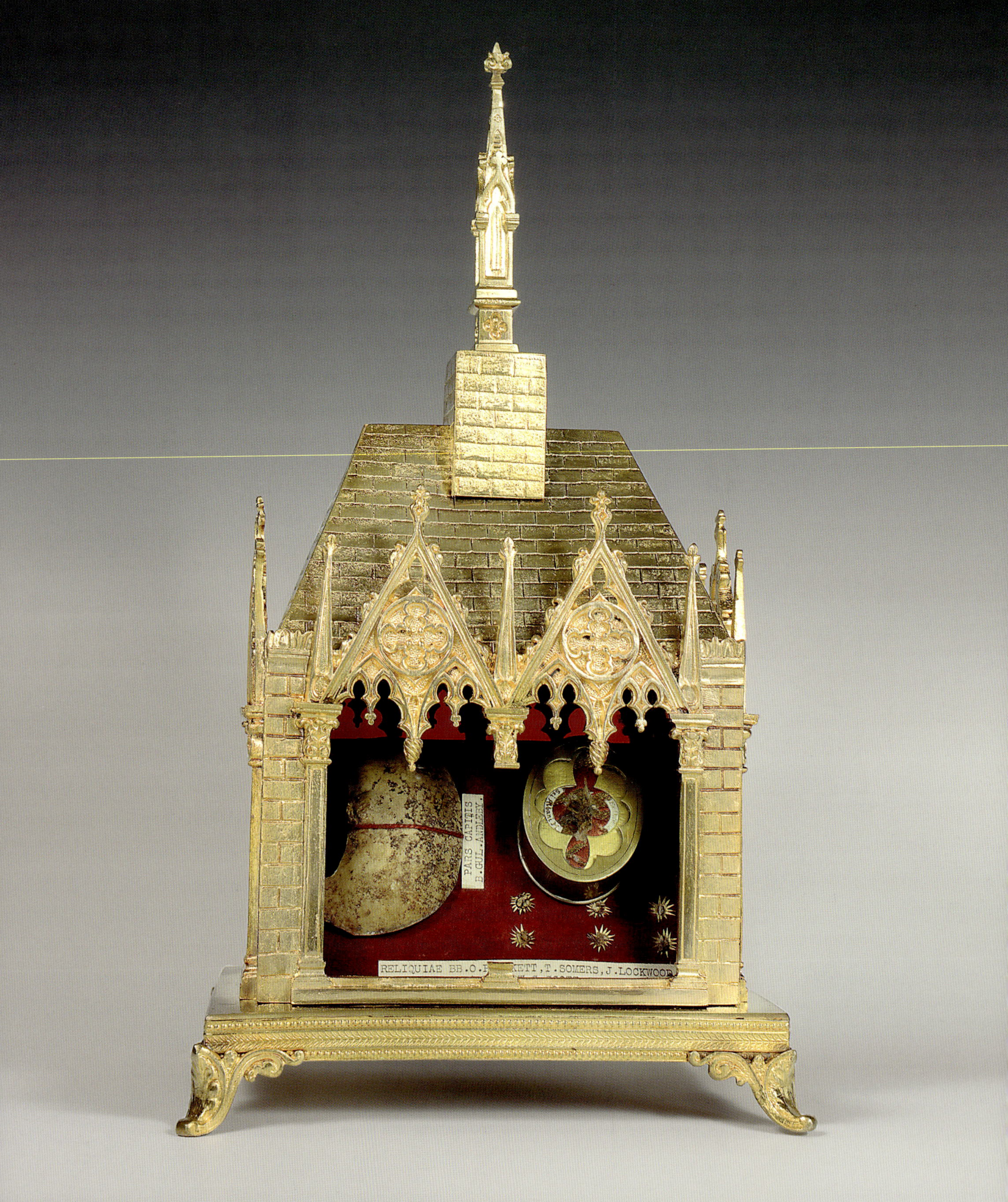
PARS CAPITIS
B.GUL.ANDLEBY.
RELIQUIAE BB.O.P
KETT,T.SOMERS,J.LOCKWOOD

Reminders of Persecution

English martyr relics, 1591–1681

Following the sixteenth-century Protestant Reformation and the Catholic Council of Trent, Counter-Reformation Europe was swept by a martyr and relic craze. Relics became a hallmark of the new Tridentine movement, a tool to counter Protestant heresy whilst simultaneously acting as a reminder of the relationship between the Catholic Church's past and present. The burgeoning martyr cult was heightened by the 1578 discovery of the catacombs in Rome, the un-leashing of the relics of early Christian martyrs bolstering Rome's claims to religious Truth and succession.

It also underlined the continuities between the martyrs of old and those of more contemporary times. As well-known victims of this new persecution, it is little wonder that the English martyrs featured prominently in the early modern European mind.

Following the accession of Elizabeth I, the Catholic faith, and particularly its priesthood, came under increasingly severe penal legislation. The 1581 'Act to retain the Queen's Majesty's subjects in their due obedience' made it high treason to reconcile, or be reconciled, to the Catholic Church. The vast majority of English martyrs were condemned under the 1585 'Act against Jesuits, seminary priests and such other like disobedient persons'. This made it high treason for a Catholic priest ordained abroad to enter the country and a felony for anyone to harbour or assist him. To be condemned as a traitor meant to be hanged, cut down whilst still conscious, and then to be drawn and quartered. The various body parts would be burnt or boiled and frequently displayed in prominent places, such as on London's Tower Bridge, as a warning to others.

However, these body parts or items belonging to the new martyrs quickly became prized relics. Some survive at Ushaw today, though by what means is currently unknown. In the oratory chapel, a gothic gasket contains parts of bone from the martyred English secular clergymen Thomas Somers (d.1610), John Lockwood (d.1642) and Montford Scott (d.1591), as well as a fragment of bone from the English Benedictine martyr Ambrose Barlow (d. 1641). Importantly for the history of Ushaw College, Somers and Scott had attended Douai College, from which Ushaw is descended. As well as a portion of the skull of William Anlaby (also of Douai, d.1597), the reliquary contains a fragment of the bone of Oliver Plunkett, the martyred Archbishop of Armagh (d.1681).

Another reliquary in the oratory chapel contains relics of the Douai-trained secular priest John Southworth (d.1654), much of whose body is preserved in the martyrs' chapel of Westminster Cathedral. Ushaw holds other relics of the English martyrs, including those of several executed at the start of the English Civil War from 1642 to 1643: the Franciscans Arthur Bell, Thomas Bullaker and Henry Heath, plus the secular priest Edward Morgan, alias Singleton.

Several of the individuals mentioned have been canonised: John Southworth is numbered among the 40 martyrs of England and Wales, canonised by Pope Paul VI in 1970, the same year that Oliver Plunkett was canonised, while the Franciscans Arthur Bell, Thomas Bullaker and Henry Heath were among the 85 beatified by Pope John Paul II in 1987.

JAMES E. KELLY

Reliquary containing the relics of six Catholic priests martyred in England during the sixteenth and seventeenth centuries: Montford Scott (d.1591), William Anlaby (d.1597), Thomas Somers (d.1610), Ambrose Barlow OSB (d.1641), John Lockwood (d.1642) and Oliver Plunkett (d.1681). The other relic is of St Alban, regarded as the first English martyr.

Ninthly as I muſt take heed of pampering my body to much and ought to take ſome ordinary corporall puniſhment of faſting, diſcipline, hearecloth, or the like: So on the other ſide, I muſt haue care of my health, and ſo temper all my ſpirituall exerciſes and bodily afflictions, with diſcretion, that I may continue in them ſtill, & not make my ſelfe vnable to perſeuer long by the vndiſcreet greedines of a ſhort time. and to vſe diſcretiō theſe obſeruations will availe.

Firſt before God to thinke whether doing this or that, I may be able to continew my vndertaken courſe in Gods ſeruice, my body, force, health, and other cares and combers or buſineſſes conſidered.

Secondly to aske counſaile of ſpirituall men long practiſed in ſpi-

A Unique Spiritual Guide

Robert Southwell, SJ, *A Short Rule of Good Life. To direct the devout Christian in a reguler and orderly course. Newly set forth according to the Authours direction before his death.* Bound with *An Epistle of a Religious Priest unto his father: exhorting him to the perfect forsaking of the world.* Secret Press, 1596/1597. Ushaw, IV.B.12.18

Robert Southwell, SJ – canonised as a saint in 1970 – was an English Jesuit, martyr (having been tortured, he was executed in 1595), and author of devotional prose and poetry read widely by both English Catholics and Protestants. Born in 1561 to Richard and Bridget (née Copley) Southwell, he left England in 1576. He boarded at the English College in Douai while studying at Anchin College, the Jesuit school in town. In 1578 he travelled to Rome, where he studied at the English College, eventually serving as prefect of studies. He was ordained as a priest in 1584 and joined the Jesuit order. Southwell returned to England as a missionary in the summer of 1586. There, he found a patroness in Anne Howard, Countess of Arundel and wife of Philip Howard, Earl of Arundel (d.1595 and canonised at the same time as Southwell). According to Anne Howard's anonymous Jesuit biographer, *A Short Rule* was first written for her spiritual direction.

Southwell's *Short Rule* is a guide to daily pious living. Designed for the laity, it adapts the intellectual foci of Ignatius Loyola's *Exercitia Spiritualia* and devotional works such as Gaspar Loarte's *The Exercise of a Christian Life*, to the life of a busy Elizabethan householder. *A Short Rule* discusses Christian principles by which to organise one's life, considers the implications of those principles for daily behaviour and offers an overview of an ideal day for a devout secular person. Drawing heavily on Loarte, the text proposes, for instance, 'An Order How to Spend Every Day', including hours for rising, times and methods for prayer, and daily examinations of conscience. Southwell also offers guidelines for virtuous eating, the supervision of servants and the religious education of children.

The work circulated in manuscript among a readership comprising Catholics and Protestants. Sometime in 1596 or 1597, Fr Henry Garnet, SJ, then the Jesuit superior in England, wrote a preface praising Southwell's work as 'a most perfecte mirrour of his godly life' and printed the work on his second secret press. Ushaw College's volume is the only known surviving complete copy of this early printing.

The Ushaw volume is also important for its readers' marks. At least one reader has made spelling corrections, underlined important phrases and inscribed key phrases from the text in the margins. Occasionally, the reader takes issue with the text. For example, on the page depicted, one can see that when Southwell advises devotees not to allow the discipline of the body to damage one's health, the reader has remarked, 'But the souls health must be preferred when danger is.' The annotations evince careful attention to Southwell's work.

Southwell's *Epistle* was written to his father, Richard Southwell, who had conformed to the national Church; the letter urges him to return to the Catholic Church for the sake of his soul. The *Epistle* probably dates from shortly after Southwell's return to England in 1586. It circulated widely in manuscript and, later, in print; the letter's advice from a devout son to an aged father was praised, imitated, adapted and printed by Protestant as well as Catholic readers. This volume contains the letter's earliest printing.

SUSANNAH MONTA

Robert Southwell, SJ, *A Short Rule of Good Life*, printed in 1596 or 1597. Detailed reader annotations underline how closely the book was read.

Francis Joseph Sloane's 'Testimony of Gratitude'

Sloane chalice and vestment, 1605–21, 1730–50

Francis Joseph Sloane (1795–1871) was among the first students to attend the newly established Ushaw College in 1808. He formed a strong bond with the college when President John Gillow arranged to pay his tuition fees after the failure of his father's business investments. As an adult he became a successful tutor in the family of the Russian Count Boutourlin in Florence and went on to own copper mines near Volterra. He is best remembered in Florence for funding the completion of the marble exterior of the church of Santa Croce.

In gratitude to his alma mater he sent Ushaw a number of fine gifts. This chalice of seventeenth-century silver chiselled work arrived at the college in 1840. It was commissioned for Pope Paul V, who was in office from 1605 to 1621, and given to the Florentine Guicciardini family. After being acquired by Sloane he asked Cardinal Wiseman to present the chalice to Pope Gregory XVI for consecration and it was used at Mass in the Vatican on 16 March 1840. High relief medallions depicting detailed scenes of the Agony in the Garden, the Apparition of the Risen Christ, the Supper at Emamaus and Ecce Homo decorate the silver gilt cup; these are surrounded by acanthus leaves and surmounted by cherub heads. The base depicts Samson and the Honeycomb, Elias receiving food from the angel, the Manna in the desert, and David and the loaves of proposition. In the hollowed-out centre of the knop is a miniature representation of the Last Supper. This is of such detailed work that the very clothes and hair of the apostles are clearly defined.

The cope of French silk brocade (1730–50; see Introduction: Historical, page 30) is part of a solemn High Mass vestment set given to Ushaw by Sloane to be worn at the opening of the Pugin Chapel in 1847. Unfortunately, A.W.N. Pugin intensely disliked them for their Roman form, arguing that, 'This stuff and this style of vestment will not suit the new church at Ushaw, and if sent there all my ideas will be deranged, and the unity of my plans will be destroyed.' After heated debate, agreement was reached to use them once a year.

As a wealthy and knowledgeable Catholic living in Florence, Sloane probably selected these vestments with great care. Despite this, the brocaded fabric is entirely secular. Luscious red and blue flowers, grapes and lemons are supported by a deeply ribbed shell above a tiny vignette featuring Italianate buildings. A woven lace-like ribbon links the cornucopia-shaped floral motifs. The copes are woven from silk alone. However, the dalmatics, stole and maniples are woven in silk using the same design in a slightly smaller scale but lavishly highlighted with silver thread. These are expensive luxury fabrics similar to those designed by Jean Revel (1684–1751) and woven by highly skilled weavers in Lyons. The vestments, ornamented with silver lace, were possibly made up later. The morse which fastens the cope has been repaired showing that, despite Pugin's views, this vestment has had considerable use.

MARY BROOKS AND CLAIRE MARSLAND

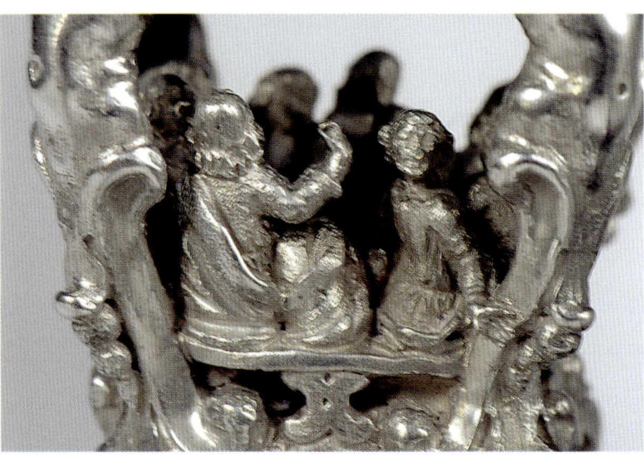

Left: The miniature representation of the Last Supper in the chalice's hollowed-out knop.

Right: The Sloane Chalice was given to the college in 1840, having been originally commissioned for Pope Paul V at the beginning of the seventeenth century.

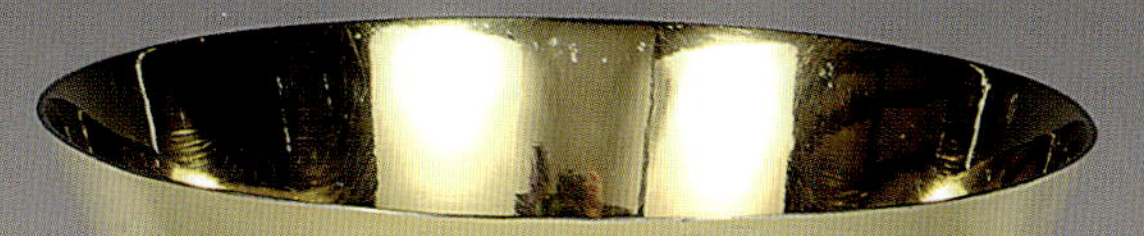
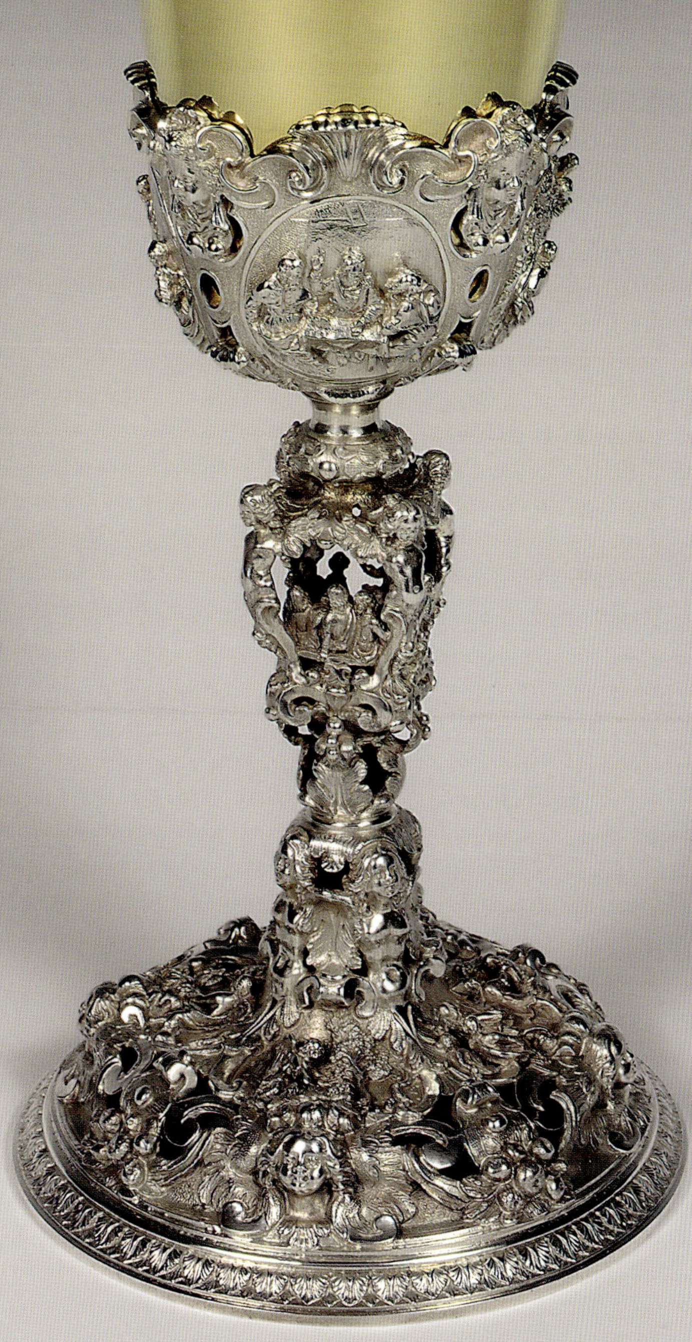

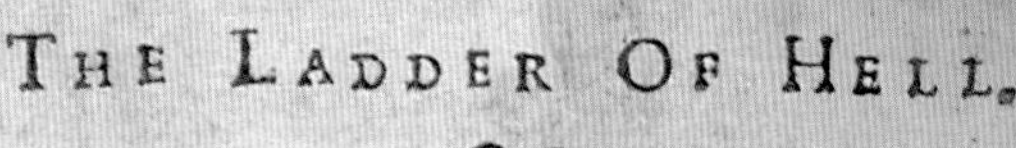

THE LADDER OF HELL.
OR
THE ~~PROTESTANTS~~ puritans LIBER-
TINE DOCTRINE, BEING
THE BROAD WAY WHICH
leadeth the followers of it to
their eternall ruine and
destruction in
Hell.

Set foorth in *Prose* and *Verse*.

ISAI. 5. 20.
Woe vnto you who call euill good, and good euill; putting darknesse light, and light darknesse.

Ex lib.
Harf.

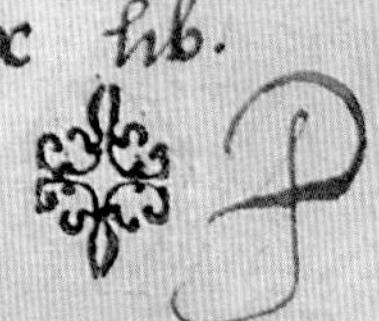

P

Permissu Superiorum.

Title page of a unique copy of *The Ladder of Hell*, printed on a secret press in England. The word 'Protestants' has been crossed out and replaced with 'Puritans'.

England's Secret Presses

Cranmer Coubridge (pseudonym), *The Ladder of Hell or the Protestants Libertine Doctrine*. Birchley Hall secret press, 1618. Ushaw, XIX.G.8.11

Post-Reformation Catholic and Protestant polemicists frequently appropriated each other's voices, quoting opponents' own statements against themselves, or printing each other's works framed by hostile marginalia. *The Ladder of Hell* owes something to both of these strategies.

It presents itself as a Catholic tract framed by a Protestant minister named 'Cranmer Coubridge'. Coubridge explains that *The Ladder of Hell* was written by a Catholic, 'to the great disgrace (as he conceived) of our Protestant religion'. But, he adds 'in regard it containeth nothing but a collection of certaine sentences set down in the publike bookes of twelue principall Pillars of our Church', so Protestants will hardly dislike it. This indicates the tract's actual purpose, to compile a list of what the author considers particularly damning quotations from his opponents' work. As the subtitle (*the Protestants Libertine doctrine*) indicates, the main charge is that Protestant doctrines of justification by faith alone, predestination and lack of free will encourage people to sin: this was a fairly common anti-Protestant trope. Along the way, he jibes at other alleged Protestant characteristics.

The pseudonym 'Cranmer Coubridge' alludes to two Protestant martyrs in John Foxe's *Acts and Monuments*: Thomas Cranmer, author of the Book of Common Prayer, and William Cowbridge. The latter was a slightly embarrassing 'martyr'. Catholic polemicists had pointed out that he had denied Christ's divinity and thus was not an advertisement for orthodox Protestantism. The choice highlights the disunity of 'heresy' and suggests that there is little difference between mainstream Protestants and extreme fanatics. 'Cranmer Coubridge' also assures himself that Protestants will not be shaken by this Catholic compilation, since 'every zealous Protestant can with the dexterite of his reformed spirit turne all, though never so plainly seeming ill, to at least a seeming good sense'. Put simply, this is the Catholic charge that Protestants twisted Scripture to suit their theories.

Ushaw's *The Ladder of Hell* is a unique copy. It bears no date or place of printing, but has been identified as the work of the secret Catholic press at Birchley Hall, Lancashire, which operated from 1608 to 1621. This press also produced the works of 'John Brereley'. Who Brereley was has been disputed, but a convincing identification has been made with James Anderton (d.1613), a Catholic layman. His books, printed between 1608 and 1624 (after his death), included *The Protestants Apologie for the Romane Church* (1608) and *Luthers Life Collected from the Writinges of him Selfe, and other Learned Protestants* (1624), which use the technique of quoting opponents against themselves. *The Ladder of Hell* is a compact and satirical example of the same thing, although it is not clear whether its author was Brereley/Anderton.

There is one further layer of appropriation: some owner has replaced the word 'Protestants' with the apparently derogatory term 'Puritans' in the title, indicating that to his or her mind, the *Ladder* is an apt rendition of a particular type of Protestantism. Whether this owner was a Catholic, or a non-Calvinist Protestant exploiting Catholic polemic against his Reformed enemies, is not known.

Finally, the author of *The Ladder of Hell* prints on his title page the same biblical verse used by Richard Topcliffe to describe William Allen in his copy of Allen's *Defence of English Catholics*, also held at Ushaw (see page 76): 'Woe unto you who call evill good, and good evill' (Isaiah 5:20). This is a detail which captures the tragic irony of the Reformation.

LUCY UNDERWOOD

Mapping the World

Philippe Briet, SJ, *Parallela geographiae veteris et novae*. Three volumes, Paris, 1648–49. Ushaw, XIII.C.4.11-13.

This work by the French Jesuit Philippe Briet (1601–88) represents one of the major achievements of seventeenth-century geographical study. In terms of its contemporary popularity, reflected in healthy sales and extensive educational usage, it bears comparison with Philipp Clüver's *Introductio in universam geographiam* (1624).

It is, however, a somewhat puzzling text so far as authorial intent and the volume's place in seventeenth-century intellectual culture are concerned. Briet's fellow Jesuit, Joseph de Jouvancy, famously stated that chronology and geography were the 'two eyes of history' and the disciplines of history and geography were intimately connected at this period, not least within the Jesuit intellectual milieu. This is certainly reflected in the *Parallela* with its focus on the ancient world. Still, we should not forget that Briet once scolded Sebastian Münster for including too much history and not enough geography in his celebrated *Cosmographia* of 1544, and it is significant that Briet makes full use of his era's advances in cartographical technology (for example, Mercator and Ortelius) as well as relying on medieval and classical sources (Ptolemy, Pliny and so forth).

As suggested by the title, one of the goals of Briet's volume (in all likelihood part of an ambitious global project that never came to full fruition) was comparison between old and new. The volumes might also be seen as a typical product of one stream of Jesuit intellectual enquiry, not least in the pursuit of a Ciceronian model of eloquence. The text was as important as the image for Briet – indeed, he regarded them as inseparable – and his aim was to use words which, as he once put it, 'translate reality in the most expressive manner'. In his cartographic work, philosophical speculation was not a significant part of Briet's agenda. It would be anachronistic to mistake this for a symptom of latter-day empiricism, but the volumes – unusually well decorated in Ushaw's copies – can still be seen as forward-thinking.

This was a widely circulated text and there is a hint regarding how this particular copy made its way to Ushaw. Annotations on the third front endpieces of each volume read: '*Dono dedit adolescens nobilissimus Ludouicus Franciscus de Neufbourg de Sarcelles.*' ('This was given as a gift by the young and most noble man, Louis Francois de Neufbourg de Sarcelles').

With notable exceptions, Briet has generally suffered from scholarly neglect. This is regrettable because he appears to have played a significant role in seventeenth-century intellectual and pedagogical life, both within and beyond the Society of Jesus. These volumes also remind us of the crucial Jesuit contribution to early modern geography. It is telling that Antonio Possevino, one of the architects of the *Ratio Studiorum*, which guided Jesuit education for centuries, held the subject in the highest regard and even produced a guide for how to teach geography: the *Methodus ad geographiam tradendam*. It is interesting to speculate on how Possevino, who died long before the publication of Briet's volumes, would have regarded this hybrid and groundbreaking work.

JONATHAN WRIGHT

A beautifully decorated map of North and South America in volume one of *Parallela geographiae veteris et novae* by the French Jesuit historian and cartographer Philippe Briet.

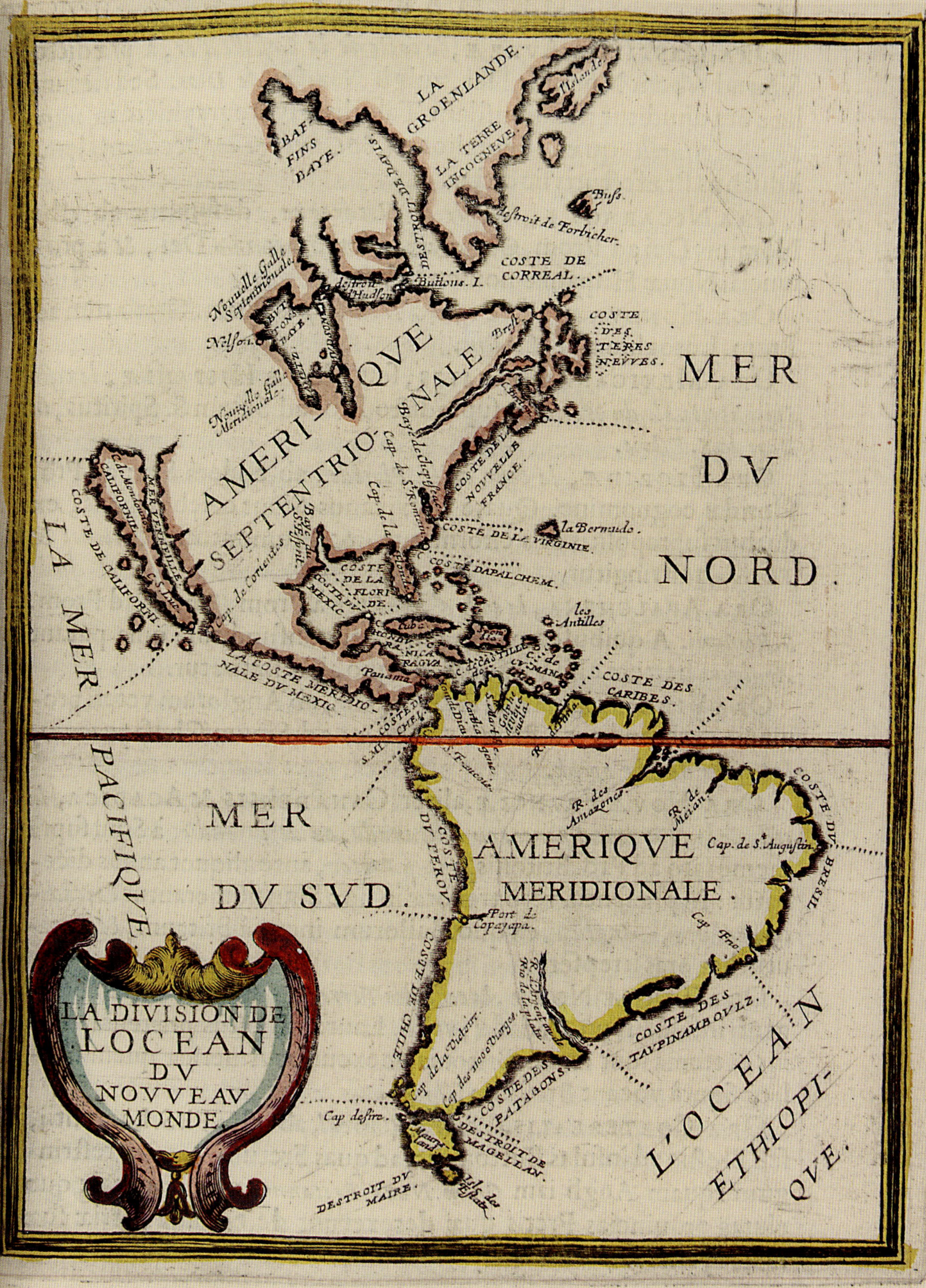

LA DIVISION DE LOCEAN DV NOVVEAV MONDE.
LA GROENLANDE.
LA TERRE INCOGNEVE.
BAFFINS BAYE.
destroit de Forbicher.
COSTE DE CORREAL.
destroit de Hudson
Buttons. I.
Nouvelle Galle Septentrionale
Nelson
Nouvelle Galle Meridionale
COSTE DES TERES NEVVES.
MER DV NORD.
AMERIQVE SEPTENTRIONALE
COSTE DE LA NOUVELLE FRANCE.
COSTE DE LA VIRGINIE.
la Bermude.
COSTE DAPALCHEM.
les Antilles
COSTE DES CARIBES.
COSTE DE CALIFORNIE
LA MER PACIFIQVE.
Cap. de Corientes
LA COSTE MERIDIONALE DV MEXIC.
Panama
MER DV SVD.
AMERIQVE MERIDIONALE.
R. des Amazones
Cap. de S.t Augustin.
COSTE DV BRESIL
COSTE DV PEROV
Port de Copayapa.
COSTE DE CHILE
COSTE DES TAVPINAMBOVLZ.
COSTE DES PATAGONS
Cap desire.
DESTROIT DE MAGELLAN.
DESTROIT DV MAIRE.
L'OCEAN ETHIOPIQVE.

A Hidden Faith: Recusant Liturgical Objects

Recusant chasuble and chalice, mid-seventeenth century

England's Catholics were often forced to practise their religion in secrecy and fear. Under the 1559 Act of Uniformity, failure to attend the nominally Protestant state church was an offence resulting in fines or imprisonment, giving rise to the term 'recusant', from the Latin *recusare* (to refuse). These punishments were enforced to varying degrees for over two hundred years until the process of emancipation began in the late eighteenth century. Laws passed in the 1580s also made it a treasonable offence for a Catholic priest, ordained abroad, to return to the country and perform his ministry, while those sheltering such individuals faced being charged and executed as felons. The importance of concealing both their priests and their Mass accruements thus resulted in recusant Catholics developing unique types of liturgical objects and vestments.

This set of Mass vestments, comprising a chasuble, stole and chalice veil, was apparently found in 1811 concealed in a priest's hole in a house belonging to the Duke of Norfolk, a leading member of a family regularly in trouble for its members' recusancy. Although rose-pink (*rosacea*) has sometimes been used as a liturgical colour on Laetare Sunday in Lent and Gaudete Sunday in Advent, this relatively unusual colour might have been intended to disguise the vestments. Other recusant vestments make use of unusual colours such as the multi-coloured late seventeenth- or early eighteenth-century 'pedlar's vestment' in white, red, green and purple striped silk held at York's Bar Convent. Another set of early seventeenth-century vestments found in a 'pedlar's chest' walled up in Stamlesbury Hall and now kept at Stonyhurst College are made from secular dress fabrics. Like the 'pedlar's vestment', the Ushaw Mass set reverses to a different colour, in this case a brownish-black – the liturgical colour for saying a requiem Mass – underlining its multi-purpose. Officially, Catholic families could not be buried in Anglican churchyards so funerals took place in secret or at night. Under these circumstances, multi-functional vestments made from several different 'liturgical colours' could be extremely useful.

Unusually made from wool in a plain weave fabric with shiny finish, these vestments have simple appliqué ornamentation. The broad creamy-white band orphrey on the chasuble's front extends over the shoulders to form a wide cross on the back. In contrast, the black face only has an outline cross and narrow strips suggesting an orphrey, similar to the crosses on the chalice veil. The current fiddle-shaped front, neck-opening and green-gold braid edging are probably later alterations.

In complete contrast to the abundant decoration used for continental Mass vessels, this silver recusant chalice is small and lightweight, with basic but elegant decoration. Its hidden feature is that it can be un-screwed into three pieces for easy conveyance by a travelling priest. During times of high persecution recusant silversmiths did not mark their work for fear of arrest. This chalice therefore bears no hallmarks. However, stylistically it can be linked with the workshop of Andrew Moore, which used cherubs with wings raised above the head as its signature, so it probably dates to the 1650s. This insular English style of church plate lasted to the end of the seventeenth century when silversmiths again looked to mainland Europe for inspiration.

MARY BROOKS AND CLAIRE MARSLAND

Recusant silver chalice, probably dating from the mid-seventeenth century.

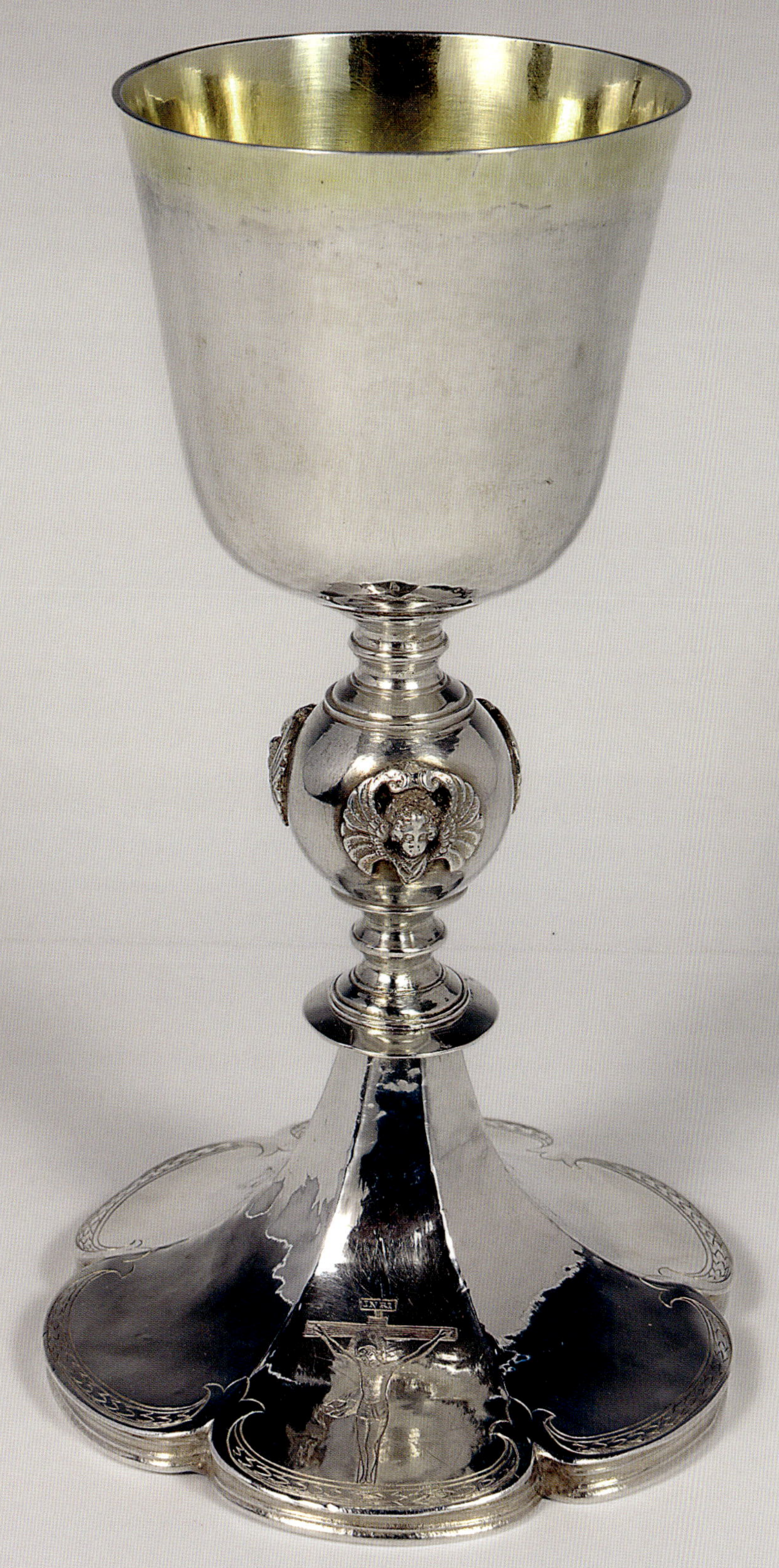

Recusant chasuble, seventeenth century. Made from wool, plain weave fabric with silk appliqué. The chasuble's various colours meant it could be used at several different points of the liturgical calendar.

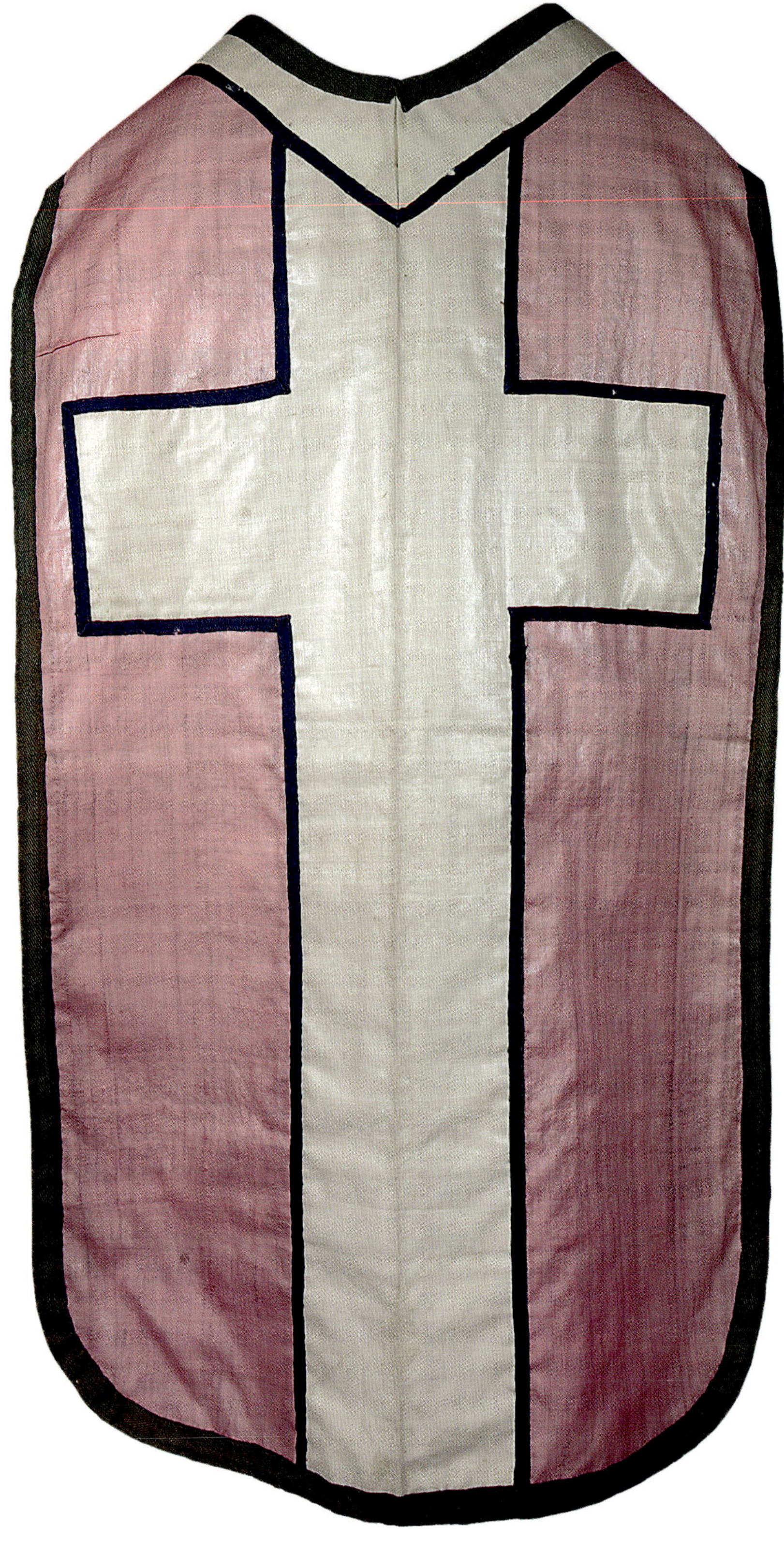

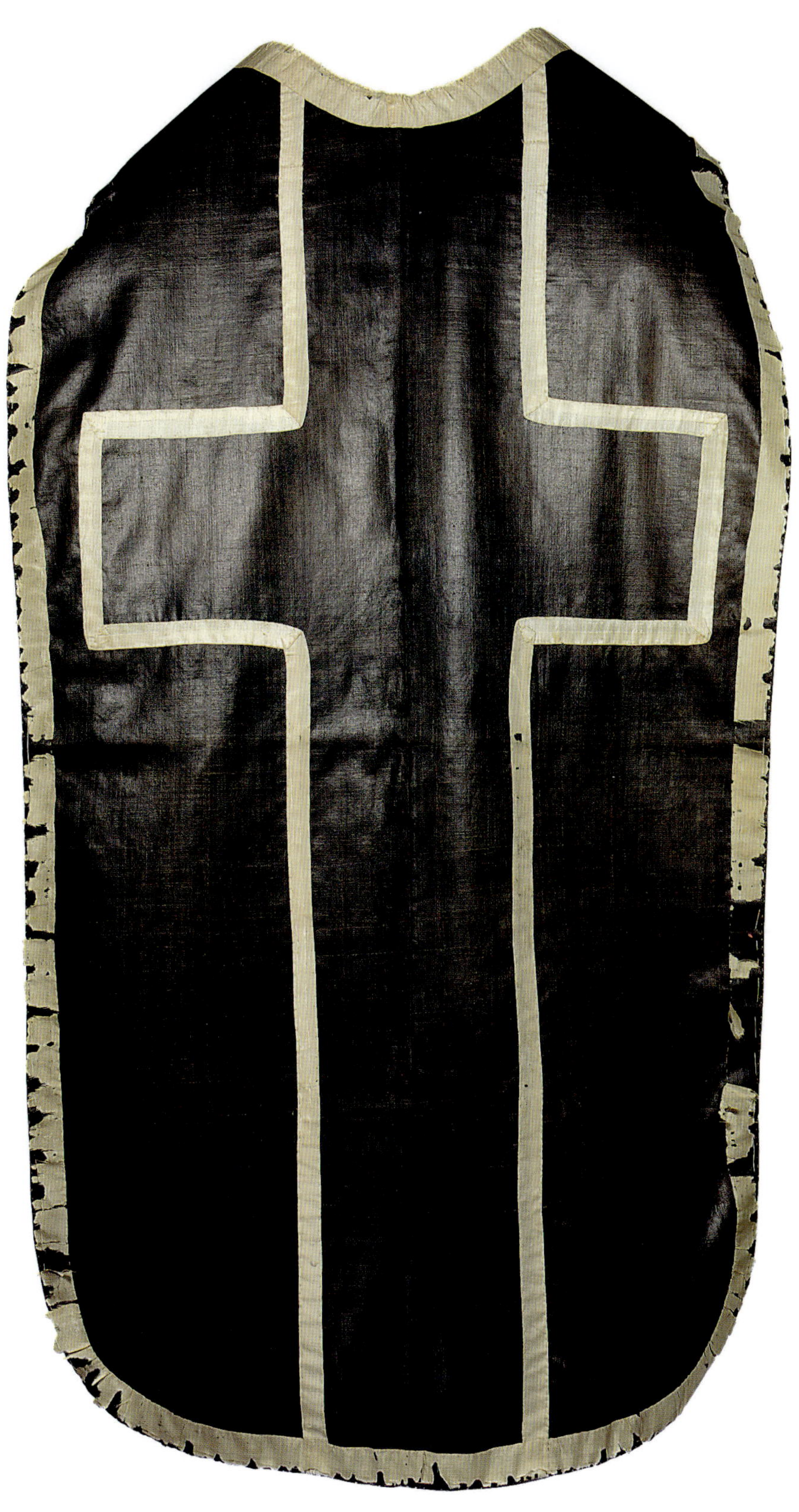

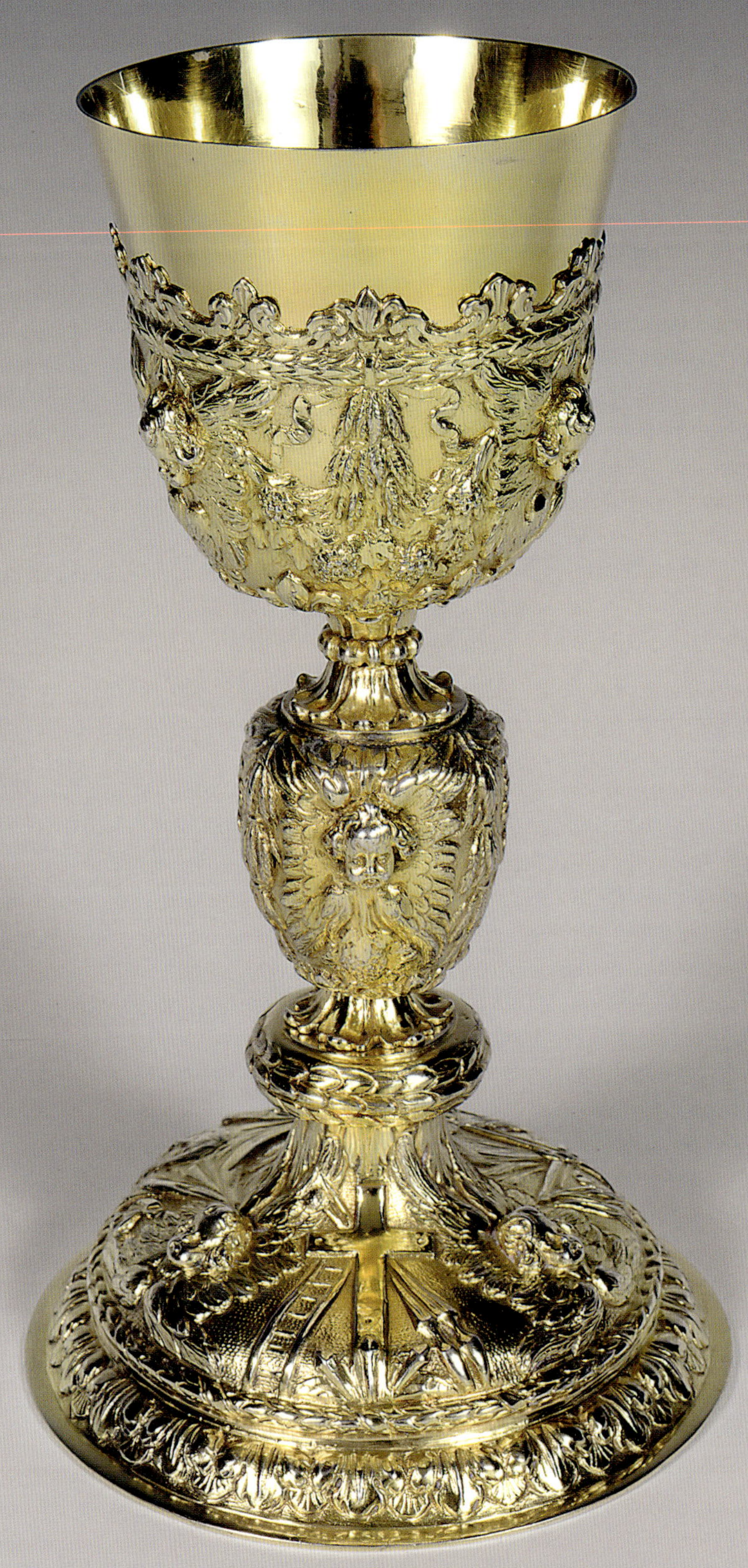

The Fermor Chalice

Silver-gilt chalice, 1659

This baroque silver-gilt chalice is not hallmarked but inscribed beneath its base in Latin are the words, '*Deo Assumptaeq. Virgini dicarunt Henricu & Ursual Fermor Coniuges Anno Dominii* 1659'. This translates as 'To God and the Virgin assumed Henry and Ursula Fermor, husband and wife, dedicated this chalice in the year of Our Lord 1659'. The inscription relates to the marriage of Henry Fermor of Tusmore, Oxfordshire, to Ursula, the daughter of Sir Peter Middleton of Stockheld, Yorkshire, and a great-granddaughter of Charles Neville, last earl of Westmorland.

It is a tall chalice, ornamented with winged cherub heads on the cup, the node and the base. The base is further decorated with a cross, ladder, spear, reed with sponge, scourges and a palm – the signs of Christ's Passion. It is of continental design, possibly French, and reflects the more elaborate tastes prevalent in Counter-Reformation Europe. As such, it seems unlikely that this was made for a secret house chapel, but perhaps given as a benefaction to one of the English colleges or convents in exile.

It was first recorded in the collections at Ushaw in 1826 and was presented to the college, along with other vestments, by a Mrs Blount who was a friend of the president, John Gillow. The Blounts were an old recusant family resident at Mapledurham, not far from the Fermors in Oxfordshire. It is possible that Mrs Blount acquired the chalice when the Fermors left the area in 1810.

The Fermors acquired the estate of Tusmore, near Brackley, Oxfordshire, in 1625 when the father of the Henry Fermor in question – Richard Fermor – oversaw its becoming the centre of a clandestine Catholic community where his descendants lived for the next 200 years. In 1665, Henry Fermor confirmed that the house at Tusmore had a chapel, not to mention 19 hearths, a walled garden and fish pond with a pleasure garden and hedges. It is not known whether the chapel was built by the Fermors or formed part of the original medieval house. By the early eighteenth century, the house was said to have a priest's hole. If the chalice was not used abroad, then another possible answer for its provenance may be that it was used in the family chapel at Tusmore for 150 years until the Fermors left the estate in 1810.

Certainly the family was strongly Catholic, the resident priest frequently being a Jesuit and several members entering holy orders. Of the couple under consideration – Henry and Ursula – three of their daughters became nuns and two sons entered the Society of Jesus. The chapel at Tusmore served seven generations of Fermors until the nineteenth century and the eve of Catholic emancipation. Besides Henry Fermor and his wife, the cook, the dairymaid and the chambermaid were all listed as papists in 1644. It was common policy amongst Catholic families during the penal period to employ Catholic servants and staff in an effort to avoid being reported to the authorities about goings-on at their residences. Indeed, in 1706 six of the servants were listed as Catholics and by 1808 all the registered parishioners were of that faith.

TESSA MURDOCH

The Fermor chalice, dedicated in 1659, commemorates the marriage between Henry Fermor and Ursula Middleton.

Jacobite 'Relics'

Items from the Radcliffe Reliquary, 1661–1745

The Derwentwater 'relics' at Ushaw College offer a unique glimpse into the political and religious allegiances of the storied Radcliffe family of Northumberland. This influential and wealthy family, well established even before James II raised Sir Francis Radcliffe (1625–97) to the earldom of Derwentwater in 1688, became allied with the House of Stuart when Francis's son, Edward, married Lady Mary Tudor (1673–1726), daughter of Charles II and his mistress Mary 'Moll' Davis. This connection was strengthened in the next generation, when the three Radcliffe sons, James (1689–1716), Francis (1691–1715) and Charles (1693–1746), were sent to be educated alongside Prince James, the future 'Old Pretender', at the exiled court of James II in Saint-Germain-en-Laye, France.

The family's personal loyalty to the Stuarts, combined with their dedication to Roman Catholicism, set them in opposition to the Hanoverian succession that eventually displaced James II and the royal Stuart line following the Glorious Revolution of 1688. Francis Radcliffe refused to take the oaths of loyalty to William and Mary, and his grandsons James and Charles were both involved in the failed Jacobite rising of 1715. James (styled third Earl of Derwentwater) led a company from his Northumberland estates and was subsequently beheaded at Tower Hill for his part in the conflict. Although Charles was also condemned to death, he managed to escape to mainland Europe. Remaining a fervent supporter of the Stuart cause, he was captured at sea on his way to participate in the second Jacobite rebellion in 1745. Charles was condemned according to his former sentence and executed the following year.

The Radcliffes had acquired the manors at Dilston, between Corbridge and Hexham, Northumberland, through marriage in the fifteenth century. Francis and his wife Isabella made additions to the estate, including a private chapel. Many items from Dilston Chapel and Dilston Hall (a manor built by James Radcliffe after his

MISSALE
ROMANVM
EX DECRETO SACROSANCTI
CONCILII TRIDENTINI RESTITVTVM,
PII V. PONT. MAX. IVSSV EDITVM,
ET
CLEMENTIS VIII. PRIMVM, NVNC DENVO
VRBANI PAPÆ OCTAVI
AVCTORITATE RECOGNITVM,
In quo MISSÆ propriæ de SANCTIS omnes ad longum positæ sunt ad maiorem celebrantium commoditatem.

ANTVERPIÆ,
EX OFFICINA PLANTINIANA
BALTHASARIS MORETI.
M. DC. LXI.

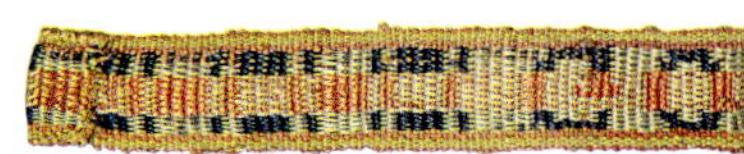

A 1661 Roman Missal from the Radcliffe chapel at Dilston.

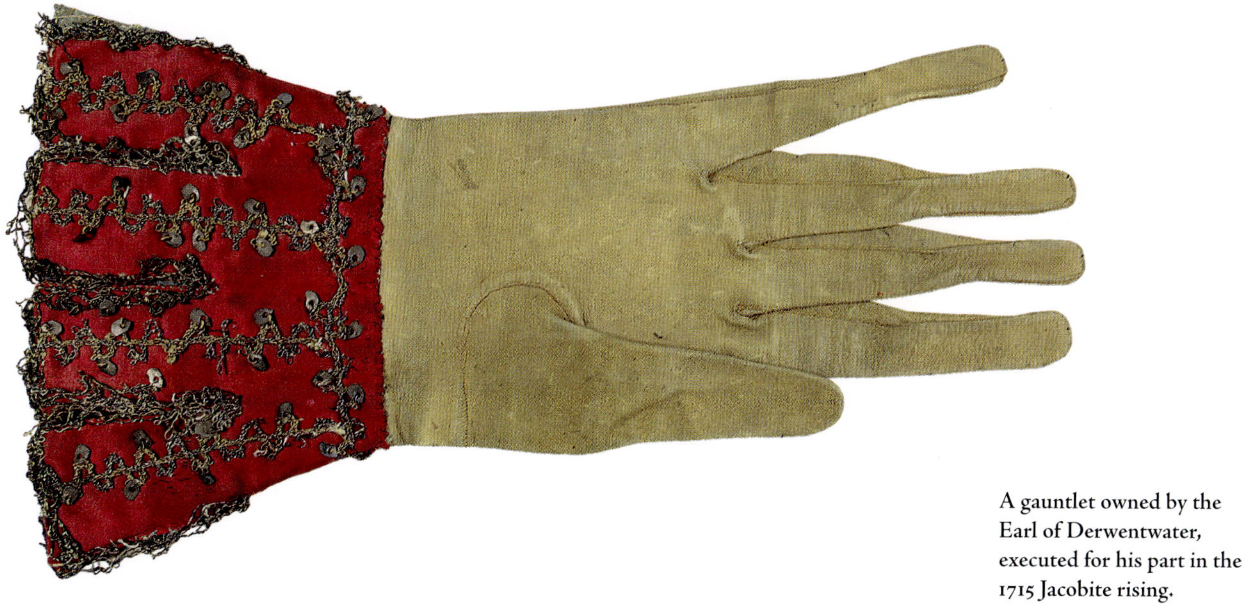

A gauntlet owned by the Earl of Derwentwater, executed for his part in the 1715 Jacobite rising.

marriage in 1712) were entrusted to Ushaw College and housed in what became known as the Radcliffe Reliquary. Items of interest range from a beautiful 1661 Roman Missal to engravings of the Radcliffe and Stuart families. Other items include a handsome Charles II pear wood chair with a cushion embroidered with the Radcliffe family crest (English needlework from the time of Queen Anne) and a delicately detailed seventeenth-century cradle. Additionally, there is a relic of flesh and blood from James II.

The pincushion here illustrated is one of two in the collection, embroidered with 'God Bless P.C. and down with the Rump', the 'P.C.' standing for 'Prince Charles' and the latter a common Jacobite call for a second Stuart restoration. Another pincushion (not pictured) is embroidered with the names of those executed for their involvement in the 1745 rebellion. Among the collection are also two gauntlets thought to have been owned by the executed James Radcliffe. The leather glove illustrated – with a red satin cuff embroidered with gold and silver thread with silver spangles – is English and particularly fine, dating from the late seventeenth or early eighteenth century.

SUSAN ROYAL

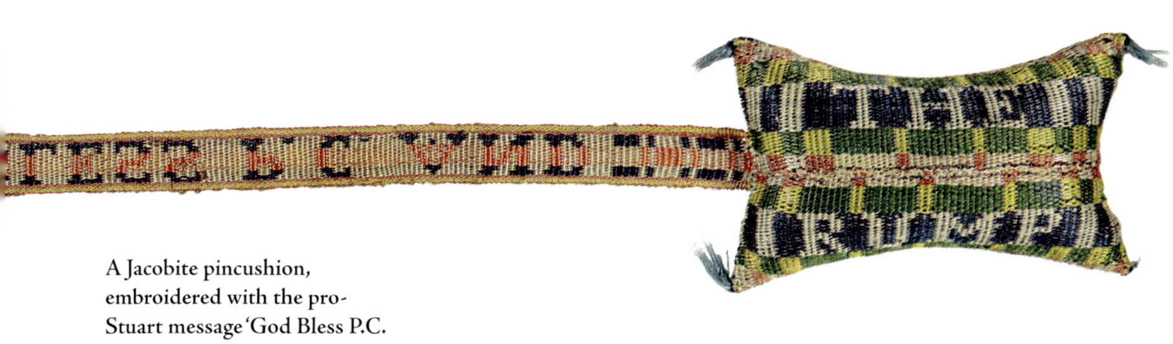

A Jacobite pincushion, embroidered with the pro-Stuart message 'God Bless P.C. and down with the Rump'.

Links to the Queen of England, Scotland and Ireland

Alban Crowther and Thomas Vincent, *Jesus, Maria, Joseph: or The devout Pilgrim of the ever blessed Virgin Mary in his Holy Exercises upon the sacred names of Jesus, Maria, Joseph. With the charitable Association for the Relief of the Souls departed. Published for the benefit of the pious rosarists by A.C. and T.V. Religious Monks of the Holy Order of S. Bennet.* Amsterdam, 1663. Ushaw, IV.D.8.18

This is the work of two Benedictine monks – in religion Alban Crowther (1588/9–1666) and Thomas Vincent, born Sadler (1604–81) – and is a shortened version of 301, rather than 648, pages of a work first printed in 1657. The most striking additions to this 1663 edition are a dedication to Charles II's Portuguese queen, Catherine of Braganza (1638–1705), together with a significant extra to the title page ('... with the charitable association for the relief of souls departed').

The two monks were also the co-authors of a best-seller in Catholic circles, *The daily exercise of devout Christians*, which ran through 15 editions from 1657 to 1793. All their work shows the influence of the mystic Dom Augustine Baker (1575–1641), as well as the Jesuit provincial and martyr Henry Garnet (1555–1606).

Doms Alban and Thomas were priests closely associated with the creation in the mid-1650s of the Confraternity of the Holy Rosary, established with the blessing of both the Pope and the General of the Dominican Order (and very clearly modelled on Henry Garnet's 1593 'Society of the Rosary'). The confraternity thrived without difficulty under the blind eye of, surprisingly, Oliver Cromwell and the indulgent eye of Charles II. It was suspended *sine die* during the Popish Plot crisis of the late 1670s.

The confraternity was centred around the home, in Lincoln's Inn Fields, of Robert Brudenell, second Earl of Cardigan (1607–1703), with a chapel, an altar dedicated to 'Our Lady of Power' and some important relics, including the Glastonbury Thorn and a splinter from the True Cross once displayed in Westminster Abbey. The confraternity priests also served at the Queen's chapel in Somerset House. The book contains a copy of the rules and statutes of the confraternity (pp.8-44), together with detailed guidance on how to pray the rosary (pp.44-129) and then an extended series of meditations on the sacred names of Jesus, Mary and Joseph. The final section consists of intercessionary prayer for the faithful departed, 'for the charitable relief and assistance of the souls in purgatory'. This is a significant addition to the 1657 edition.

Why was it reprinted in 1663? Perhaps it was intended simply to popularise the confraternity. More likely it was to make clear that the Queen was now its patron. But the addition to the title (and of prayers for souls in purgatory) might just be part of the stand-off between ultramontanes and Gallicans about concessions that could be made in order to secure freedom of Catholics from the penal laws. The liberals ('Blackloists') were pushing at just this time for toleration in exchange

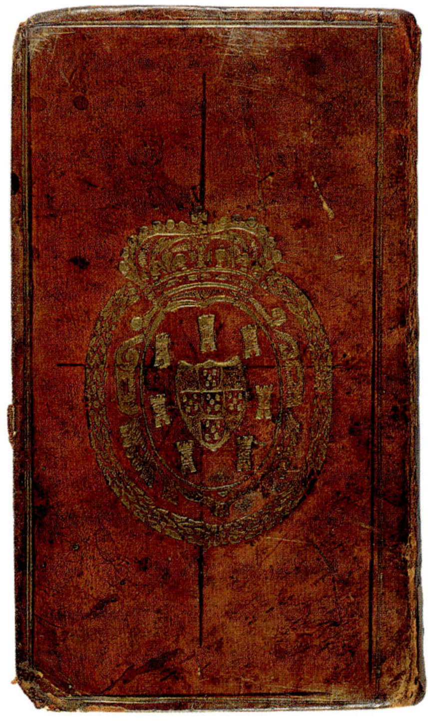

The coat of arms representing Catherine of Braganza.

Part of the Lisbon collection, this coded letter was sent during the secret negotiations surrounding Catherine of Braganza's marriage.

for a new oath of obedience together with promises that priests would stop preaching on those doctrines most obnoxious to Protestants. Purgatory was at the top of the list. Perhaps the Queen was being enlisted in the internal disputes about these proposed 'concessions'.

The Ushaw copy of *Jesus, Maria, Joseph* was almost certainly one of those presented to Queen Catherine. Although bound in plain calf, it has gilt stamps of the title phrase on the front cover and the arms of Portugal under the English crown (representing Catherine of Braganza) on the back. But there is a much grander copy in gold-tooled morocco bearing her coat of arms in the British Library, which is a copy formally held in the royal library. At some point, most likely on her return to Portugal in 1699 or at her death in 1705, the Ushaw copy was presented to the English College in Lisbon (ironically, a stronghold of Blackloism in the mid-seventeenth century) and from there it made its way to Ushaw in the nineteenth century.

The book is not the only link to Catherine of Braganza in the college's collections. Particularly noteworthy is a coded letter (dated 11 December 1665) from King Alfonso VI to the English priest, Richard Russell, relating to the secret negotiations behind the ceding of Bombay to the British as part of Catherine of Braganza's dowry.

JOHN MORRILL

A Unique Sailors' Guide

Gerard vander Vluyn, *The North-sea, containing the demonstration of the coast of Holland, the Texel streame, the Mase, the Channel of Goeree, the river of London, and from the same to the river of Edinbroug. With all courses, distances, and streames: as also the purtraictures of the lands.* Rotterdam, 1669. Ushaw, XIII.B.3.19

The most revealing views into the past are often in those items which were commonplace in their time but by their mundane nature have become very rare indeed. This nondescript sailor's guide to the coasts bordering the North Sea is a unique example, no other copy being known.

Coastal navigation in the seventeenth century was very much at the mercy of wind, tide and the sands, which as the guide says 'do alter and shift oftentimes much within a short time, so that ther is no certaintie to be written of it, wher unto man migt trust'. The text provides a description of the appearance of the coastline and the approaches to harbours, together with a set of woodcuts of 'how these lands doe shew themselves at sea' with important features such as beacons, woods, church towers and conspicuous sand dunes. These are supplemented by a collection of nine charts covering the coast of southern Denmark, the Netherlands including the Zuyder Zee and the approaches to Amsterdam, the Maas, the Flanders and English coasts. Bearings are recorded as compass points rather than degrees, a practice common until the nineteenth century. Due to their irregular numbering, it is possible that the charts were sold separately; vander Vluyn is known to have dealt in maps.

The book is bound in limp vellum with two leather ties remaining and is divided into two parts of 44 and 64 pages respectively, each with its own title page, although intended to be issued together. Unfortunately, the chart covering the east coast of England has been torn out leaving only a stub. Pages three to six of the first part are also wanting.

The text is in English but includes many Dutch-looking spellings suggesting that the compiler, Gerard vander Vluyn, may not have been a particularly fluent English speaker. The directions for entering the north east of England's River Tyne give a flavour of this: 'From the point of Tinmouth shooteth off a ledge of rocks, men must sayle in by it, leavingh it one the starboard side. The markes there of are two firebeakons, standingh up the north shoare, & bringh them one in the other, saile so right in alonghst by the foresaid ledge of rokes one the north side ... Coming within runne alongst by the north shoare, untill past the litle town Sheals, edge then over to the other shoare.'

The directions accord closely with a chart of the River Tyne in the *Atlas maritimus & commercialis* of 1728 (Ushaw, XVIII.G.1.6). This shows the two lights on the north shore which must be lined up 'one in the other' to cross the notoriously dangerous Tynemouth Bar while also avoiding the equally lethal 'ledge of rokes' known as the Black Middens. One can imagine that such a practical book of instructions might be worked to destruction but, sadly, there is no indication as to how this unique surviving copy arrived in the Big Library at Ushaw.

ALASTAIR H. FRASER

Title page of Gerard vander Vluyn, *The North-sea ...*, published in Rotterdam in 1669.

THE SECOND BOOKE,
Off the
NORTH-SEA,

CONTAIGNING

The Deſcription of the North-Sea, the Coaſt of Holland, the Texel Stream, the Maſe, the Channell of Goeree, and the River of London.

With a Courſes and Diſtances & Streames. Gathered by

GERARD vander VLUYN.

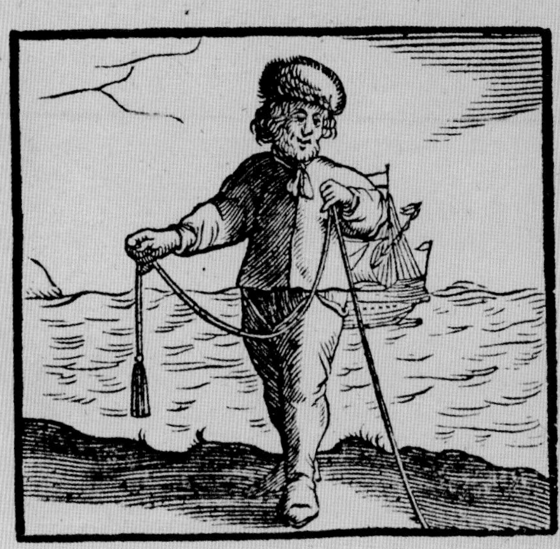

At ROTTERDAM,

Printed for GERARD vander VLUYN, Bookſeller, dwelling hard by the Iron-bridge in the Paſcart, 1669.

The Glorification of a King: Louis XIV and the *Cabinet du Roi*

Cabinet du Roi, 16 volumes from 1669 onwards. Ushaw, XI.E.1.2–15

One of the treasures of the Big Library at Ushaw is the set of plates known as the *Cabinet du Roi*, which was issued from 1669 under the direction of Jean Baptiste Colbert (1619–83), Louis XIV's finance minister, not to mention Minister of Fine Art and a patron of the Académie Royale.

At a meeting of the Conseil du Roi in December 1667, Louis 'decided to have engraved the plans and elevations of the royal houses, their decorative paintings and sculptures, the paintings and old illustrations of His Majesty's cabinet, in which are found illustrations of plants and animals of all kinds and other rare and unusual things'. Colbert's aim in the production of the series was the glorification of Louis XIV's reign both then and in the future. In the *avertissement* to the volume of royal tapestries he stated that the plates would be 'precious monuments to all that is achieved today [...] those who come after us will be spectators to the marvels that we witness'.

The Ushaw copy is the first edition, identifiable by

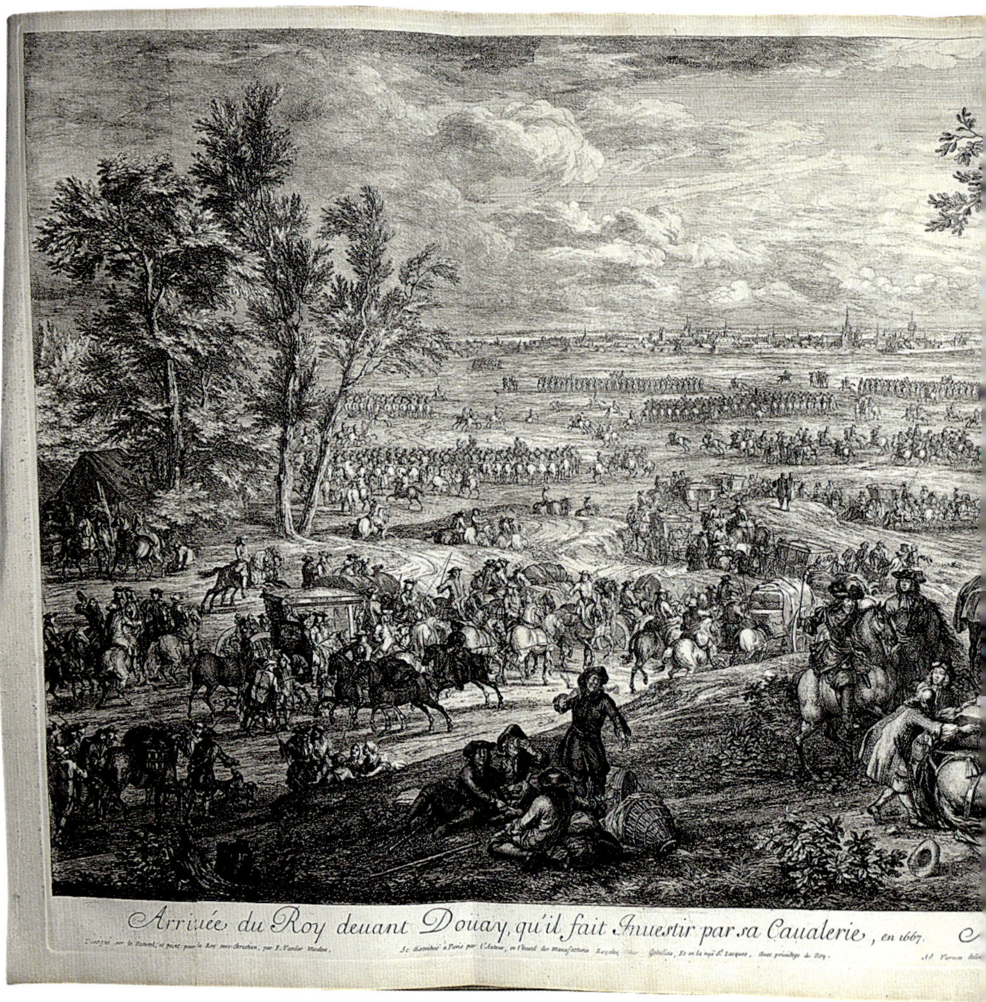

The skyline of Douai in 1667 as portrayed by van der Meulen, whose original drawings survive in the Louvre. The most identifiable feature is the belfry of the Hotel de Ville on the right with the squat tower of St Pierre and the steeple of St Albin to its left. Despite the detail of Jansonn's maps and the artist's sketches, other buildings are surprisingly hard to distinguish. Unfortunately the English College is on the far side of the town and so not visible; the twin towered building in the centre may be the monastery of the English Benedictines although it is not quite correctly positioned in relation to its near neighbour, the parish church of St Albin.

the varying size of the volumes, unlike the reissues of 1723 and later which are of uniform dimensions. It is in sixteen volumes and is bound throughout in red morocco with Louis XIV's arms in gold on the front of each volume.

Many volumes were issued without title pages and the bibliographical history of the work is complex. The set comprises plans and views of towns; sieges and battles; festivals, processions and fêtes; the palaces of Versailles, the Louvre, Vincennes, the Tuilleries, St Germain-en-Laye, Fontainbleu and their interior decoration and paintings.

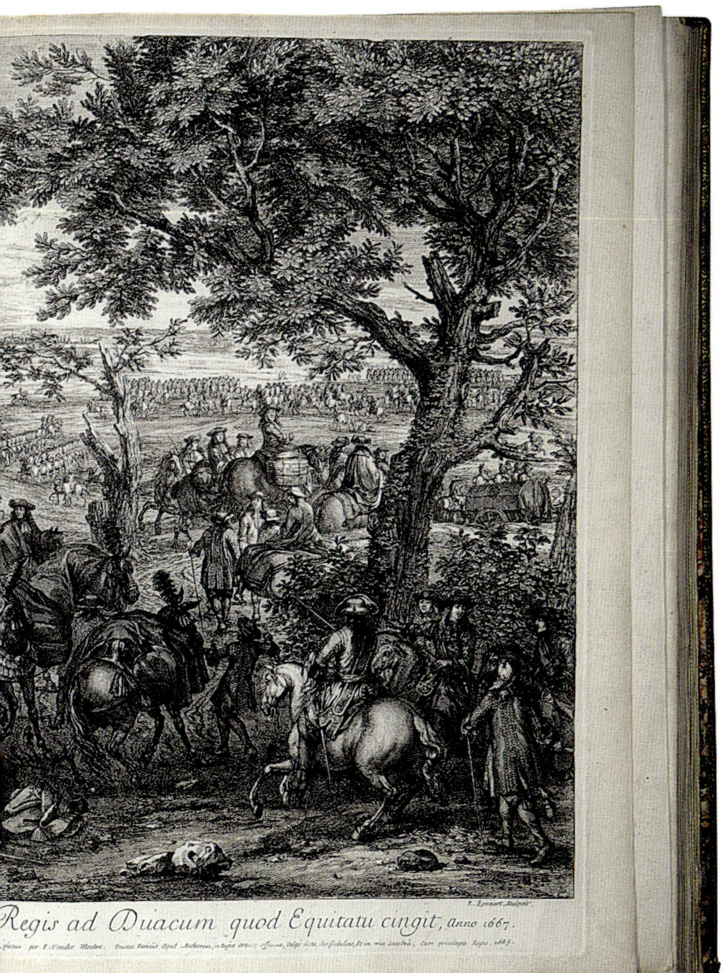

Many visitors to Ushaw will be familiar with the plate showing Louis' army before Douai reproduced here. The *Cabinet* in fact contains three plates of this event, which took place in 1667 during the War of Devolution between the French and the outnumbered Spanish forces in the Spanish Netherlands and Franche Comté. A second plate in the same volume shows the French camp in front of the Notre Dame gate. Louis was accompanied by two official artists and the views of Douai are from paintings by Adam Frans van der Meulen (1632–90). Comparison with plans of Douai in Jan Jansson's *Urbium totius Belgiis seu Germaniae Inferioris* ... of 1657 (Durham Chapter Library, L.3.A.10) indicates that the view is from the north-east as the French cavalry established a cordon around the town. Trenches were opened on 3 July and the town surrendered five days later once the French had gained a lodgement in the fortifications. Louis directed operations from the front-line and an engraving of another van der Meulen painting (Ushaw, XVIII.E.1.15) shows a horse being killed in front of him.

A medal was produced portraying Louis in the trenches to emphasise his credentials as a combat-hardened soldier and is reproduced in *Medailles sur les principaux evenements du regne de Louis le Grand*, printed at Paris in 1722 (Ushaw, XI.E.1.19).

ALASTAIR H. FRASER

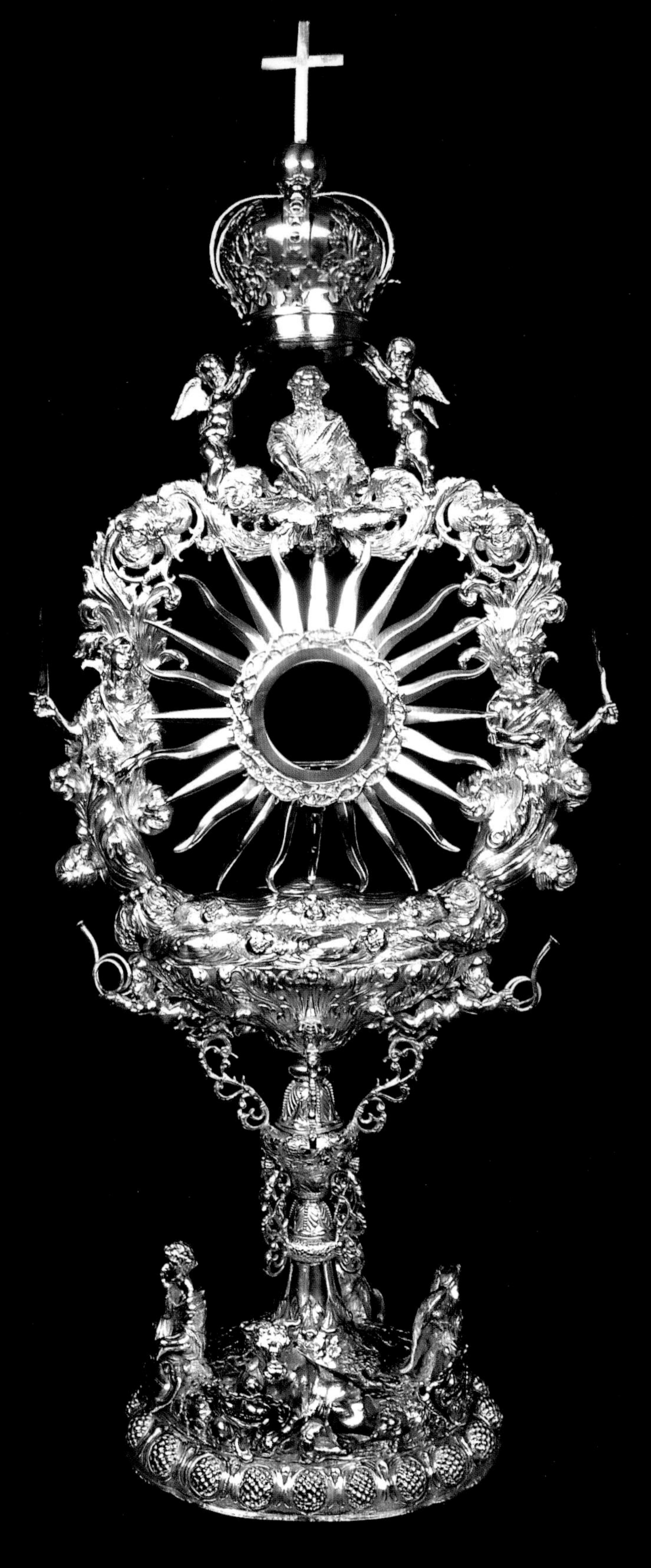

The Antwerp Monstrance

Silver monstrance, *c.*1670

This large silver monstrance, which stands 92 centimetres high, bears hallmarks for the Netherlands and the town mark of Antwerp. The date letter is obscured but the monstrance can be dated on stylistic grounds to about 1670.

The monstrance is surmounted by a royal crown, orb and cross, symbols of the authority of the Holy Trinity. Surrounding the lunette is a crown of thorns from which spring rays of light. These are flanked by two draped figures bearing swords. Above is a dove representing the Holy Spirit and higher still a seated figure of God the Father. The base is carved with foliage and on it stand the symbols of the four evangelists: a man for St Matthew, a lion for St Mark, an eagle for St John and an ox for St Luke. Each of these symbols bears a shield on which are inscribed the words '*Hoc est Corpus Meum*' ('This is My Body'), which recall the words of Jesus at the Last Supper and are uttered by the priest during the Mass at the moment of consecration.

The function of a monstrance is to display the Blessed Sacrament, that is the wafer which, according to Catholic belief, becomes the body of Christ when consecrated by a Catholic priest during the celebration of Mass. The Host would have been placed inside the window in the crescent-shaped holder called a 'lunula'. This size of monstrance may have been placed on the altar as a focus for worship during the service of Benediction, or carried aloft during church processions for all the congregation to see, such as on the feast of Corpus Christi.

The example at Ushaw was spotted in the 1830s in the window of a Liverpool jeweller's shop, where it was described as a second-hand watch stand! The eagle-eyed 'spotter' consulted with Ushaw's then-president, Charles Newsham, and the monstrance was subsequently presented to the college by a group of benefactors. It was certainly in use at Ushaw by 1839. The re-identification of this spectacular monstrance a few years after the emancipation of Catholics in 1829 demonstrates the increased popular awareness of the Catholic tradition. Its re-dedication for use in the college chapel also illustrates the emergence of a more confident Catholicism after the lifting of over two centuries of prohibition.

Catholic sacred silver that survived penal times, such as this example, frequently has an interesting, if concealed, history of ownership. Later embellishments frequently bear witness to the continued respect lavished on precious objects originally created – and once again restored – for sacred purposes.

Another fine example is an early sixteenth-century monstrance made in the Spanish Netherlands, which was embellished with jewels in the mid-seventeenth century and given to the English Augustinian convent at Louvain by its prioress, Magdalen Throckmorton, in 1662. It was subsequently acquired by the Catholic diocese of Plymouth and is currently on display at London's Victoria and Albert Museum.

TESSA MURDOCH

This large, seventeenth-century silver monstrance was spotted in a jeweller's shop in the 1830s, where it was being advertised as a second-hand watch stand.

Learning at Douai and Ushaw

Douai dictates and disputations, 1679. Ushaw, XVIII.D.1.9

From its earliest days, the English College at Douai employed the common European educational methods of teaching philosophy and theology. The extant sources now at Ushaw are particularly plentiful from the 1690s onwards and amply demonstrate these approaches.

Students were taught in the college by the institution's own lecturers. What the students wrote down in lectures were called 'dictates', but it is plain that they were expected to refer to the lecturer's own texts in the library as well. The result was that each student had in his own hand a reliable summary of his courses in philosophy and theology to guide him through his work as a missionary priest serving in England. Ushaw holds over 90 of these dictates; some of them are on permanent loan from old mission bases, while others form part of the Lisbon College collection, which arrived at Ushaw in the 1970s. Occasionally there are passages reflecting controversies raging at the time, for instance over Jansenism. The tradition of dictation tailed off following the death of Ushaw's first president, Thomas Eyre.

The item featured here is a fairly typical example of a Douai dictate from 1679 and includes a treatise on the Catholic doctrine of grace and its mediation through the sacraments. The student, Peter Bryan Tunstall (alias Scargill), took the missionary oath at Douai ten years later on 15 August 1689. He remained at the college as prefect general for several years, confessor for a further eight and procurator for two more years before going on the mission in 1715, a dangerous time for Catholics following the failure of the Jacobite rising. He became missioner of York and died there on 3 June 1742.

Disputations were also a staple of teaching and intellectual exercise within the English College at Douai. The contents of a course can be recovered from the printed posters advertising public disputations, to which other colleges at Douai were invited. These public displays of learning were a form of publication: the task of ensuring the orthodoxy of the teaching devolved in the first place on the lecturer himself, but also on the college's prefect (director) of studies. These public demonstrations of orthodox learning provided a natural occasion for inter-collegiate rivalry – particularly with members of the Society of Jesus – as one can glean from occasional letters or remarks made in lectures.

The tradition of printed public disputations continued after the college's relocation to England, first at Crook Hall and then at Ushaw, though the 'public' was limited to alumni and other friends of the college. From 1830, lectures on natural philosophy (soon to be renamed 'science') were in English. Despite the misgivings of John Lingard and Robert Tate, the rest of the philosophical disputations and all the theological disputations continued to be in Latin, until this long tradition died a natural death in 1896.

Scholars visiting the Ushaw libraries today will find complete hand lists of all the dictates and printed disputations from the college's past.

MICHAEL SHARRATT AND JONATHAN BUSH

Dictates were a staple form of learning at the English College at Douai, as shown here by the 'Treatise on Grace' from 1679 by student Peter Tunstall.

Tractatus de Gratia:~:

Prima 2ae q 79 & deinceps usque ad finem.

Quicquid de graa tradi solet illud deo iuvante visum est duabus disputationibus comprehendere, quarum altera erit de naa & necessitate graa, altera de hostibus illius Pelagianis & semipelagianis.

Disputatio 1ma.

De Natura & necessitate Gratiae divinae.

Q 1

Quid & quotuplex sit Gratia. q.111

§ 1.

Gratia in coni.

Graa inde nomen accepisse quod gratis detur, observavit *Apost. ad Rom 11 v 6 si a graa iam non ex operibus, alioquin graa iam non est graa. & S Aug.* l de spiritu & litera c 8 graa non

*in pl 43 T8. ser 61 de verbis Dni c 1 T10

The Lisbon chasuble

Chasuble and maniple, late seventeenth century

Probably made in Italy, this chasuble is thought to have been used at the English College at Lisbon before it was brought to Ushaw.

Chasubles are worn by priests during the celebration of Mass. This lavishly sequined, creamy-white silk damask example would have made a dazzling impact, reflecting the candles lit for the saying of Mass in the late seventeenth century. White liturgical vestments, such as this example, were worn at Christmas and Easter, as well as for the feasts of the Virgin Mary, angels and non-martyr saints since the thirteenth century.

The dominant cross on the chasuble's back is made up of a geometrical grid of sequins interspersed with small knots and bars worked in metal threads. The rayed roundel at the centre of the cross contains an image of the bleeding crucified Christ imposed over the embroidered letters 'IHS', signifying Jesus's name in Greek (*iota-eta-sigma*). Ignatius Loyola, founder of the Jesuits, used various versions of this Christogram in his letters and, at his wish, it appears conspicuously on Jesuit churches, though in the early modern period Lisbon College never had any contact with that order. Naked angels in clouds, worked in metal threads highlighted with blue and red silk embroidery, hover on either side of the main cross. One holds aloft a crown and the other a chalice.

The rest of the chasuble is embroidered in metal threads in a design of stars with short and long wavy rays alternating with drops of blood or tears. Sequins stitched in groups of five fill in the remaining spaces. The cross and the chasuble's edges are bordered with a band of alternating stylised blue flowers and leaf sprays linked by small red hearts, echoing the heart embroidered below Christ's feet.

The same border design appears on the matching maniple, a doubled length of fabric stitched together to form a loop so it could be worn over the left wrist of the Mass celebrant. This was used to prevent a priest's hand making direct contact with the sacred Mass vessels. Symbolically, the maniple has been associated with the chains which bound Christ's hands, with penitential tears and with the weight of sin. The vesting prayer said by a priest when putting on a maniple links it with the burden of priestly office: '*Merear, Domine, portare manipulum fletus et doloris: ut cum exultatione recipiam mercedem laboris*' ('Lord, may I worthily bear the maniple of tears and sorrow so as to receive the reward of my labour with rejoicing').

MARY BROOKS

Overleaf: Angels in clouds, worked in metal threads highlighted with blue and red silk embroidery, hover on either side of the main cross.

Late seventeenth-century chasuble from the English College at Lisbon, made from silk damask with silk and metal thread embroidery and sequins.

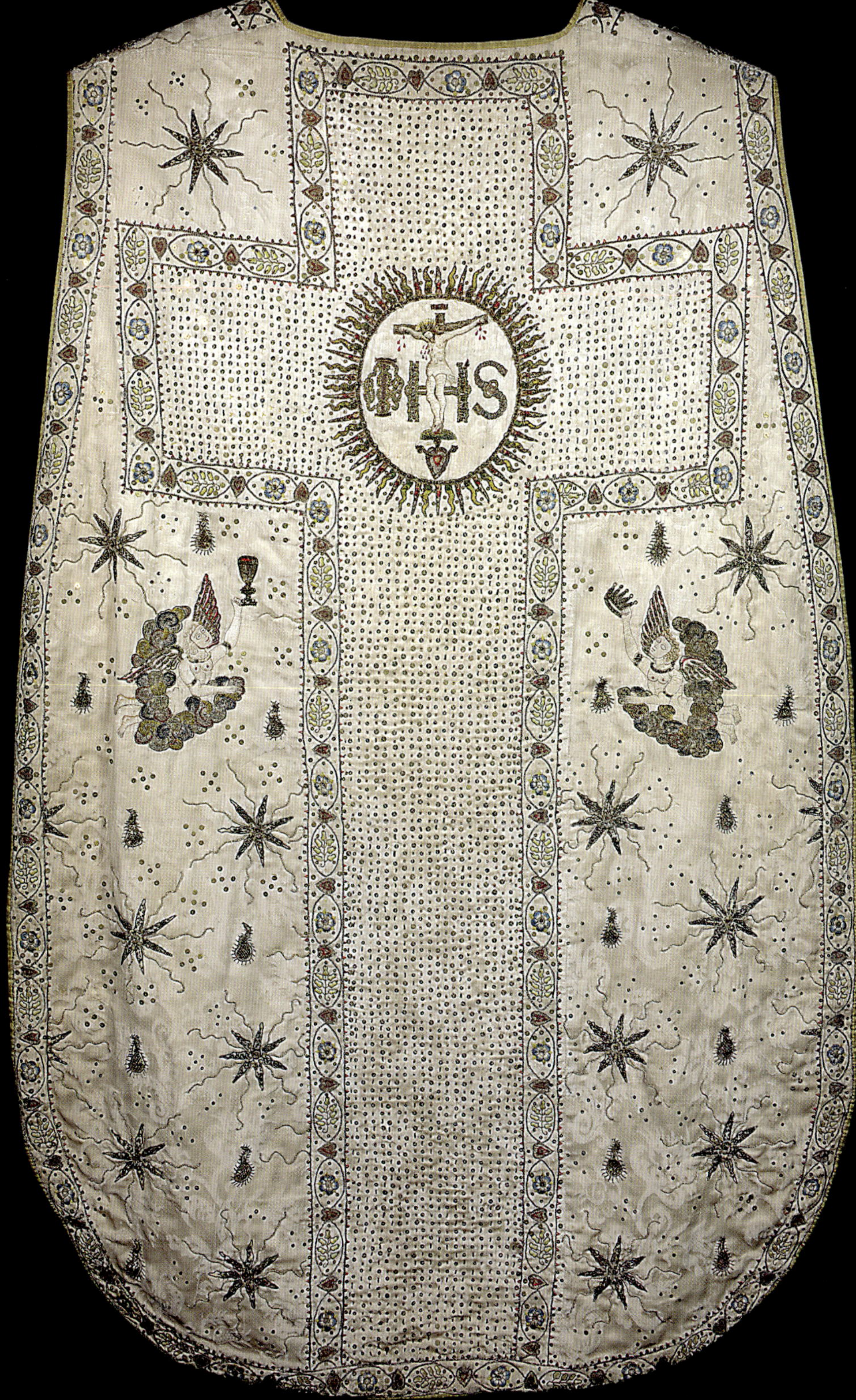
IHS

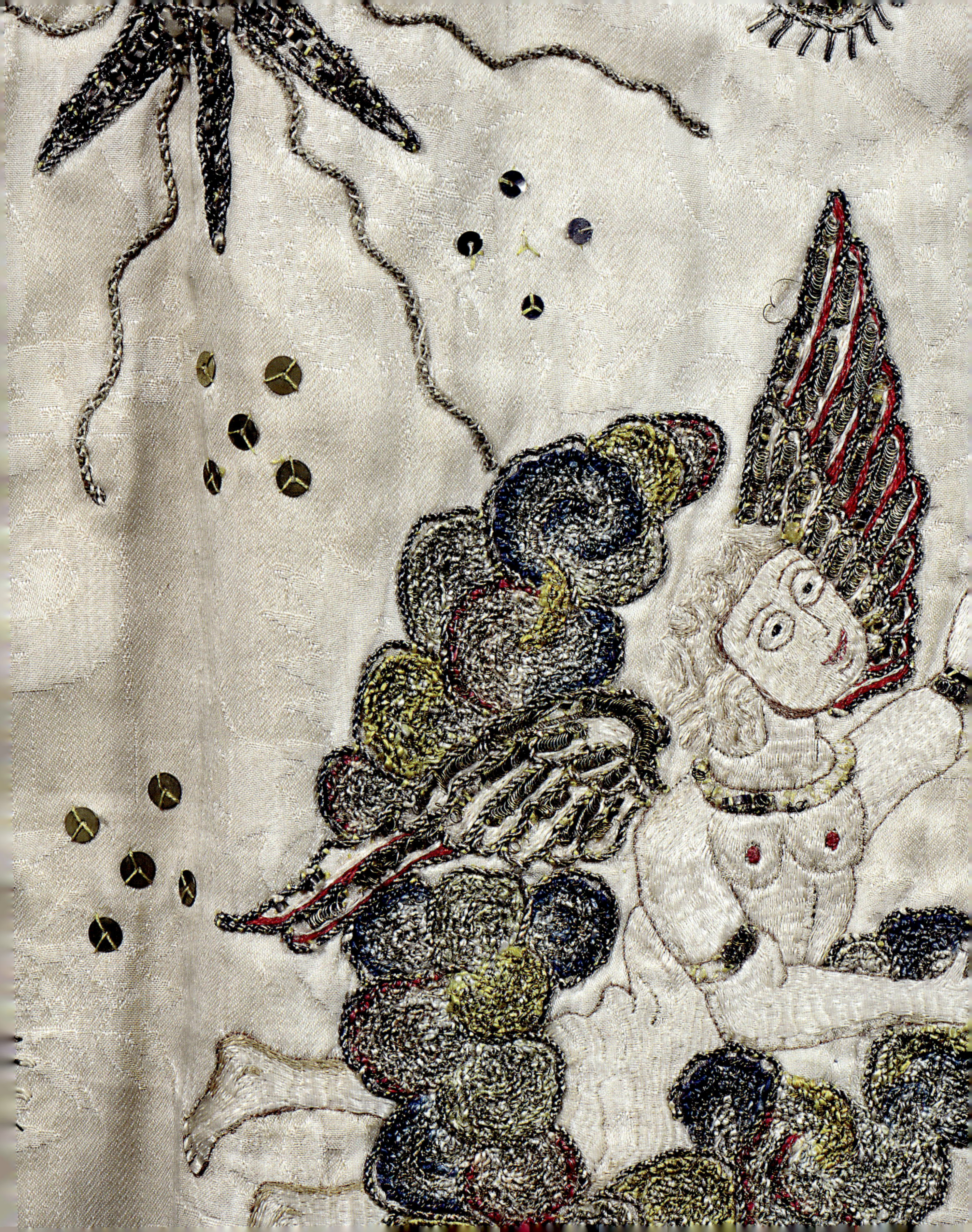

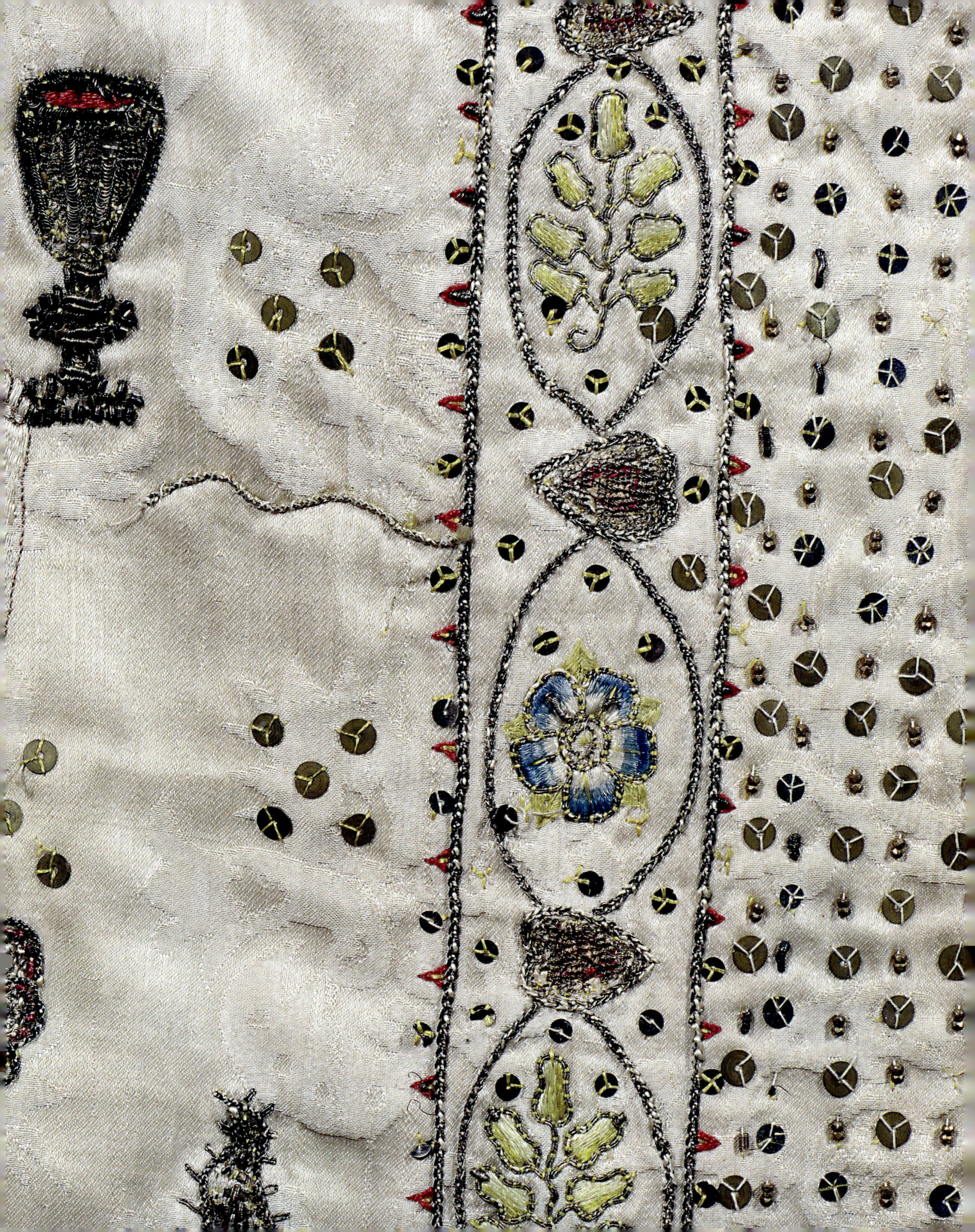

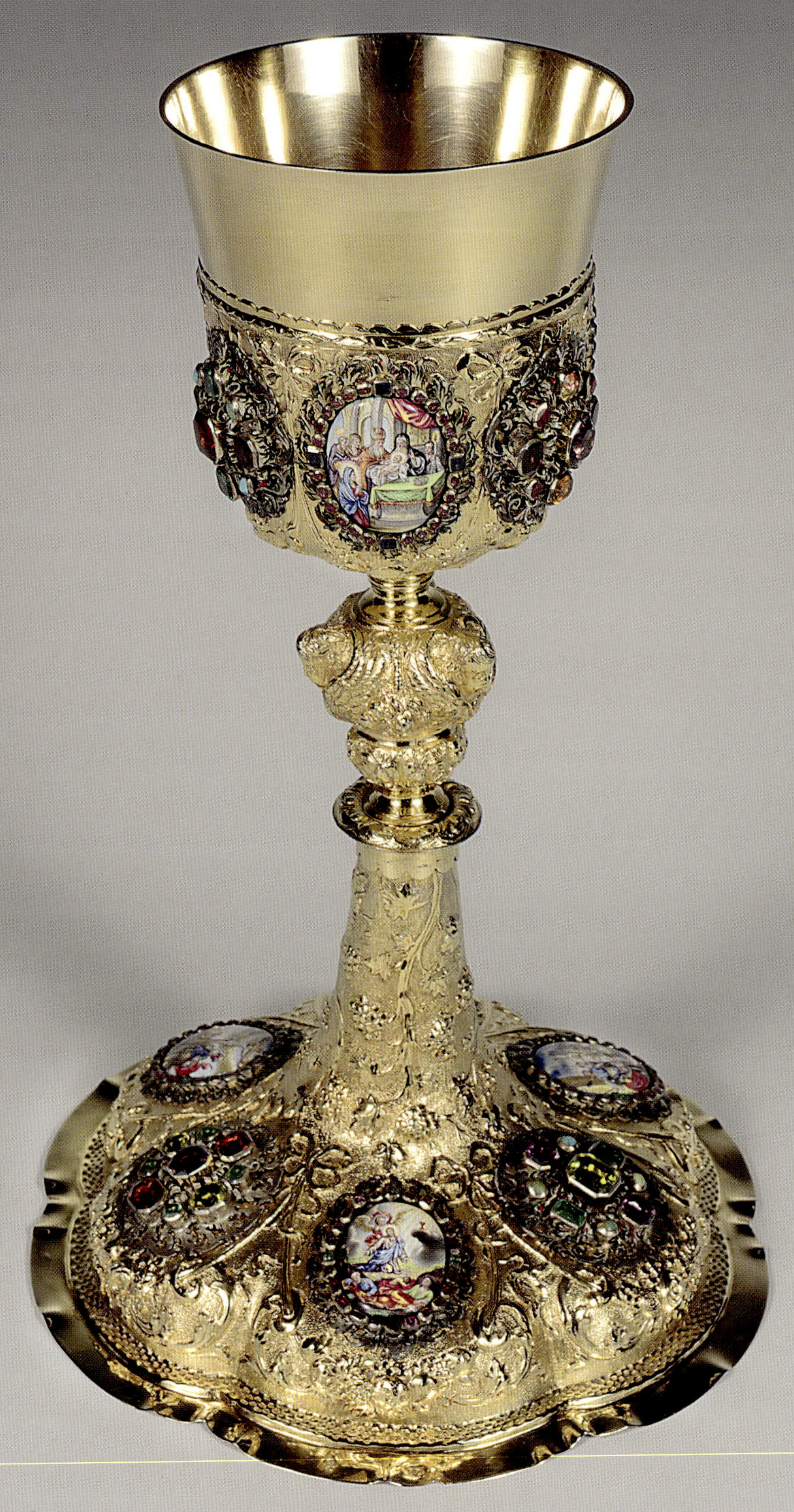

The Augsburg Chalice

Silver-gilt chalice, *c.*1700

This silver-gilt chalice, Roman in shape and standing nearly 30 centimetres high, with a knopped stem chased with cherub heads and vines, was a gift to Ushaw College from Mgr Witham of Lartington Hall, Yorkshire. Mgr Witham was actually a member of the Silvertops, an old recusant family resident at Minsteracres in Northumberland, but his father changed the family name to Witham when he succeeded to the Lartington estate. The earliest record of this chalice being at the college is in a sacristan's guide of the 1830s, meaning it would therefore have been used in Ushaw's original 1808 Georgian chapel. The chapel was a modest room with no decoration except for a few paintings and two monumental tablets; the wooden altar was designed so that the inner case of the tabernacle could be lowered out of view, thus protecting the Blessed Sacrament from potentially sacrilegious intruders. One can imagine that the ornate beauty of this chalice would have been quite striking against the simplicity of a chapel designed for the penal days.

The lower half of the cup is chased with bows and flowers, and bears three clusters of stones set in enamelled silver mounts and three enamel plaques representing the Annunciation, the Nativity and the Presentation in the Temple. The base is also mounted with enamels representing the Agony in the Garden, the Scourging of Christ and the Crucifixion, all set between clusters of table-cut stones, chased with garlands of flowers. The chalice is hallmarked for the well-known Augsburg silversmith, Johann Zeckel, and retains its original leather case embossed with gold.

Zeckel was active in Augsburg from 1691 until his death in 1728 and, as a Catholic, specialised in making sacred silver for Catholic use. This chalice relies on figurative enamel plaques for appropriate theological symbolism. Silver from Augsburg was exported across Europe and this chalice may have been acquired for use in England during the eighteenth century, although there is no evidence to confirm its history of ownership.

Augsburg was at the time a leading centre for goldsmiths and the jewellery trade. Contemporary workshops specialising in secular silver included that run by the Lutheran Biller family, Lorenz (working 1664–85) and his three sons, Johann Ludwig (1656–1732) Albrecht (1663–1720) and Lorenz (working *c.*1678–1726), as well as the Drentwett family, represented by Abraham Drentwett (1647–1729) during Zeckel's lifetime.

In contrast to the Augsburg chalice, a silver and partly gilded monstrance marked by Johann Zeckel for 1705, elaborately decorated with imagery in relief associated with Christ and the Eucharist, is preserved in London's Victoria and Albert Museum. The plaque beneath the window shows the Last Supper. The apostles are seated around the table but Christ himself is absent, to be represented by the Host when the monstrance was in use. The imperial crown at the top represents God the Father. The cornucopias on either side, containing grape vines and ears of corn, symbolise the wine and bread of the Eucharist, the blood and body of Christ, underlining Zeckel's taste for symbolism.

TESSA MURDOCH

This chalice was made by Johann Zeckel in Augsburg between 1691 and 1728, and stands almost 30 cm high.

For 'the veneration of the faithful'

Relics in the Oratory of the Holy Family, eighteenth century

Ushaw College is home to one of the largest collections of religious relics in the United Kingdom. Resting in specially built cabinets in the Oratory of the Holy Family, it was hoped that the saints represented would 'redouble their prayers for the conversion of the English'.

The acquisition of relics in the Christian tradition peaked in Europe during the medieval period; from the fourth to the sixteenth century the veneration of relics became a powerful tradition within the Church. Considered more valuable than gold and silver, they influenced power struggles and helped form community identities. Their importance lay in their perceived direct connection to the saints in heaven, who would then intercede on behalf of the individual, thus bridging the gap between the living and the dead. Thought to possess the power of the living saint, relics became associated with miracles of healing and became the focal point of pilgrimages. Elaborate reliquaries were crafted to enshrine such sacred objects and are now recognised as artworks in their own right.

This large-scale trade in relics, however, led to some being of questionable authenticity and the Ushaw relics are no exception to this.

Numbering around eight hundred individual relics set into two hundred beautifully ornate reliquaries, the Ushaw collection includes relics of the True Cross and Crucifixion, hair of the Blessed Virgin Mary and relics of bone from Ss Joseph, Mary Magdalen and John the Baptist. The majority of the collection is of early Christian saints, including a relic of blood from the Church's first martyr, St Stephen, the skull of St Felix and relics of bone from Ss Perpetua, Lucy, Cosmas and Damian. Also included are early European saints such as Elizabeth of Hungary and Edmund of Canterbury, not to mention St Ursula and her followers.

This impressive range of holy relics was gathered by a private collector in early eighteenth-century Naples. Don Nicola Antonio de Bonis, advocate in the court of the Archbishop of Naples, used his connections within the Vatican and across southern Italy to acquire – and sometimes swap – relics. Housing them in his personal oratory, de Bonis set his precious acquisitions in the same striking baroque reliquaries in which they are still enshrined today.

On hearing that President Charles Newsham was seeking a collection of relics for Ushaw's new chapels, Mgr George Talbot, chamberlain to Pope Pius IX, wrote to Newsham about de Bonis's collection, which he had travelled to Naples to see. Talbot's letter of 1859 states that he did 'not know a place in which so magnificent a collection of numerous relics would be more appreciated than at Ushaw, where a *reliquia insignis* might be exposed for the veneration of the students on all the festivals of the Great Saints'. As it was illegal to buy and sell relics, Newsham phrased it as a transaction for the reliquaries, costing £1,000. Their arrival at the college in May 1860 was met with the jubilation of the student body; the relics were led in procession to the chapel where the *Te Deum* was sung in thanksgiving.

CLAIRE MARSLAND

A sample of the relics housed in the Oratory of the Holy Family. In the foreground stands a phial of St Teresa of Avila's blood (1515–82).

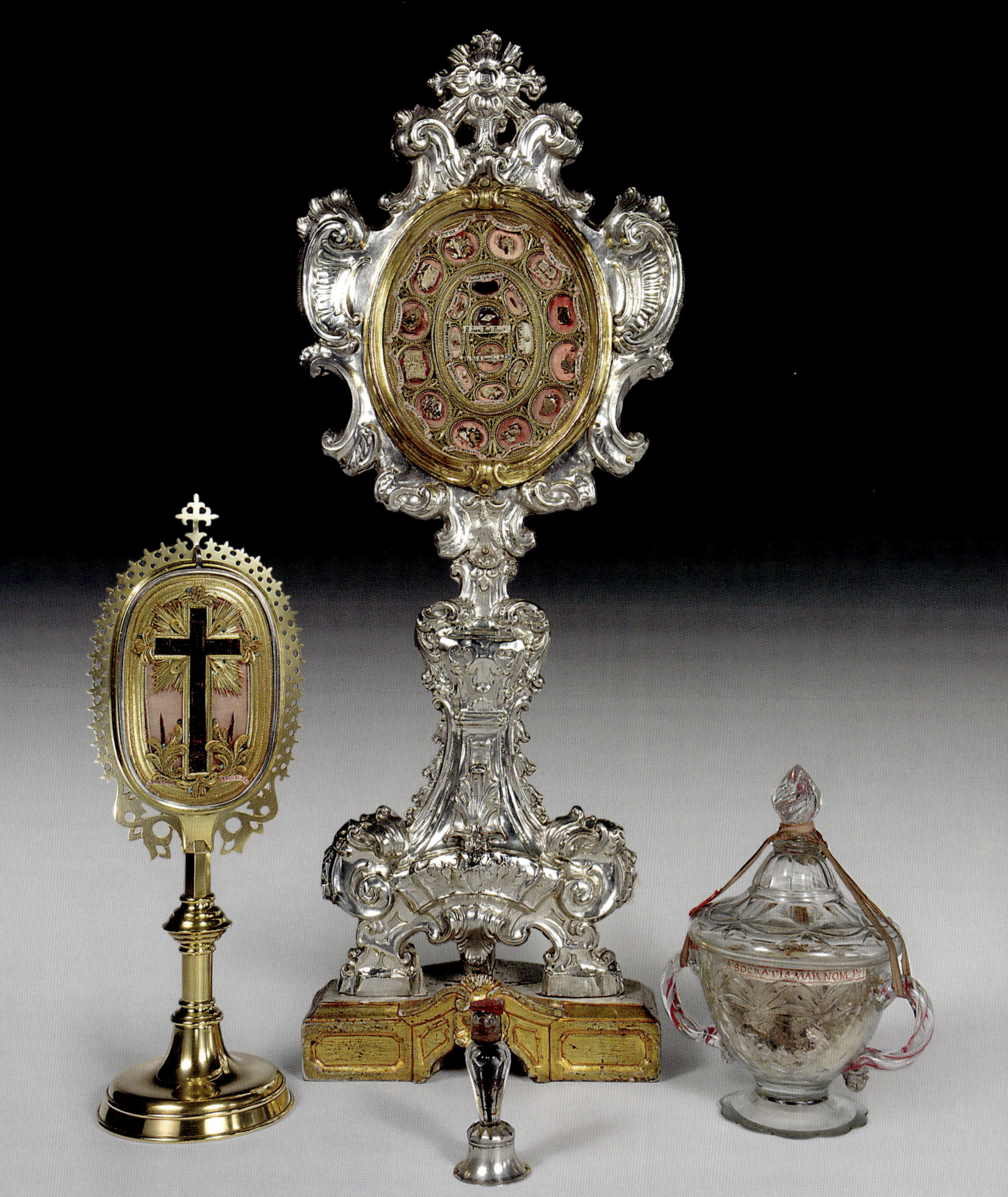
S SOCRATIS MAR NOM P

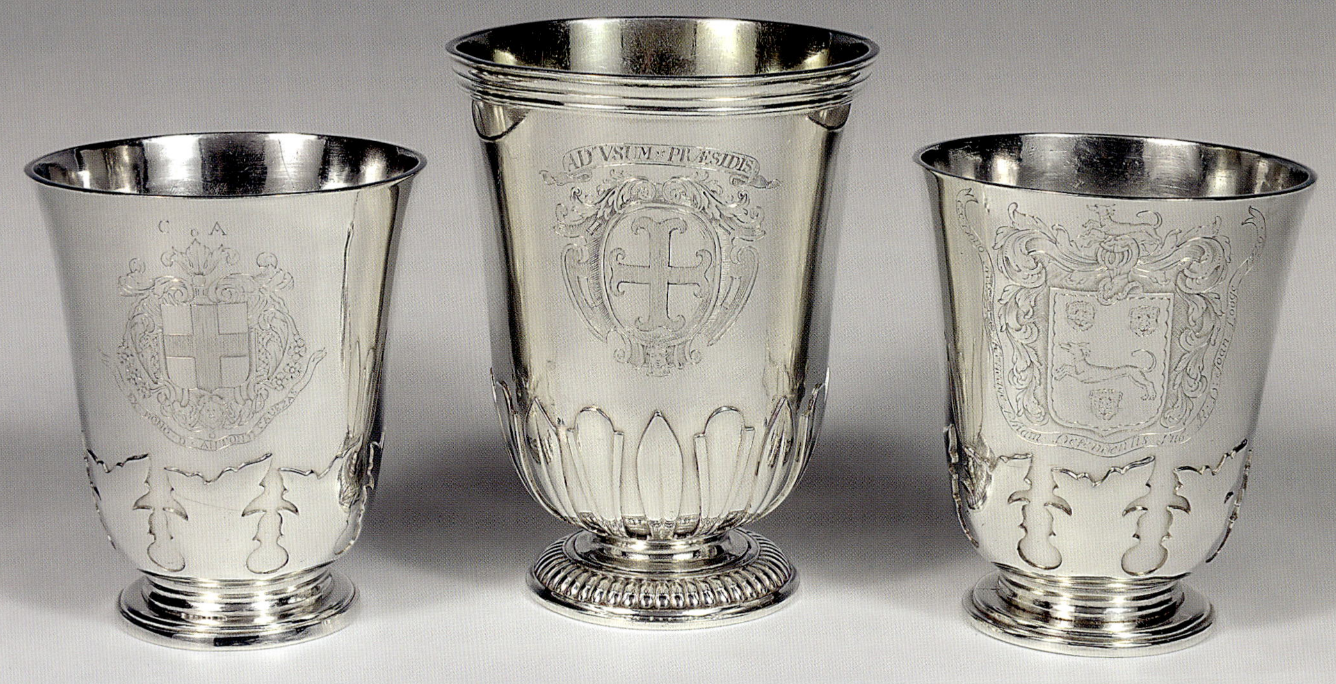
C. A
AD VSUM PRÆSIDIS

The Douai Silver

Silver beakers from the English College, Douai, 1721–50

Founded in 1568 by William Allen, the English College at Douai flourished until the French Revolution and its associated violence forced the institution to close. The students were interned by the authorities in an upper room of the college but they managed to rescue the college silver housed in the president's room by climbing down the chimney. Silver and scientific instruments were packed into two boxes and then lowered to the ground floor. One of the boxes was buried under a flagstone in a ground-floor classroom; the other was buried outside the walls of the town. However, the contents of the latter were soon sold to feed the students and to meet their travel costs back to England. It is believed that this box contained the sacred silver, as only a set of altar cruets and a single chalice survive from Douai College.

The English College buildings were confiscated by the revolutionaries and converted to a military hospital, a cotton factory and a barracks. As staff and students were forced to leave, they were only able to bring back to England with them a few objects. The college silver that had been buried for safe keeping under the classroom floor was only reclaimed following its re-discovery in Douai by students from Ushaw in the nineteenth century. One of the four students who had hidden the silver, Fr R. Thompson, returned to Douai in 1841 and reported that the box was still intact.

It was 22 years later that Mgr Francis Searle obtained permission from Napoleon III to search for the treasure and, with the assistance of notes from the last survivor of Douai, Thomas Penswick, finally discovered the box. The contents was divided on reaching England between Ushaw and its 'sister' in the south, St Edmund's College, Ware. The silver allocated to Ushaw includes several beakers, of which three are here illustrated from a total of 19 survivors. Each beaker is engraved with the names and armorial crests of prelates and students at the college. In addition, some cutlery is also held at Ushaw, as well as a chocolate pot, candlesticks and salt cellars.

One of the earliest of the surviving silver beakers, illustrated here, commemorates the role of the president of the college and was made in 1721–23, when Robert Witham held the position. It is marked for Lille with the maker's mark – a Medusa's head – which has not been identified. The base is adorned with cut card work (cut from sheet silver and soldered to the vessel). The beaker is engraved with the coat of arms of the English College and the legend '*Ad usum praesidis*' (for the use of the president).

The students of the English College at Douai were mostly sons of the English nobility prevented as Catholics from attending English 'public' schools or the universities of Oxford and Cambridge because of the religious oaths required for entry. They were sent to Douai either for a general education or for specific training for the priesthood. The illustrated beakers commemorate Anthony Cauzas, a student from 24 June 1747 to 9 November 1750, and George Heneage, who studied at Douai from June 1745 to 1749 under the philosophy tutor Fr John Lodge. Both the Cauzas and Heneage beakers were made by local Douai goldsmith, Charles Louis Gerard.

TESSA MURDOCH

From left to right, the beakers of Anthony Cauzas, the college president – who at the time was Robert Witham – and George Heneage.

Scientific Enquiry at Lisbon

Bronze sundial, 1732

John Shepperd (1678–1761), a canon of the English Chapter (a body of senior clergy which helped oversee the management of the English Catholic mission), served as agent for the English College at Lisbon from 29 January 1733 to his death on 27 October 1761. The position of agent or 'London procurator' was one of great influence and even greater burdens. Shepperd's agent accounts (1733–61), held at Ushaw as part of the Lisbon collection, give an economic narrative of buying and selling that details the interests of Lisbon College at the time and the state of the English Catholic community in England. In addition, the letter books of presidents Edward Jones (1707–29; 1732–38) and John Manley (1729–32; 1739–55), as well as the correspondence papers of President Gerard Bernard (1755–77) – all held at Ushaw – supplement the agent accounts to reveal a network of patronage and clientage crucial to the college's survival.

Shepperd's role was somewhere, in modern parlance, between a logistics agent and a development officer. He was responsible for procuring material for the college in Lisbon and responding to orders from the three mentioned presidents, as well as from members of the college's council of superiors. These orders included anything from reading material to spectacles, onion seed to wine, mustard grain to musical instruments. Shepperd, based for most of his office at Hammersmith in west London, controlled a web of networks that he utilised for the good and promotion of his alma mater. Bernard, in his entry in the college's annals, wrote that Shepperd, 'spares no effort in promoting the College's welfare, as is evident from his account books'. There are 236 of his letters in the Lisbon collection at Ushaw; most are addressed to Jones and Manley.

Shepperd's interest in sundials was taken up by a contemporary Lisbonian, the Anglo-Portuguese Jerome Allen (1730–1815). Allen, a client of the Marquis of Pombal, attempted to build an observatory on the college's third floor and in correspondence to Nicholas Williams of London (20 November 1792) details his request for a sundial for the Bishop of Porto as a gift from the college. The 'observatory' was built in the 1790s and reflected a healthy interest in scientific learning that flourished in the college at the time.

This sundial, previously situated in the college's gardens, has been part of the Lisbon collection at Ushaw since the closure of the English College in Lisbon in 1973. It is made of bronze and was commissioned by President John Manley and dated London, 1732. It is 46 centimetres in diameter and is engraved '*ex dono Joannis Shepherd*'. The sundial displays astronomical terms and is the work of Thomas Wright (1711–86), instrument maker to King George II. Wright, of Byers Green, County Durham, was apprenticed to the instrument makers Thomas Heath and Jonathan Sissons of London. He was still an apprentice when he made this sundial after the 'school' of his teachers, Heath and Sissons. Wright later became more widely known for his astronomical publications, most notably *An Original Theory of the Universe* (1750). From the 1750s he turned his skills to landscape architecture. His most celebrated designs include the pinnacles for Durham Cathedral.

SIMON JOHNSON

The bronze sundial, made in London in 1732, was situated in the gardens of the English College at Lisbon. There was a strong tradition of scientific enquiry at the college.

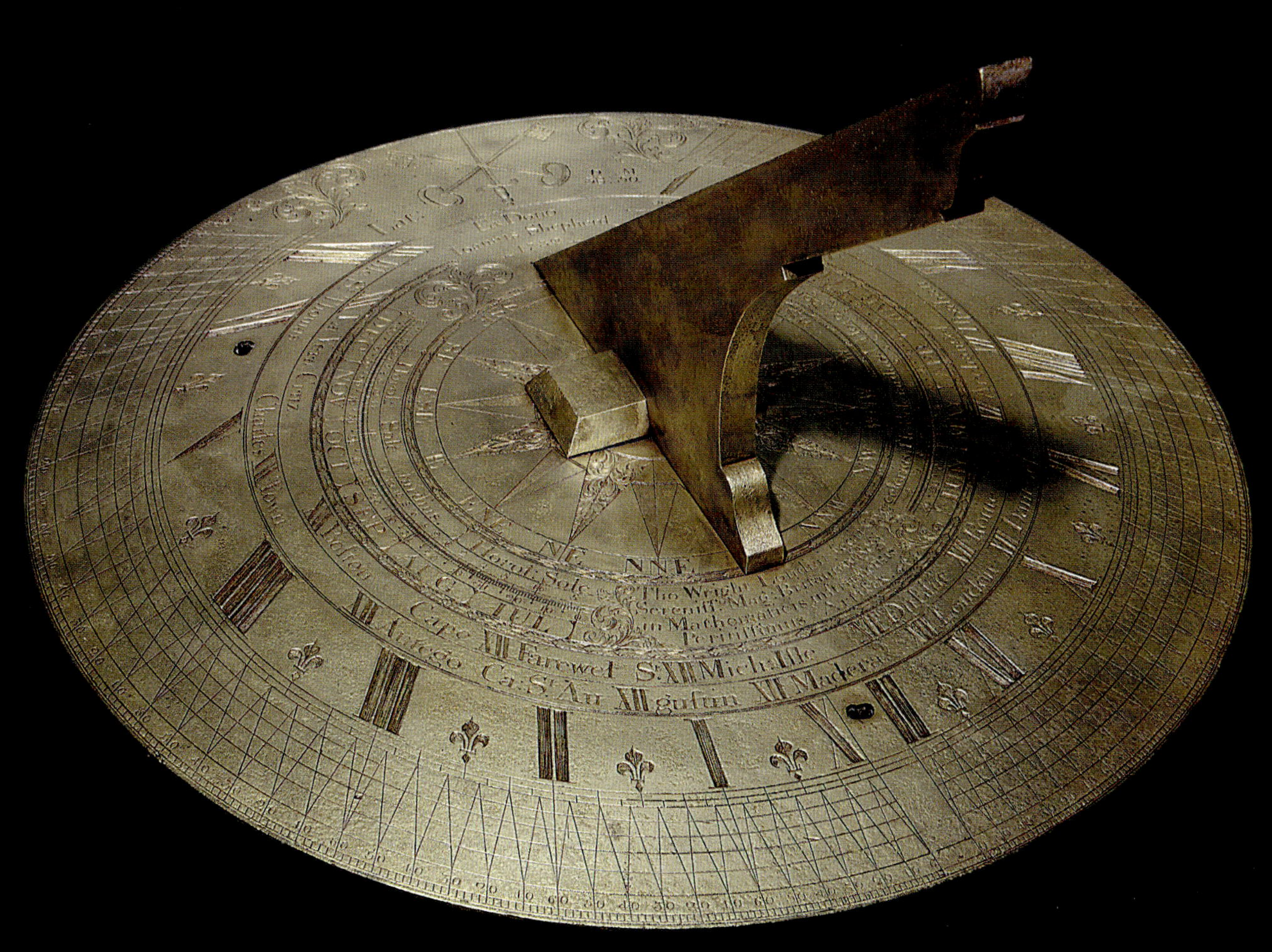

NE
NNE
Horol. Sole
Cape
Farewel
Antego
Madera

The Lisbon Sanctuary Lamp

Sanctuary lamp, 1739

This massive eighteenth-century silver baroque sanctuary lamp – 137 centimetres in height – once hung above the high altar of the chapel at the English College in Lisbon. The lamp embodies the liturgical splendour English Catholics experienced in mainland Europe, but which they rarely found in the small clandestine English chapels where they worshipped under the penal laws. The lamp came to Ushaw in the 1970s with a range of objects, vestments, incunabula and early printed books following the closure of the English College in Lisbon.

The metalwork includes a crowned 'L' mark, indicating that it was made in Lisbon between 1721 and 1750. Indeed, records held at Ushaw show that a sanctuary lamp was commissioned for the college in 1739. The silversmith was Antonio Amado Sanches, born in Leiria around 1700. He held several positions in the Brotherhood of St Eloi, a fraternity of silversmiths, but unfortunately ended his career in poverty and died around 1772.

The receipt for the lamp, dated 28 August 1739, records that Sanches received 111,820 Portuguese reis as payment for his work. This roughly translates to £2,697 in modern money, such an expense underlining the value that was placed on creating a beautiful artwork that would be prominent in the college chapel.

Damage to the sanctuary lamp indicates that it was probably caught up in the destruction caused by the 1755 Lisbon earthquake and may have fallen from its hanging. The earthquake took place at around ten o'clock on the morning of All Saints day, 1 November 1755, and killed over 20,000 people, causing massive destruction in the city as a whole. The college chapel was certainly damaged in the earthquake; indeed, the president, John Manley, was killed by the collapse of the church belfry whilst preparing for Mass.

A sanctuary lamp burns continuously before the tabernacle to signify Catholic belief in the real presence of Christ in the reserved consecrated Hosts. In England before the Reformation, many cathedrals and abbeys possessed sanctuary lamps of silver. They were not ordered again for private, clandestine Catholic chapels until after the Restoration of the monarchy in 1660.

Two early examples are on display in the sacred silver galleries at London's Victoria and Albert Museum. A late seventeenth-century lamp in silvered brass formed part of the furnishings of the Catholic Petre family's chapel at Thorndon Hall, Essex. It bears the coat of arms of Thomas, 6th Baron Petre and his wife Mary Clifton and can be dated to between 1685 and 1690. It is on loan to the museum from the Catholic Diocese of Brentwood.

A silver sanctuary lamp marked for London-based goldsmith Charles Kandler is inscribed 'The Gift of James Aveline who died ye 7th of April 1726' and is identified with James Aveline of Steyning, West Sussex, although it is not known for which chapel the lamp was made. Kandler, of German birth and training, supplied sacred and secular plate from his shop at the Mitre, St Martin's Lane, Charing Cross. Kandler's clients included Thomas Howard, 8th Duke of Norfolk, who was educated at Douai College.

TESSA MURDOCH

This silver sanctuary lamp, commissioned in 1739, once hung in the chapel of the English College of Ss Peter and Paul at Lisbon.

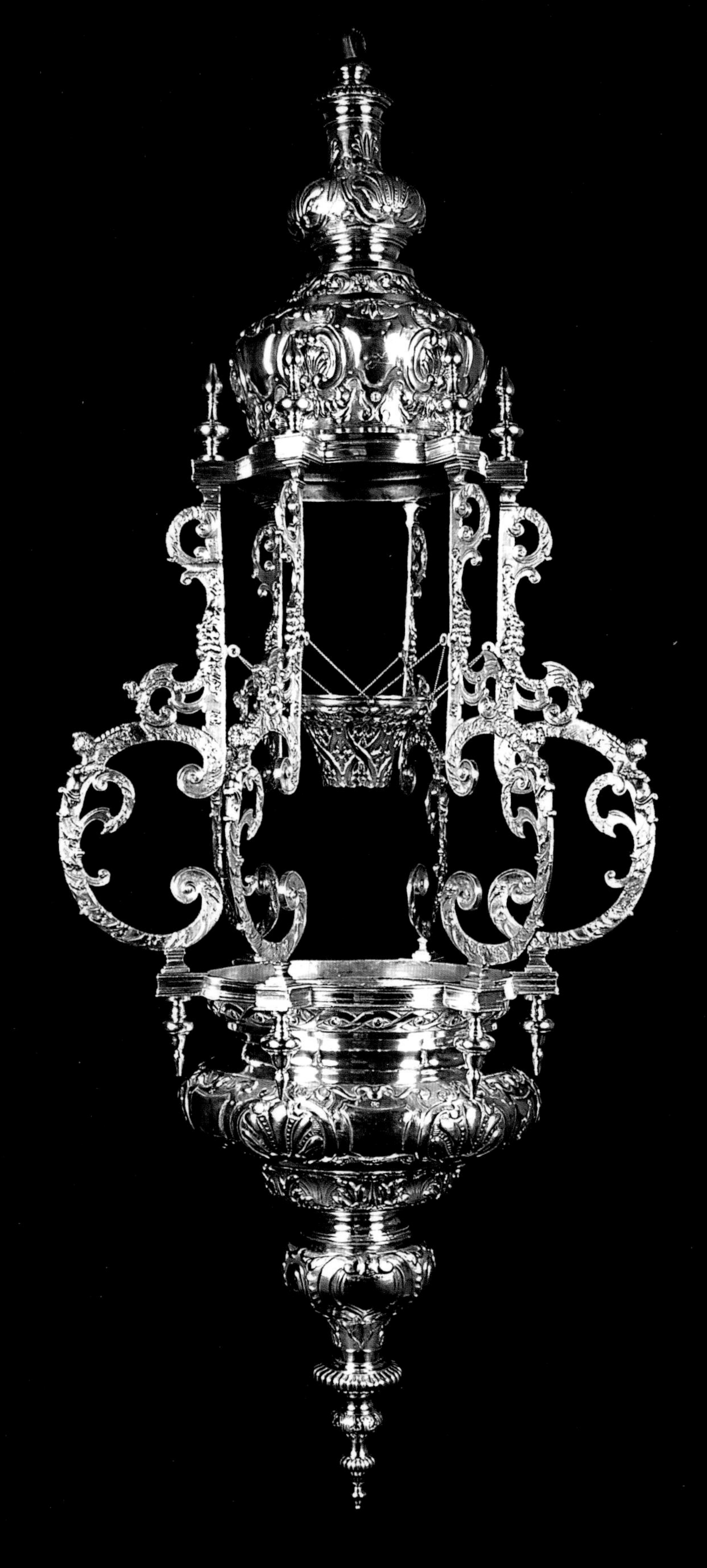

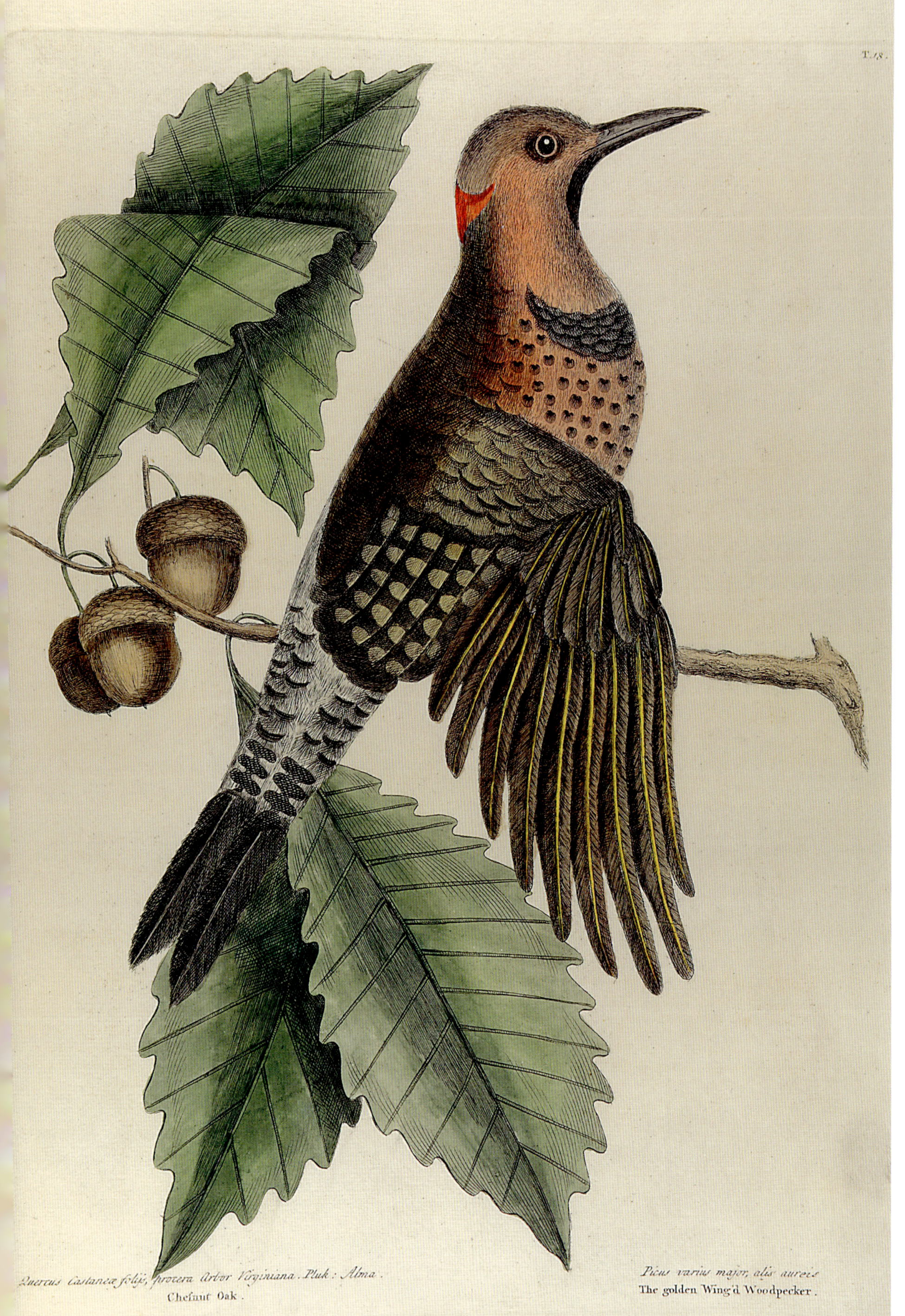

Quercus Castaneæ folijs, procera Arbor Virginiana. Pluk: Alma.
Chesnut Oak.

Picus varius major, alis aureis
The golden Wing'd Woodpecker.

Natural Science at Ushaw

Natural science books, 1747–*c.*1890

It is no surprise to anyone that Ushaw's library holdings are strong on scripture, dogmatic theology, patristics, moral theology, canon law and church history. What is unexpected is the fact that secular subjects, particularly the natural sciences, are so well represented. Much of the credit for this is due to Thomas Wilkinson, Bishop of Hexham and Newcastle from 1889 to 1909 and concurrently president of Ushaw. From early in his life Wilkinson made it his business to provide a worthy successor to the library of Douai College, which had been almost entirely lost when the college closed following the declaration of war between Britain and France in the aftermath of the French Revolution. Wilkinson lived to see his collection of some 12,000 volumes installed in the custom-built Big Library at Ushaw in the 1850s.

In the 1880s the college's holdings of works on science and philosophy of science were significantly increased by the addition of the library of Henry Logan. For a short time he had been rector of the seminary at Oscott but, through no fault of his own, was removed by the incoming Bishop of Birmingham, William Ullathorne. Ushaw welcomed Logan as a guest, albeit a paying one, in the 1860s and this policy of economically casting bread on the waters paid off when Logan left his library to Ushaw in 1884. Nevertheless, it has always been the default position of Ushaw librarians to assume that Wilkinson, who never put his name to any of his gifts, was the benefactor of many of the library's treasures.

Included among the numerous science-themed works in the Big Library are the three volumes of Robert Dudley's *Dell'arcano del mare* from the late Italian Renaissance, complete with its moving paper volvelles to enable artisans to make actual instruments of navigation. There is also a fine copy from the same period of the first published translation into English by Thomas Salusbury of Galileo's famous *Dialogue on the Two Chief World Systems* (1661).

One of the most beautiful works is Mark Catesby's two-volume *Natural History of Carolina, Florida and the Bahama Islands* (1747), presumably given by Wilkinson.

Less imposing is the battered copy of an unquestionably scientific work: a first edition of Charles Darwin's 1859 *On the Origin of Species*. This famous work sold out immediately, so one has to give credit to Ushaw's professor of philosophy, William Wrennall, for being alert enough to spot a significant development in the field of science. However, his interest – and that of his brother – was to use Ushaw's annual public disputations to dismiss Darwinism altogether.

Such a reaction was not inevitable, as is shown by comments made by the nineteenth-century cardinal, John Henry Newman. Documents at Ushaw show that in the 1880s Newman was very critical of the way the notorious Galileo case had been handled in 1615 and 1633. It is not that Newman espoused Darwinism; rather, in a letter of 1868 to an Ushawman, William Walker, he thought it might be compatible with a deeper understanding of the way providence works through secondary causes, and he had no difficulty in jettisoning the prevailing assumption that the universe could be no older than about 6,000 years.

MICHAEL SHARRATT

'The golden Wing'd Woodpecker' on a 'Chesnut Oak' [sic] in Mark Catesby's *Natural History of Carolina, Florida and the Bahama Islands,* published in 1747.

The English Plainchant Revival

The Ushaw *Te Deum*, 1783. Ushaw, XVIII.F.1.20

On 8 September 1783 one 'J.P.C.' sat down to copy a manuscript of Gregorian chant from a Dominican processional once used at the English congregation's house at Bornhem in Flanders. Little did he know that his unassuming manuscript would hold the key to the origins of the English plainchant revival, the movement which saw the full-scale return of chant to both Catholic and Anglican worship centuries after the Reformation.

The Ushaw *Te Deum* was copied by J. P. C., presumably James Peter Coghlan, the son of the famous recusant publisher of the same name. Coghlan the elder (1731–1800) was arguably the most important Catholic publisher of his day, feeding a recusant community hungry not only for Catholic literature and liturgical books, but for music as well, especially the traditional music of worship, Gregorian chant. Based in London, Coghlan was at the epicentre of English cosmopolitan recusancy, with a host of aristocratic connections and easy access to London's many foreign embassy chapels. Because embassy chapels technically occupied foreign land, they became the only places in England where Catholic worship could be conducted legally. As such, the embassy chapels – the Sardinian, Portuguese, Spanish, Bavarian, French, Venetian, Austrian, Neopolitan, Polish, to name but a few – became home to a flourishing Catholic counter-culture. Coghlan was at the very heart of this underground church.

Flaunting their freedom, the embassy chapels revelled in the spectacle of liturgical display, and music was an integral part – especially Gregorian chant. Never slow to grasp an opportunity, Coghlan observed a gap in the musical market and commissioned the first plainchant treatise published in England, *An Essay on the Church Plain Chant* (1782), to be followed by a number of other, equally important books of chant. *An Essay* was almost certainly written by the composer and organist Samuel Webbe the Elder, using the plainchant manuscripts of John Francis Wade (1711/2–86), the father of the English plainchant revival.

Known popularly today as the composer of the Christmas carol *Adeste fidele*, Wade was, incontestably, the central figure in the production of eighteenth-century recusant chant. Over more than a 40-year period from the 1730s he hand-copied upwards of 20 manuscripts and published several liturgical books with handwritten chant notation. His staggering level of productivity is matched only by the exquisite quality of his very distinctive calligraphy and illumination. Evidently the son of a convert to Catholicism, Wade was very probably the son of a John Wade who helped found the Dominican chapel at Stourton Lodge. Appropriately enough, early references identify Wade as a member of the Dominican Confraternity of the Rosary at Bornhem in 1731, and in 1734 in the same confraternity in Leeds. Later references place him, married, in London from the 1760s.

Until the discovery of the Ushaw *Te Deum* there was no clear evidence linking Wade's manuscripts to any one musical tradition in particular and so the source of the English plainchant revival remained unknown. But undeniable similarities between the Ushaw *Te Deum* and Wade's manuscripts provide incontrovertible proof that the English plainchant revival started in Bornhem: the precise calligraphic style of its chant notation; the decorative illumination of its head-letter 'T'; its Dominican origins; and the initials of James Peter Coghlan's son all combine to establish provenance. The English plainchant revival originated in Belgium and the Ushaw *Te Deum* proves it.

BENNETT ZON

The Ushaw *Te Deum*, with the important 'J.P.C.' initials and its Dominican background recorded at the top of the page.

Te Deum laudamus

Copied from the Engliſh Dominican Proceſſional at Bornhem in Flanders. September 8th: 1783.

by J.P.C

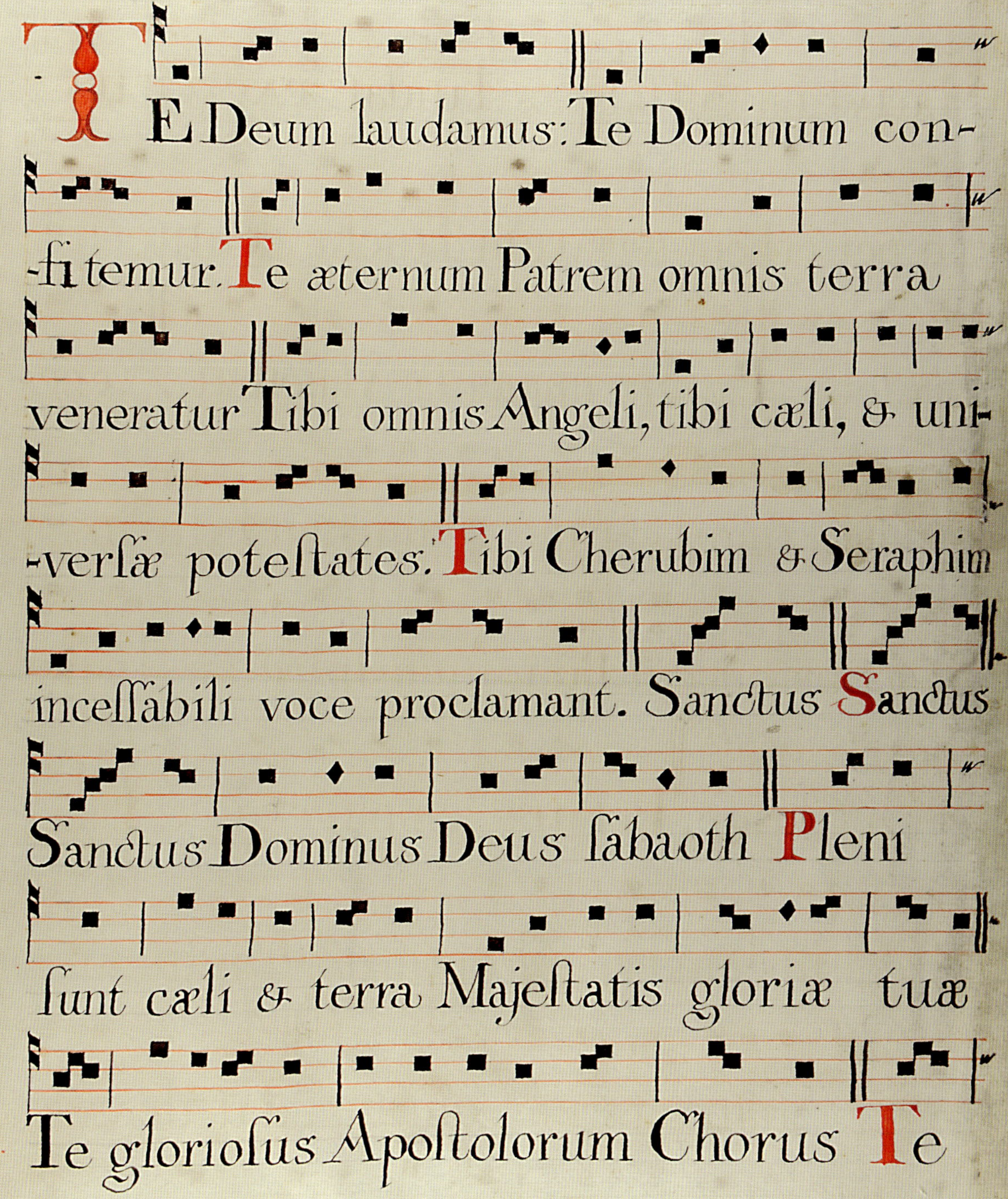

Teaching the Solar System

Orrery, 1794

Orreries are machines to demonstrate the motion of the planets around the sun and the moon about the earth. They have a prehistory including the ancient Antikythera mechanism and Arabic astrolabes, but their immediate ancestry is in clockmaking. Mechanical clocks date back to the thirteenth century; they were – and remain – wonders and tourist attractions at cathedrals including Exeter, Wells, Durham and, most famously, Strasbourg. Not only do they show the time but also the phase of the moon and other astronomical data, while on the hour mechanical figures process, ring bells, or joust.

Their elaborate gearing was a stimulus to the 'mechanical philosophy' of Galileo, René Descartes and Robert Boyle: the world seemed a great machine, 'the clockwork universe'. Scientific societies and academies were founded to carry out their programme of explaining phenomena by matter and motion. Clockmakers flourished, pocket-watches became a status symbol and society became more time-conscious. Building upon Galileo's observation that pendulums beat time regularly, clockmakers could make very accurate clocks. Thomas Tompion built pendulum clocks for Greenwich Observatory, established in 1675. A blacksmith's son, he became a rich man running a large workshop making scientific instruments as well as clocks and was buried in Westminster Abbey.

The mechanical philosophers were also Copernicans, believing that the sun was the centre around which the planets, including Earth, revolved. In 1709 Tompion, with his heir George Graham, built the first orrery. However, it was a rival, John Rowley, who made one in 1712 and named it in honour of Charles Boyle, fourth Earl of Orrery – a great-nephew of Robert Boyle, prominent in political and scientific circles. In 1715 Rowley relinquished his shop to Thomas Wright, whose trade card shows an orrery and who called his shop 'The Orrery and Globe'.

The Ushaw orrery was made in 1794 by William Jones and his younger brother Samuel, whose shop, named after Archimedes, was in Holborn: their trade card shows Archimedes with an armillary sphere. They were prominent and busy makers of scientific instruments, whose customers included Thomas Jefferson and Harvard College. 'Grand orreries' included outer planets, Mars, Jupiter and Saturn; but Ushaw's has only Mercury, Venus and Earth. When you turn the handle, the gears rotate the planets at their appropriate speeds. The moon and Venus are painted black and white so that their phases can readily be followed as they revolve: below them are the months and the signs of the zodiac through which Earth travels each year. Ushaw's is similar to one at Princeton and would have cost the substantial sum of £23. 2*s*. 0*d*.

Orreries are not for making observations, but for demonstrating the solar system to a class, as in Joseph Wright's painting of 1766 of an elaborate version in use. The clockwork cannot replicate the planets' elliptical orbits in empty space under gravity; but it shows the central sun and moving Earth powerfully and memorably, and reminds us that by 1794 the idea that had got Galileo into such trouble was no longer seen as a hypothesis but as a truth.

DAVID KNIGHT

The Ushaw orrery, used for demonstrating the Solar System. *Right:* The device pictured from above, showing Mercury, Venus and Earth. *Overleaf:* The orrery's detailed model of the Earth clearly shows the continents and oceans.

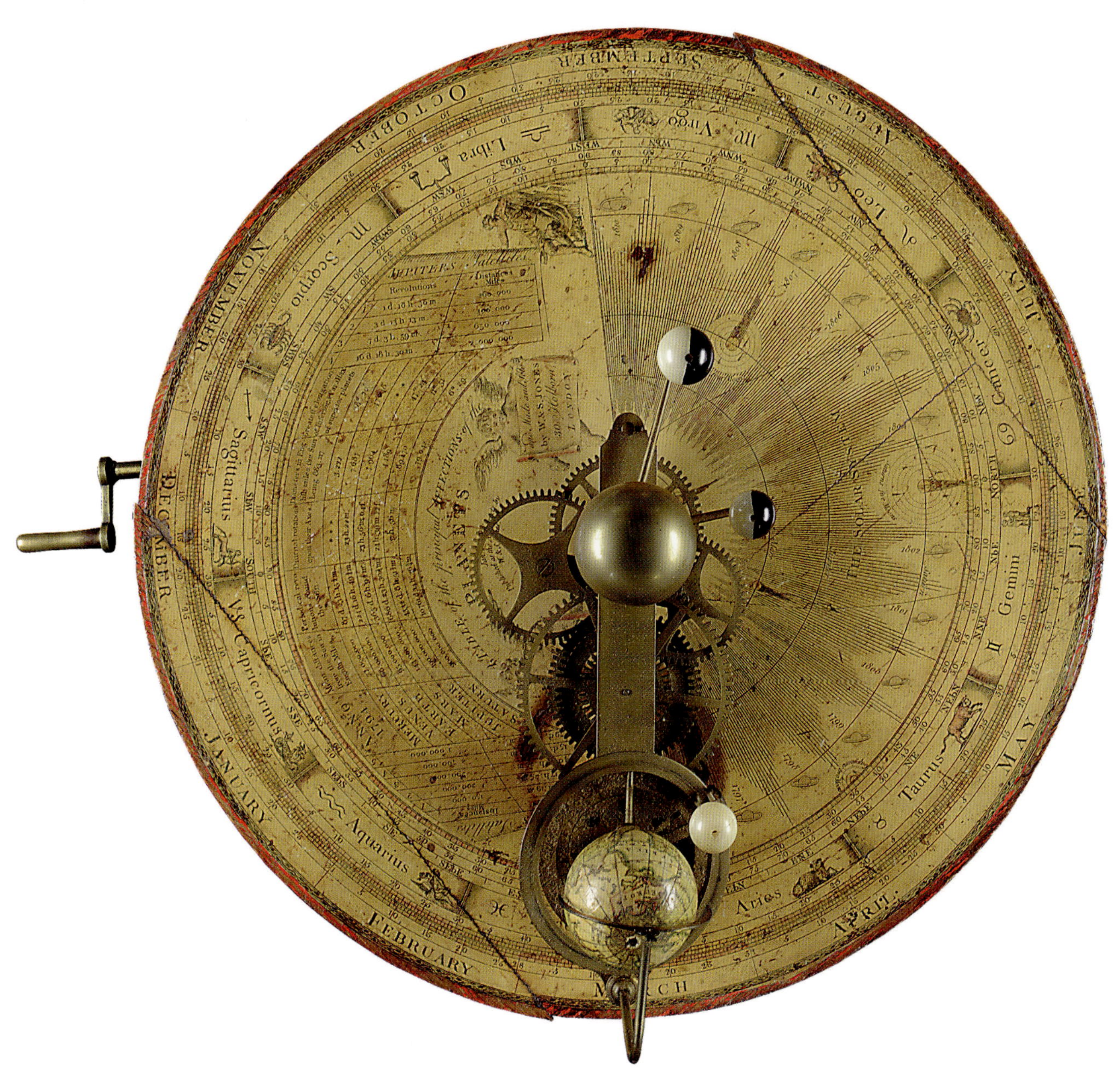
SEPTEMBER
OCTOBER
NOVEMBER
DECEMBER
JANUARY
FEBRUARY
APRIL
MAY
JUNE
JULY
AUGUST
Virgo
Libra
Scorpio
Sagittarius
Capricornus
Aquarius
Aries
Taurus
Gemini
Cancer
Leo

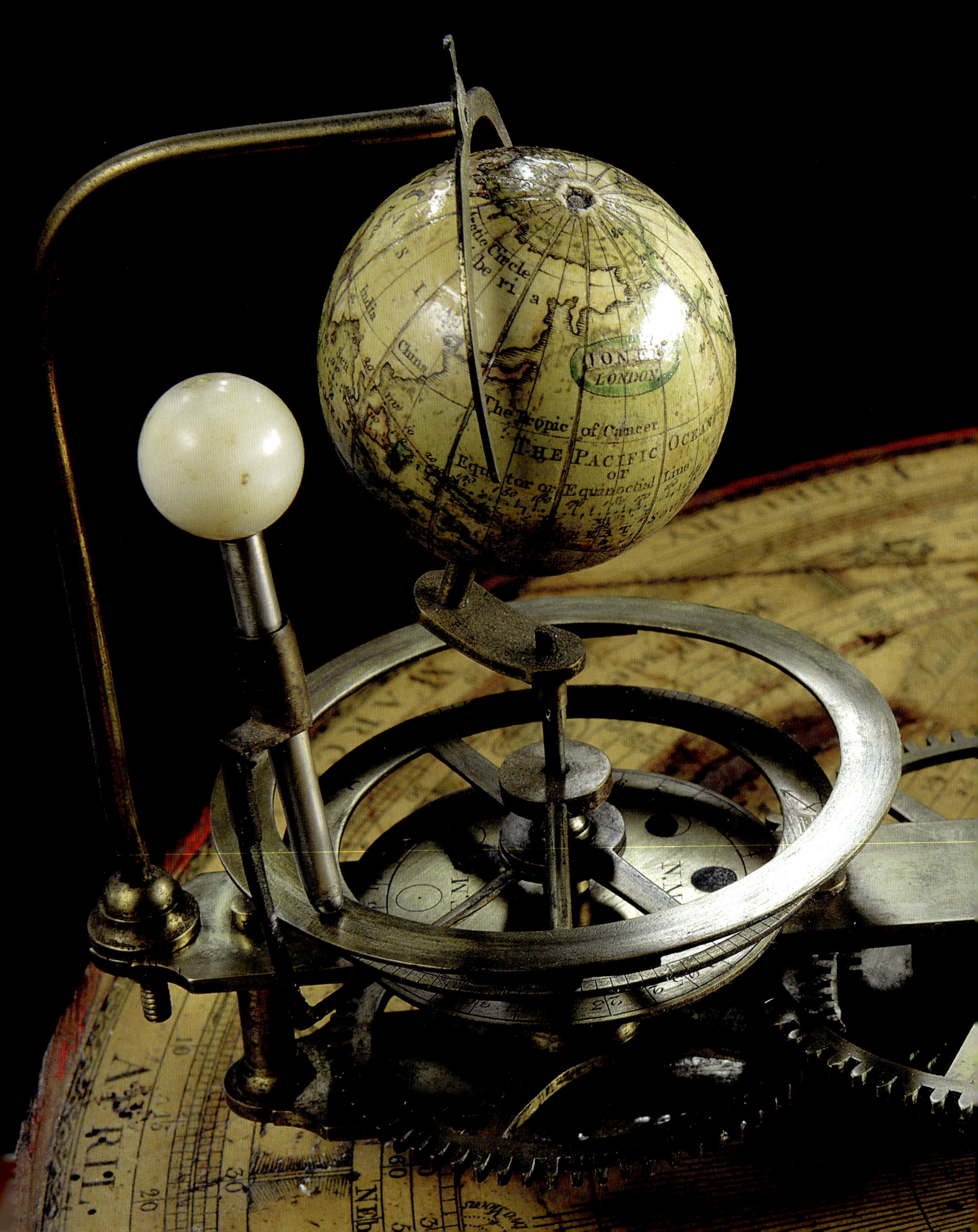

JONES
LONDON
The Tropic of Cancer
THE PACIFIC OCEAN
Equinoctial Line
China

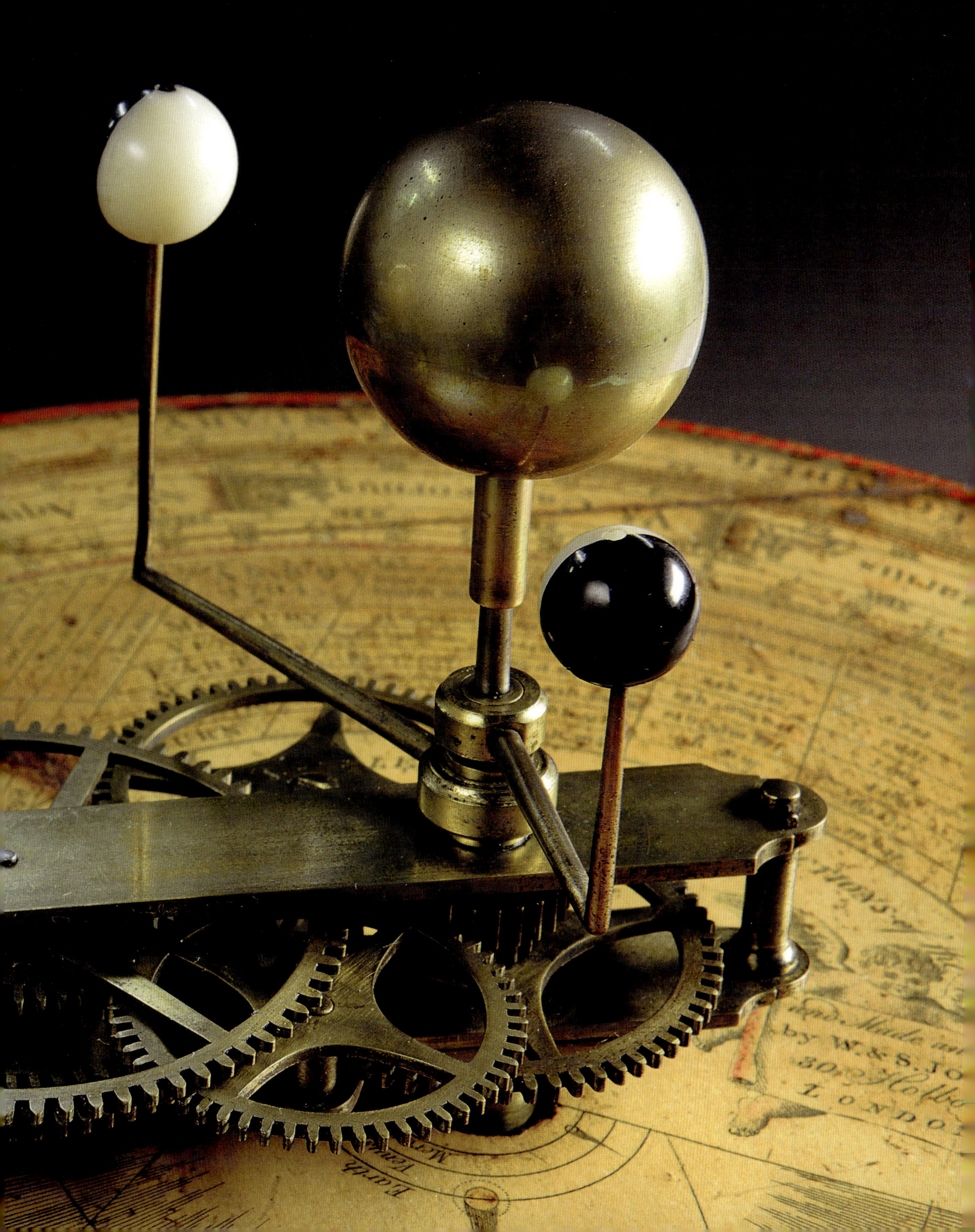

The Quintessential Ushaw Sport

The game of Cat, *c.*1808

Cat has been described as the quintessential Ushaw sport. The origin of the game is a matter of some debate but there is documentary evidence that 'Katt' was developed by students at Douai College and was likely brought from there by those resettled in England at Ushaw. Played at Ushaw continuously for nigh on 175 years, the game went into decline in the mid-1970s following the closure of the Junior College. However, the tradition is kept alive in rather less energetic form by alumni who play a more measured game at their annual reunion.

Cat features two teams of seven-a-side, playing on a circular track 70 to 80 yards in circumference ('The Ring'), marked with seven equidistant holes and elongated on two sides, with an open area of field where the fielding side take station.

The equipment required for the game may appear rudimentary; a stick, some balls and leather gloves for the close fielders. This, however, belies the influence that excellence in manufacture has on the quality of the game.

The stick begins life as a block of young ash. It is fashioned into a formidable striking implement by means of axe, spokeshave and rasp, made by the player himself to suit his own requirements of length, weight and balance. It has a shaft not unlike that of a golf club but carries a bulbous head, somewhat flattened on the striking face and some four inches in length. The striker wields the stick in one hand, in the manner of a squash racquet, not a golf club or cricket bat.

The balls, which are a little larger than a golf ball, are also 'homemade' and very hard. They have a core of *lignum vitae* (wood), wound round with hemp twine, and are dipped repeatedly into boiling pitch until the required circumference is reached. They are then taped and whitewashed.

To begin the game, the players on the 'in' side stand at the hole designated for their nominated fielding position. The 'feeder' of the opposing team delivers the ball to the player at the striking hole (which is situated in one of the elongated areas at the apex of the circle), in a particular motion prescribed by the rules and unique to the game; the striking player hits it into the outfield, allowing his teammates to run clockwise around the ring, as in the game of rounders. Their 'Corner', or captain, calls out the number of holes which he judges can be reached, based on the direction and distance of the strike.

When the striking side has completed two 'rounds' of the ring, plus an additional five holes, they will attempt to complete a 'cross'. The striker is allowed three attempts to hit the ball sufficiently well to allow all the team members to run to the middle of the ring, cross their sticks simultaneously and return safely to their holes. If they succeed, the score is marked and the innings continues; if not, no score is registered and the fielding side takes to the ring to begin their innings.

Struck sweetly, a Cat ball is a formidable projectile. The Corner of the fielding side positions himself at the opposite side of the ring to the feeder, within the other elongated area, ready to intercept any ball within reach. He wears a pair of leather gloves to help take the sting out of the ball. He is afforded no other protection, his well-being secured only by the speed of his reflexes and his fleetness of foot.

The fielding positions behind him are Behind Corner, Top Plat, Bottom Plat, Second Furthest Out and Furthest Out. The Corner is mobile, ready to take up position at the hole nearest to the incoming ball as it is thrown in and attempt to place it in the hole before it is reached by a runner, thus putting out the striking side. The striker may also be caught out.

The side scoring the most crosses is the winner at the end of the game. In the event of a tie, victory goes to the side which has accumulated the most holes towards their next cross. Under match conditions, a game is of two hours duration and is very strenuous.

CHRIS SEDDON

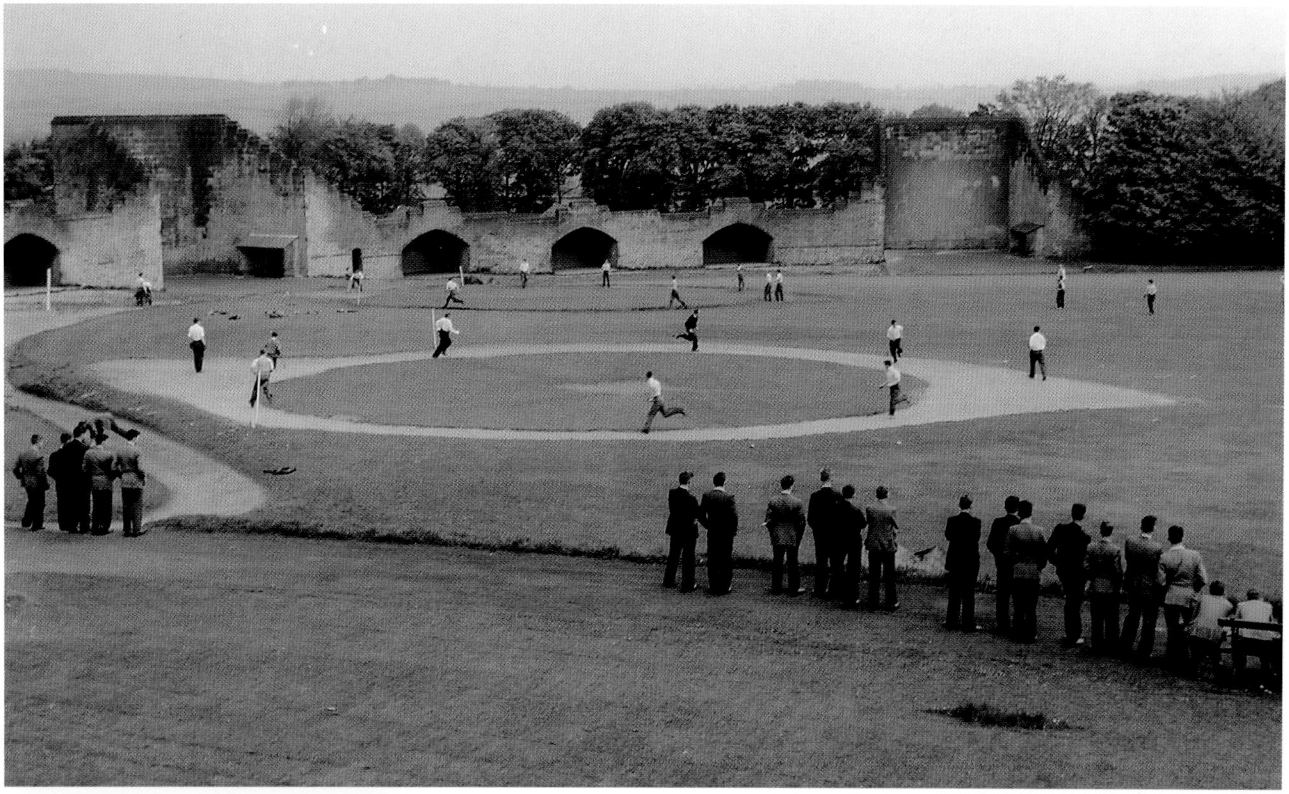

The game of Cat was developed by students at Douai College and was played continuously at Ushaw for nearly 175 years. Several games of Cat would run concurrently.

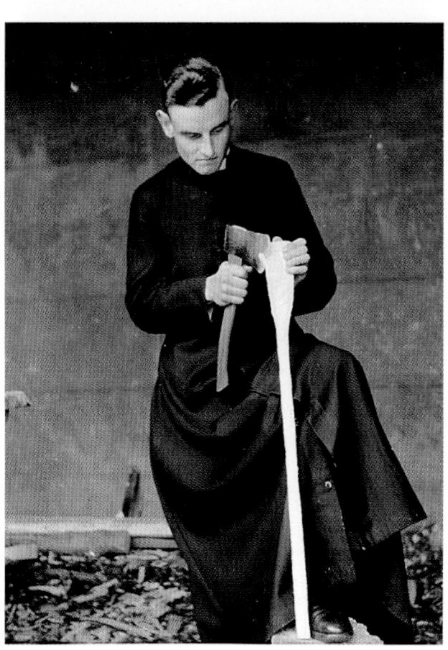

Members of the college made their own Cat sticks to fit their requirements.

A Major Historian

The Lingard collection, nineteenth century

Each year the priest and historian, John Lingard (1771–1851), celebrated his entry as an 11-year-old into his alma mater, the English College, Douai, 'with a bottle of my best wine', and recalled with affection special days in the college year such as 'Apricot Tart Day', and the 'most delicious rice puddings, better than any your housekeeper can make'. This devotion he transferred to the community of northern students which eventually settled at Ushaw in 1808. He had taught there and was acting vice-president while the community resided at Crook Hall and, after the move to Ushaw, continued in his role until 1811, when he moved to Hornby in Lancashire.

In later years he never lost his affection for the institution, remaining closely involved in its affairs. He became a trustee of the college, was generous in establishing bursaries for students, offered advice on a wealth of matters, from the storage of beer and the new gas lighting to the course of studies, and supported the initiative of allowing students to matriculate at the new London University. In spite of his dislike of Pugin's designs for the new chapel, he paid for a window (now in the sanctuary of St Cuthbert's), sending the college a copy of St Ethelwold's benedictional, as well as additional drawings of Anglo-Saxon mitres, so that the clothing would be accurate. Pugin's objections to this were an irritation, but a compromise was achieved: mitre and crosier were omitted; Alcuin was depicted in deacon's vestments, Bede with a cloak and Aldhelm with priestly vestments.

On his death, Lingard left to the college most of his possessions, from his silver fish slice to books and manuscripts. He had played a significant part in the transformation of historical scholarship in the first half of the nineteenth century. By an assiduous attention to primary sources newly rediscovered in archives at home and abroad – and often overlooked by his contemporaries – he sought to challenge the Whig interpretation of England's past and the inevitability of Protestant ascendency. He offered one of the earliest in a series of revisionist accounts of English history, which flowered in the historical scholarship of the late twentieth century. Although Lingard destroyed many letters, the college's collection includes well over eight hundred items (another collection, lent by Ushaw to Mark Aloysius Tierney, Lingard's first memoirist, and not returned, is now in the Cambridge University Library).

Lingard also presented to Ushaw the portrait commissioned by friends in 1834; it was the work of James Lonsdale. Gifts made to him over the years are also held at the college: the gold medal awarded to Lingard by Pope Leo XII in 1829; an inkstand, black inlaid with silver, formerly belonging to the poet William Cowper, a gift from Lady Throckmorton; a fifteenth-century missal, once owned by James Goldwell, Bishop of Norwich, which Lingard had inscribed, '*Collegio Cath. Ushaviensi ex bibliotecha Hornbeiana*'. A more rustic gift, but no less precious, is a clog almanac, one of only 23 known to be in existence in England.

Lingard is buried at Ushaw. He was one of its greatest alumni, a generous and loyal friend of the college which continues to treasure his memory.

PETER PHILLIPS

John Lingard's handwritten manuscript for his eight-volume *History of England* (1819–30). This page shows the start of the chapter on William the Conqueror (d.1087).

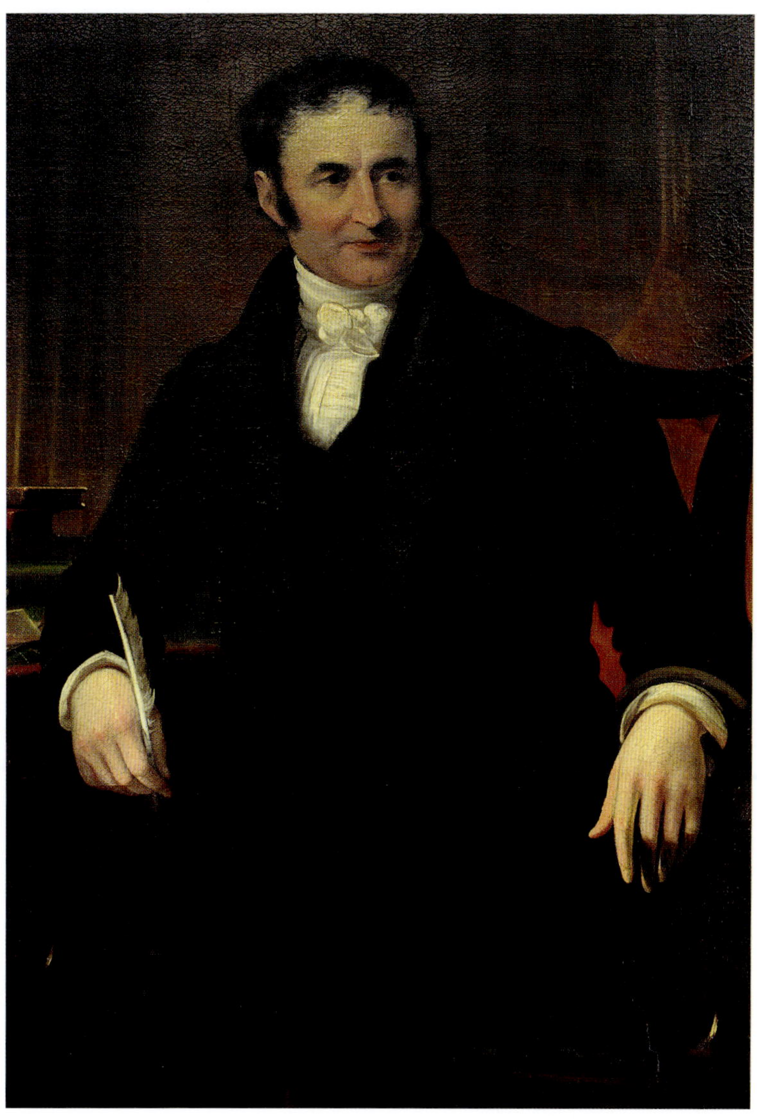

James Lonsdale's portrait of John Lingard, commissioned in 1834, oil on canvas, 142 × 109 cm.

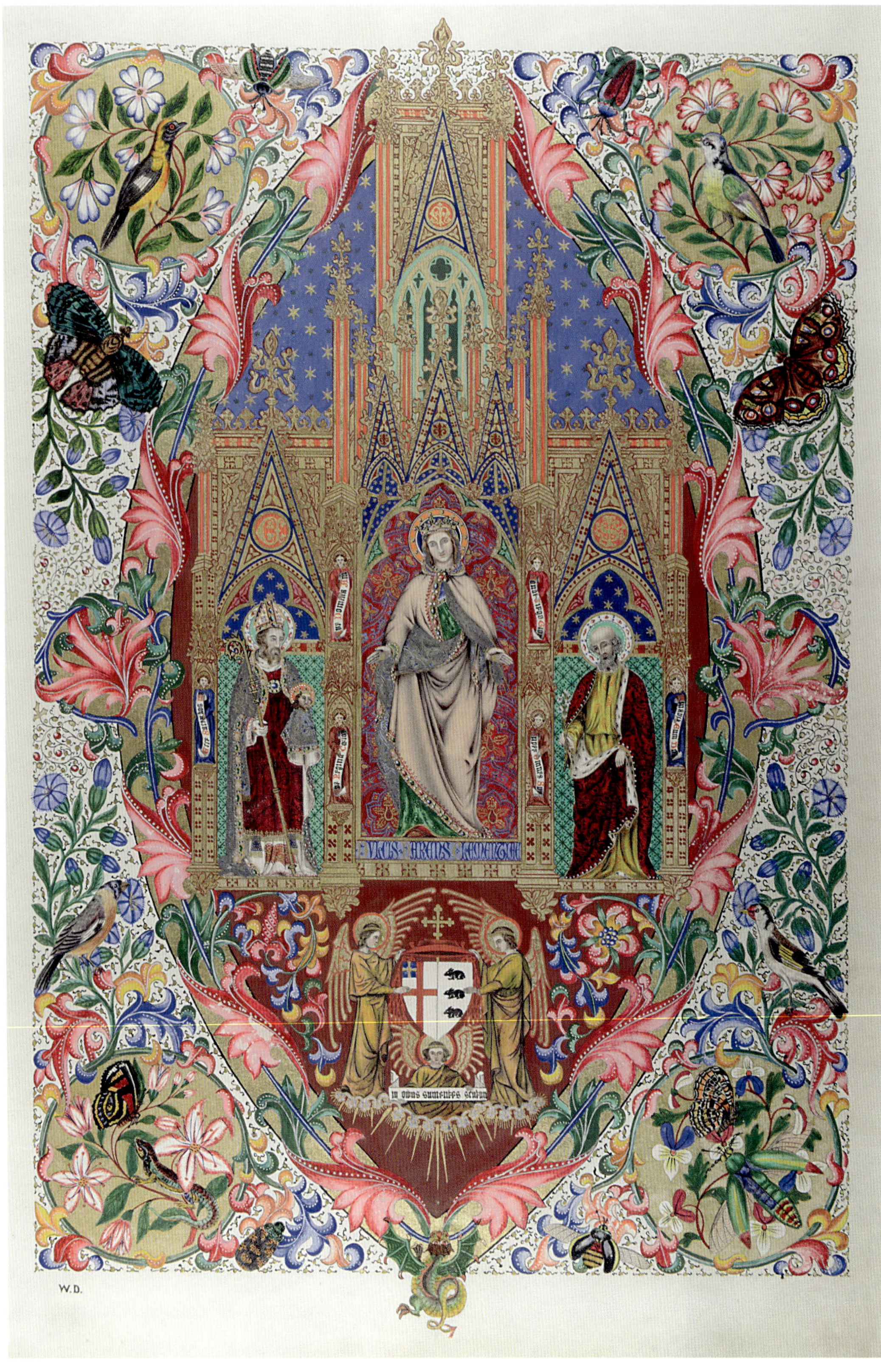

The early Reading Up books were richly illuminated, such as this example by William Dunderdale from 1842.

Developing School Customs

Reading Up books, 1842

On his appointment as president of Ushaw in May 1837, Charles Newsham insisted on a shake up among the staff so that he could initiate a policy of intellectual and economic reform. He therefore embarked on an extensive programme of building and fundraising, as well as a reorganisation of life in the school so that it might rank with the best in the country. Although St Cuthbert had been invoked as patron of the college in an 1813 Roman Brief allowing Ushaw to confer the degree of doctor of divinity, this had never been fully recognised, and by mid-century a new debate opened as to who might be Ushaw's patron. By 1839, however, 'St Cuthbert's College, Ushaw' was petitioning the newly opened London University and in May 1840 Ushaw had the privilege of educating the first Catholic students since the Reformation to be trained entirely in an English Catholic institution and awarded a degree recognised by the state.

A new course of studies was introduced to prepare students for the London degree and this was adapted still further by the prefect of studies, Ralph Platt. He proposed a classical master for each class who could look after the interests of the students, as well as introducing various masters for different subjects. Perhaps the changes were too rapid: they certainly marked a distinct break from the old Douai tradition and demanded the expense of new textbooks. Discipline and the use of the birch had also become harsher. All this led to a revolt of the students in November 1842, which lasted several days. In the end Newsham decided to abandon Platt's additional reforms and Platt handed in his resignation.

One thing which did emerge out of this period of uncertainly was the custom of 'Reading Up' and six large, red, leather-bound volumes record the practice from 1842 until 1967, each stamped with the college crest in gold. With the completion of Pugin's new chapel in 1848, the old chapel was converted into a fine exhibition hall with a painted hammer beam roof by Joseph Hansom. This proved a suitable setting for the ceremony which many former pupils remember with some embarrassment. Marks for each subject were recorded in these registers at the end of each quarter (term) and results in Latin established one's place in class. Students lined up in front of the college in their old order and sat down as their names were read out. Of course, if one had dropped place, it soon became evident as the student was left standing. His failure was made public as he eventually scurried away to hide his disgrace. The event was reduced sometime in the twentieth century to an annual occasion during Grand Week (the college reunion), with visiting old boys, priests and dignitaries as witnesses to one's shame. By 1966 a reforming regime abolished the line-up and public ignominy; the following year marks were recorded in this way for the last time.

The early Reading Up books included finely illuminated pages, produced before each set of marks was added, quarter by quarter, and details have been preserved of some of the illuminators. The first, by William Dunderdale, shows Our Lady flanked by St Joseph and St Cuthbert surmounting the arms of Ushaw held by three angels surrounded by plants, birds and butterflies in vibrant colours: blues, reds, and gold leaf. Other early illustrations are equally fine, often illustrating the opening and closing phrases of the ceremony: '*Quod felix faustumque sit locorum assignatio post confectum studiorum curriculum … Doctrina sed vim promovet insitam rectique cultus pectora roborant*' ('The assigning of places at the completion of the course is a cause for happiness and rejoicing … Knowledge encourages natural talent and hearts are strengthened by a correct way of life'). During the twentieth century the ability to provide such exquisitely illuminated pages had ceased and in the last years the lists of names were entered on ruled lines in pencil. The early volumes bear witness to a rich vein of artistic skill in the college.

PETER PHILLIPS

A.W.N. Pugin at Ushaw

Illuminated manuscript, High Mass vestments and paschal candlestick, 1842–51

The *Liber Vitae* is a manuscript list of subscribers to A.W.N. Pugin's chapel at Ushaw (1844–47). The idea behind it came from the college's president, Charles Newsham, the prime mover behind Pugin's appointment to the job. Similar lists are mentioned in the sixteenth-century *Rites of Durham* and it was to be kept, like them, next to the high altar for the commemoration of benefactors at all Masses. It is bound and cased in velvet and brass with a central boss and angle clasps.

A similar folio missal, bound in the style of Pugin 'in velvet with brass corners', was ordered from Hardman & Co in 1841 by the future vicar apostolic of the Northern District, William Riddell. However, the Ushaw *Liber Vitae* is not actually Pugin-produced but is in fact a piece of 'amateur' work, by one of the college professors, William Dunderdale, who was celebrated at Ushaw for his artistic talent; he also completed many designs for the Reading Up books (see previous pages). The frontispiece of illuminated vignettes shows the story of St Cuthbert and the migration of his body; the bottom left initial 'L' depicts a contemporary student's cell and the right-hand 'V' shows Pugin's chapel with its projected tower and spire.

Hardman's name is listed as a subscriber, with further subscribers added for the Dunn & Hansom chapel. Pugin also made a bound volume of his drawings for the first unexecuted chapel scheme of 1840. Many other unbound Pugin drawings survive at Ushaw.

Pugin wished to replace the ubiquitous Roman or French vestments with those of a larger gothic cut. On a visit to Ushaw in 1845 he had commented to Hardman: 'Large chasuble apparelled albs at Mass.'

The depicted High Mass set is made of high-quality woven silk, with a stylised pattern of red fruit and leaves on a gold ground, trimmed with silk braid and fringes. The orphrey work, with floriated IHS monograms repeated in a cross shape, is also of silk braid, but with central quatrefoil and crown terminations of velvet and silver wire and other embroidery. Pugin design-reform principles can be seen in the use of repeated flat-pattern and woven braids. St Cuthbert's cross at the apex of the stole is also found on the 'apparelled' cuffs of the rochet in Herbert's portrait of Charles Newsham (1854).

Pugin had encouraged vestment making by the firm, Mistress Powell & Daughters, set up by Hardman's sister in 1842. Indeed, a Pugin letter of 13 October 1844 ordered 'Dalmaticks for Ushaw', though Pugin did also employ other makers in London and Manchester.

A related set of vestments survives at St Chad's Cathedral in Birmingham and others are on loan to the Victoria and Albert Museum in London.

Liber Vitae manuscript by William Dunderdale of Ushaw College, bound and cased in velvet with brass mounts by Hardman & Co, *c.*1844.

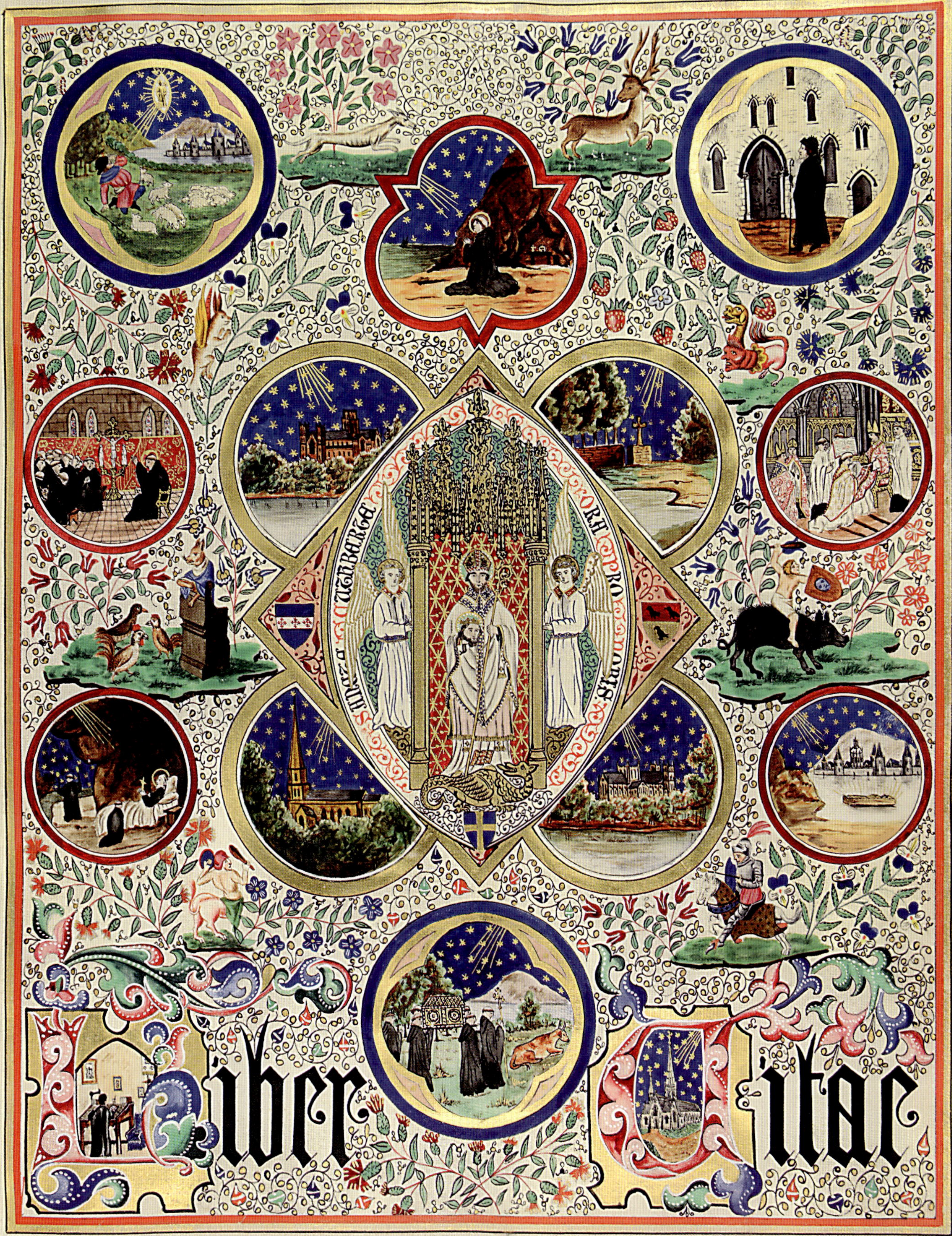
ora pro nobis
Liber Vitae

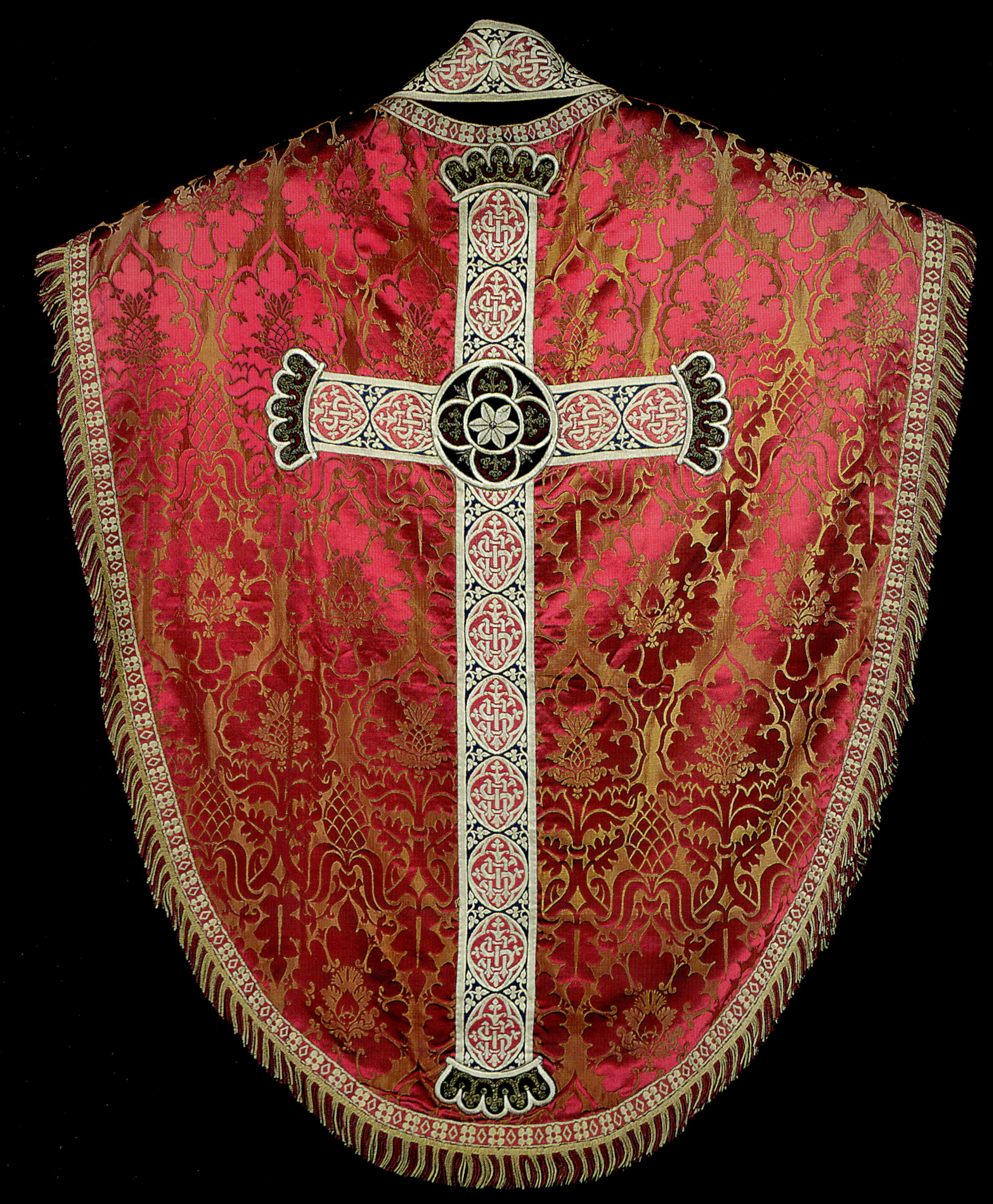

The paschal candlestick was shown at the 'Medieval Court' in the Great Exhibition of 1851 and the Dublin Exhibition in 1853. It was subsequently presented to Ushaw by Fr Thomas Wilkinson, the founder of the library which was built to balance Pugin's chapel. The candlestick is 244 cm high. It is divided into four figurative sections – supporting lions; pointing angels; the Three Maries with anointing jars under niches; and three angels in mini-pulpits announcing 'Alleluia' – through which rises the hexagonal shaft, with angled buttresses, gables, pinnacles and turned details to reach the inscribed bowl, gallery and pricket. There were originally crystal insets, though recent cleaning revealed that at some point these were removed and replaced with synthetic copies.

The unusual iconography of the Three Maries was perhaps suggested by medieval examples from which Pugin drew assiduously on his Continental travels. Pugin provided the designs for his collaborator John Hardman, most notably for stained glass and base and precious metalwork. Ushaw abounds in examples.

RODERICK O'DONNELL

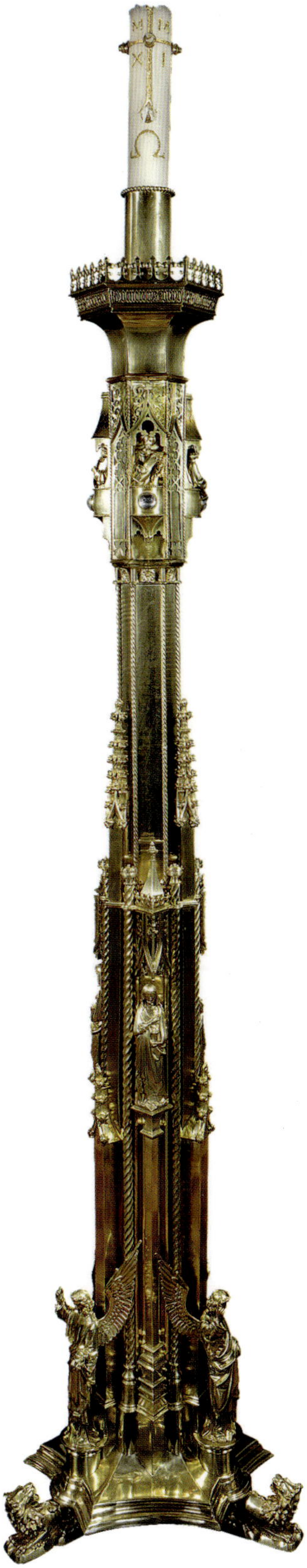

Paschal Candlestick: brass with crystal insets, by A.W.N. Pugin and Hardman & Co, 1851.

High Mass set: woven silk, silk braids and embroidery, attributed to A.W.N. Pugin and Mistress Powell & Daughters after 1842.

The Painter of Ushaw

Franz von Rohden paintings, 1851, 1852

If Karl Hoffmann deserves the title of 'the sculptor of Ushaw' (see page 145) for the truly devotional statues which came to the college from his chisel, his friend and colleague Franz von Rohden (1817–1903) deserves to be considered its painter. Ushaw houses the largest collection of Rohden paintings in the world and, together with Hoffmann's sculptures, one of the most remarkable collections of Nazarene art in the United Kingdom. The presence at the college of Hoffmann and Rohden testifies to Ushaw's commitment to looking towards Rome when commissioning sacred art and to the Nazarene school for its execution.

Founded in Rome by a group of dissident German artists in the early nineteenth century and characterised by its radical recourse to the pictorial repertoire of Italian and German pre-modern masters, the Nazarene movement exerted a tremendous influence on European Romanticism, the gothic revival and the British Pre-Raphaelites. For its controversial aesthetics, religious orthodoxy and anachronistic gestures, the Nazarenes strike today as one of the most compelling voices in modern debates on Christian art. Largely unknown to the scholarly community, the works preserved at Ushaw represent a truly hidden gem for experts and collectors alike.

The art of Franz von Rohden, or Francesco de Rohden, born in Rome in 1817 as the son of the German landscape painter Johann Martin von Rohden (1778–1868), represents a phase of Nazarene art that still waits to be fully grasped. This phase was marked by the conversion to Catholicism of its unrivalled leader, Friedrich Overbeck, and his militant adherence to the artistic politics of Pope Pius IX. In full agreement with these politics, Ushaw's president, Charles Newsham, commissioned two of the five Rohden paintings presently at Ushaw: an *Adoration of the Magi and the Shepherds* (1851) and a *Crucifixion* (1852). The remaining three reached the college later through private donations.

Rohden's splendid *Adoration* has, since 1851, tastefully adorned the Oratory of the Holy Family, specifically designed by A.W.N. Pugin to contain Rohden's picture. Rohden blends here the two standard iconographies of the adoration of the magi and the shepherds to produce a devotional prototype of the Holy Family, destined to acquire an iconic status during the pontificate of Pius IX. On the edges of the painting are the portraits of Johann Martin von Rohden (on the left) and Friedrich Overbeck (on the right), the natural and artistic fathers of the artist.

Distinct from the *Adoration*, a subject that Rohden replicated in various versions based on the prototype painted for Ushaw in 1851, his *Crucifixion* is unique in the artist's repertoire. The painting, which certainly counts as one of Rohden's finest and purest works, was kept in Newsham's office for his private devotion. After 1859 it was donated to the Junior College as a culminating piece of Alexander Rossi's (1840–1916) *Stations of the Cross*, based on the Nazarene model of Joseph Führich's one in Vienna. In its Peruginesque style, this exquisite painting had already become a sensation while still in Rohden's atelier; its first admirers called it 'a miracle of art and a most devotion-inspiring picture', and prized it as 'the finest picture of the subject that ever was painted'.

STEFANO CRACOLICI

Franz von Rohden, *Crucifixion of Our Lord, with the Virgin Mary, Saint John and Mary Magdalene*, Rome 1852, oil on canvas, 167 × 119.4 cm.

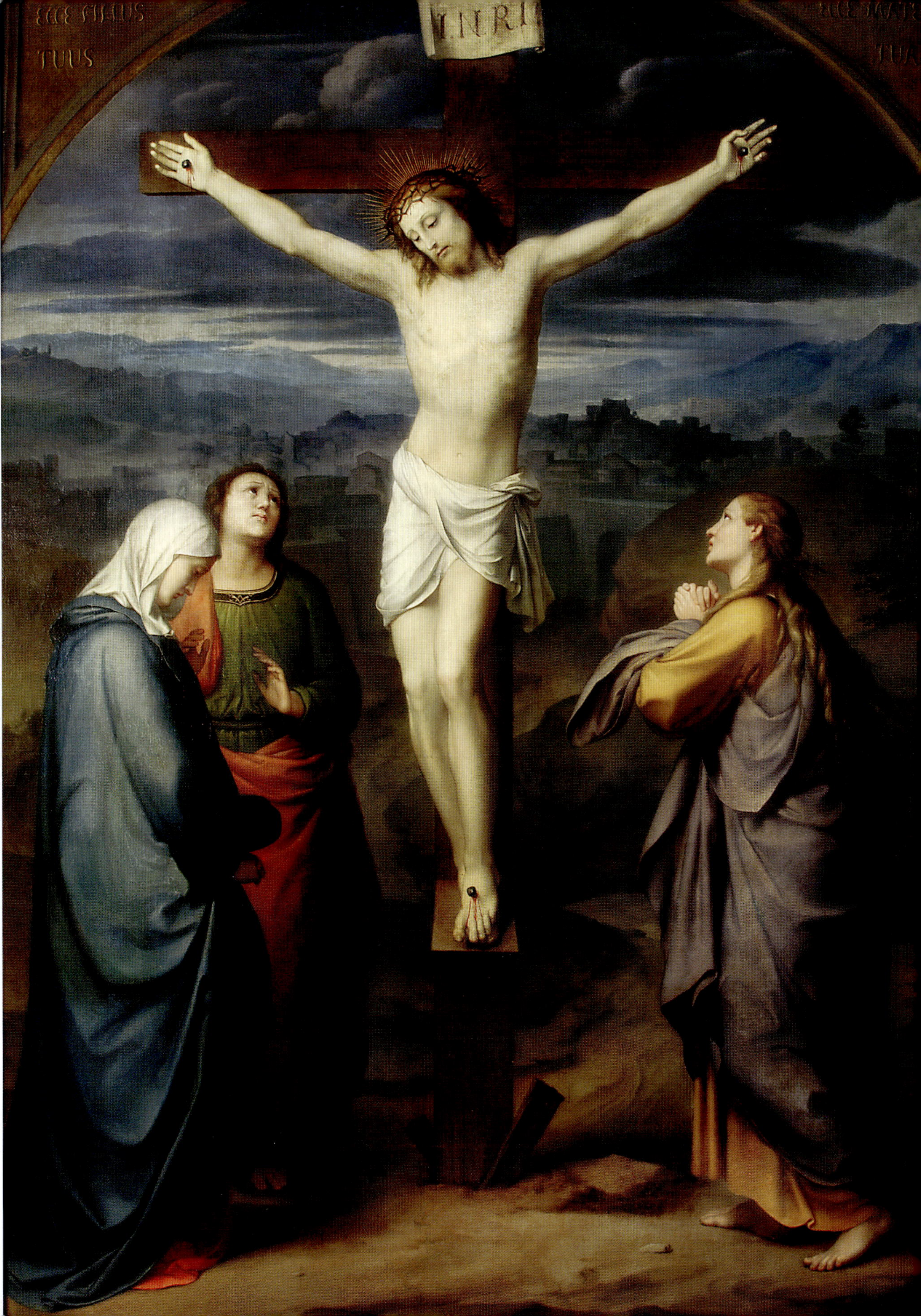
ECCE FILIUS
TUUS
I.N.R.I.

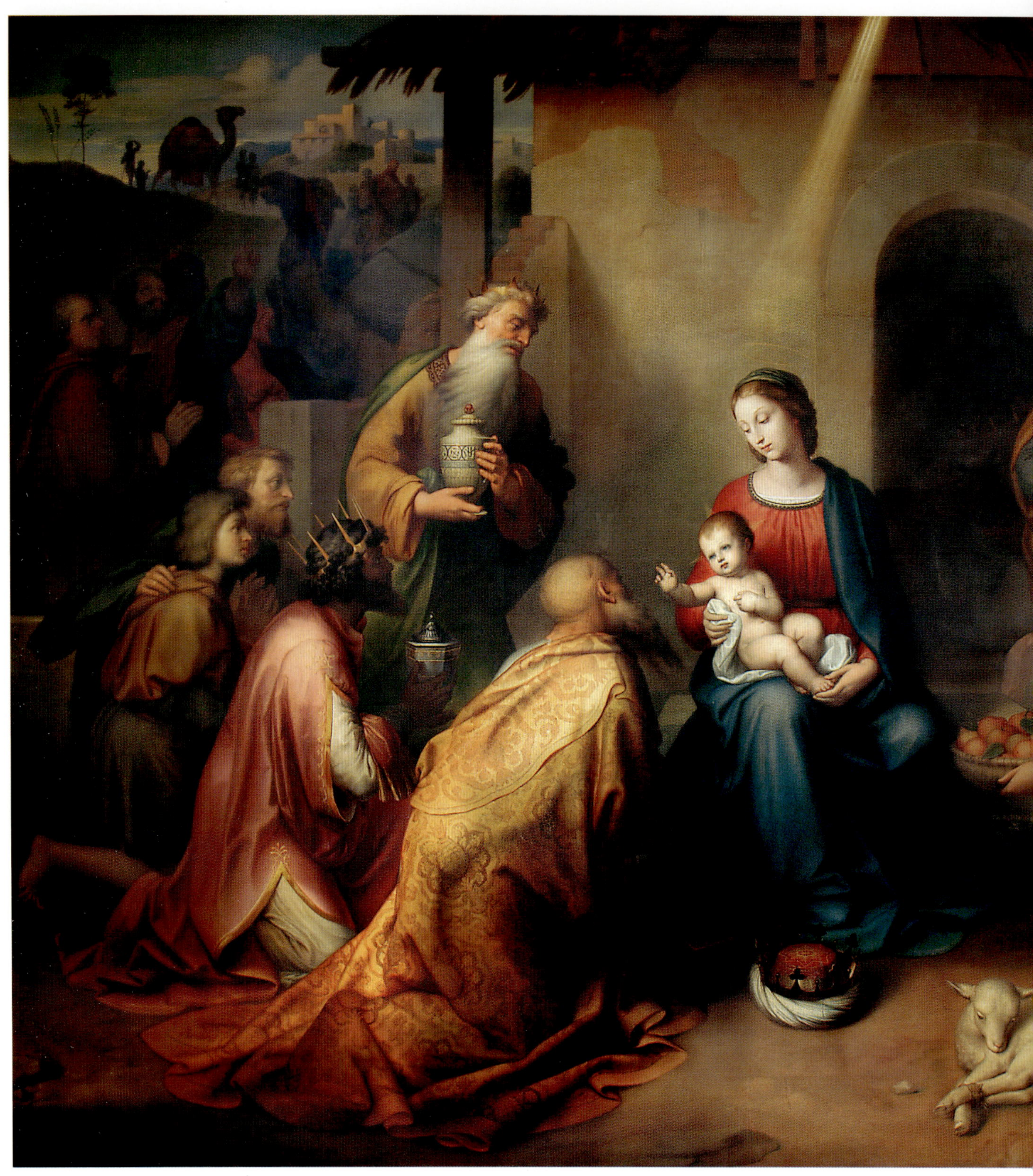

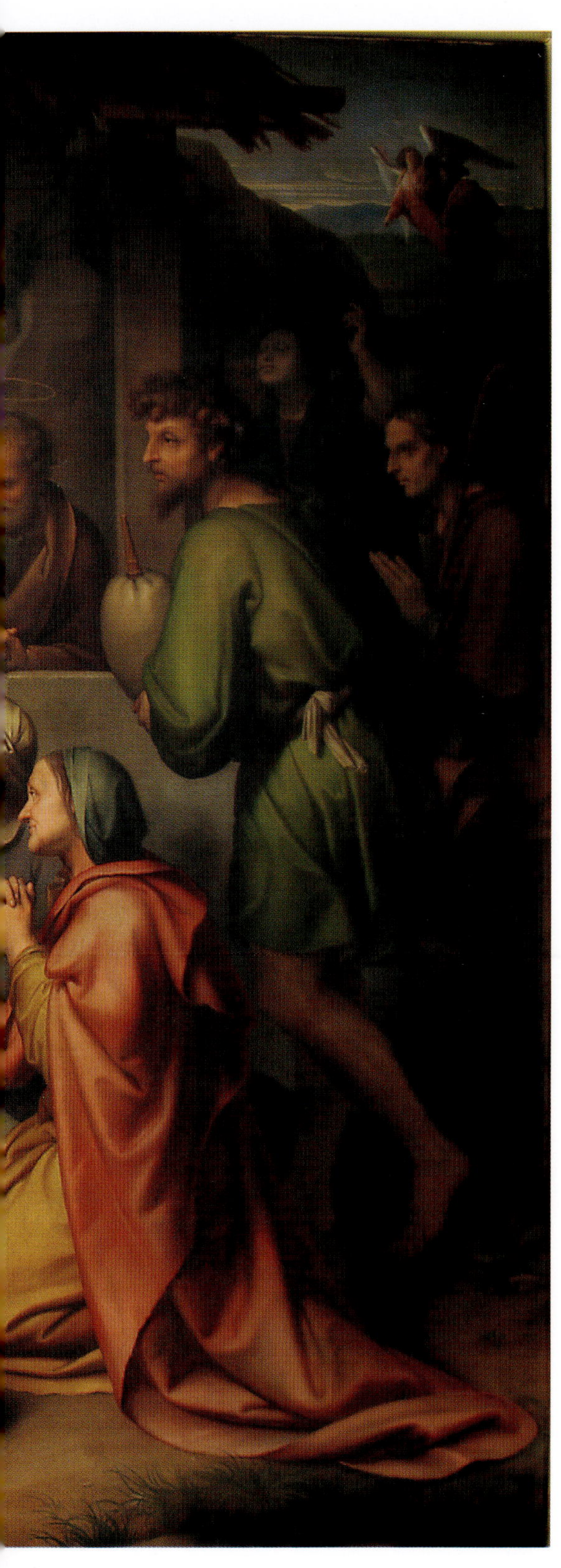

Franz von Rohden, *The Adoration of the Magi and the Shepherds*, Rome 1851, oil on canvas, 185.5 × 256.5 cm.

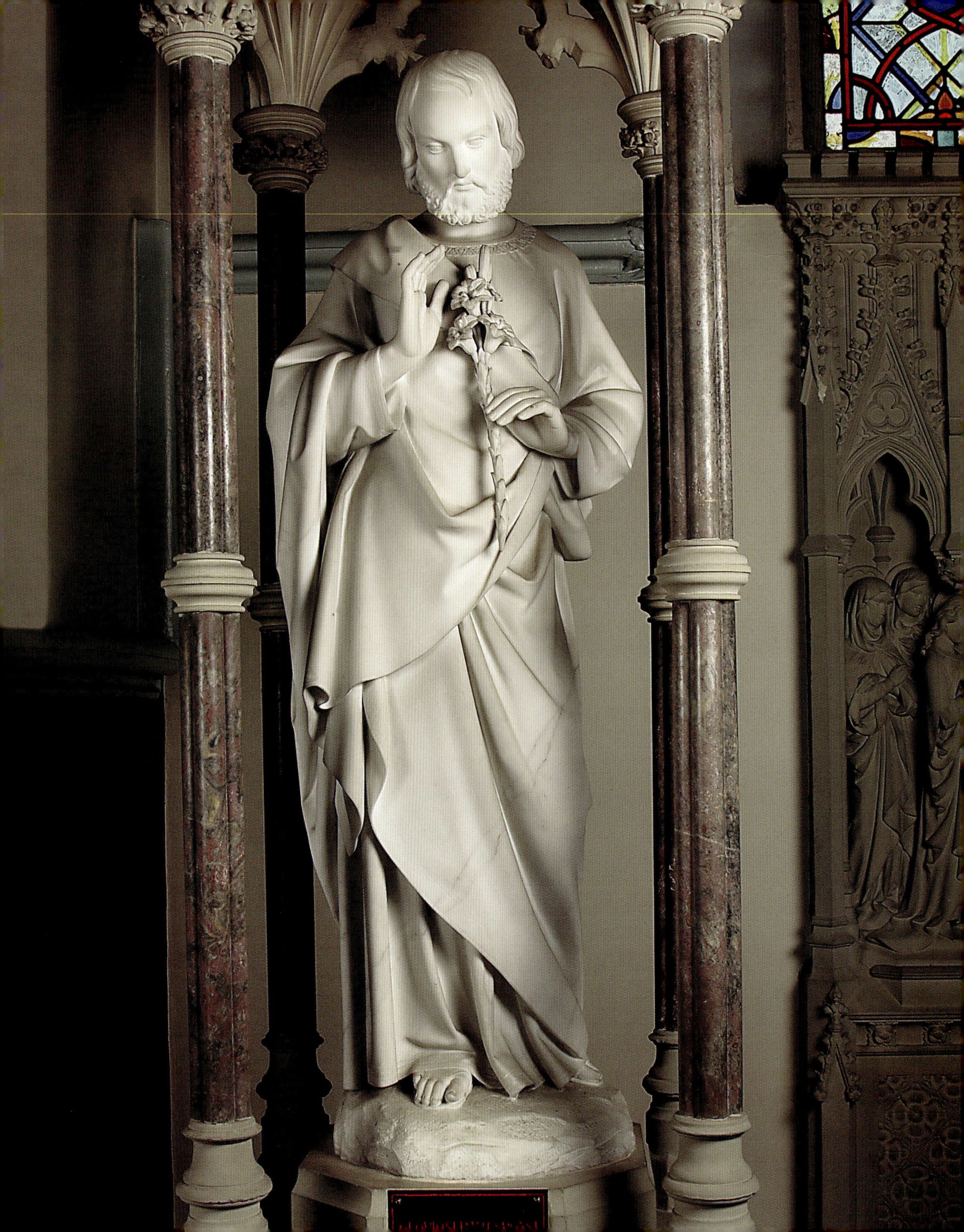

The Sculptor of Ushaw

Karl Hoffmann statues, 1852, 1853, 1855

One of the most distinctive characteristics of Ushaw's Catholic identity is its devotion to the cult of the Virgin Mary. The veneration of Our Lady featured regularly in the life of the college and was given expression in a remarkable variety of devotional rituals and religious confraternities. The core around which these practices revolved finds its monumental testimony in the magnificent marble statues executed in Rome by Karl Hoffmann (1816–72) of Wiesbaden, who justly earned the title of 'the sculptor of Ushaw'. With the later addition of Alfred B. Wall's *Our Lady, the Seat of Wisdom*, placed in the entrance to the college in 1879, Hoffmann's statues of the Virgin Mary transformed Ushaw into a Marian shrine.

Hoffman had already made a reputation for himself with the beautiful statue of *Our Lady, the Immaculate Conception* (1844), commissioned by Fr Edward Lambert in Rome for the church of St Edward King and Confessor in Clifford, West Yorkshire. The legend goes that while carving this piece Hoffmann underwent a spiritual crisis, culminating with his conversion to the Catholic faith on 14 June 1844. The great Nazarene painter Friedrich Overbeck (1789–1869) subsequently acted as his godfather. Through the recommendation of Overbeck, Hoffmann obtained in 1845 an important commission from Cologne Cathedral. It was here, in Cologne, that the indefatigable Charles Newsham contacted him in 1849 to produce a statue for Ushaw.

Hoffmann's sculpture was intended to adorn the Gospel side of Pugin's chapel (1848) and become, under the title of *Our Lady of Clemency*, the centre of devotion for Ushaw students. Newsham needed to wait three years to see his plan fulfilled, for the statue could be completed only after Hoffmann's return to Rome in 1850. Before being sent to Ushaw, Pope Pius IX consecrated the statue in the Vatican gardens on 15 April 1852, granting 300 days indulgence to all who recite the litany of Our Lady before it. The unusual pose of *Our Lady of Clemency*, chiselled in white marble and embellished with turquoises and rubies, adheres to an iconography suggested by Newsham himself: it represents the Virgin Mary as receiving the prayers of the students, handing them on to her Son in the tabernacle, where the consecrated Hosts were kept.

In 1853, Ushaw received as a gift from Fr Henry Bennet the delicate statue of *Saint Joseph with the Lily*, today in the chapel of St Joseph, under Edward Welby Pugin's charming canopied reredos. Hoffmann's statue, which was originally placed on the Gospel side of the choir screen, arrived at Ushaw together with a small figure of the Virgin and Child, also commissioned to Hoffmann by Ms Elizabeth Orrell. In 1855, a larger version of this sculpture was designed to adorn the Epistle side of the choir screen – this is the justifiably famous *Our Lady of Help*. Visitors entering the chapel could admire three statues by Hoffmann, beautifully staged to represent a *Trinitas Creata* (Earthly Trinity) – St Joseph, Mary as queen and Mary as mother.

Karl Hoffmann, *St Joseph with the Lily*, 1853, marble, St Joseph's chapel.

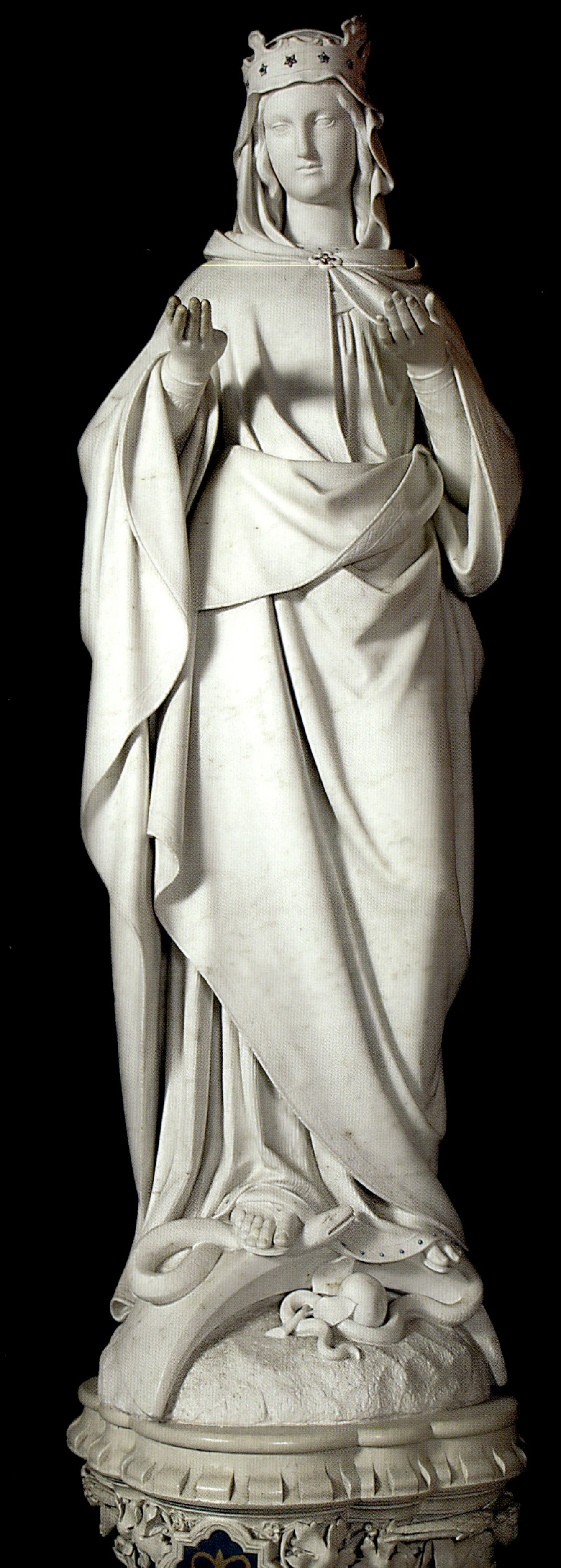

Ushaw soon treasured *Our Lady of Help* above all; popular devotion renamed it as 'Our Lady of Ushaw'. The arresting innocence of Hoffmann's statue inspired members of Ushaw to address their May prayers to her, May being the month of Marian devotion. Erected in her honour was a new confraternity, authorised in 1856 by Pius IX. When the Junior College was completed in 1859, Ms Orrell donated her version of *Our Lady of Help* to Ushaw to be displayed in the chapel of St Aloysius, where, under the presidency of Robert Tate (1863–76), another striking statue by Hoffmann, *Our Lady, the Mother of Jesus*, joined her.

This remarkable series of devotional sculptures, all carved in white marble, constitutes today the largest collection of Hoffmann's works in the world.

STEFANO CRACOLICI

Karl Hoffmann, *Our Lady of Clemency*, 1852, marble, St Cuthbert's chapel.

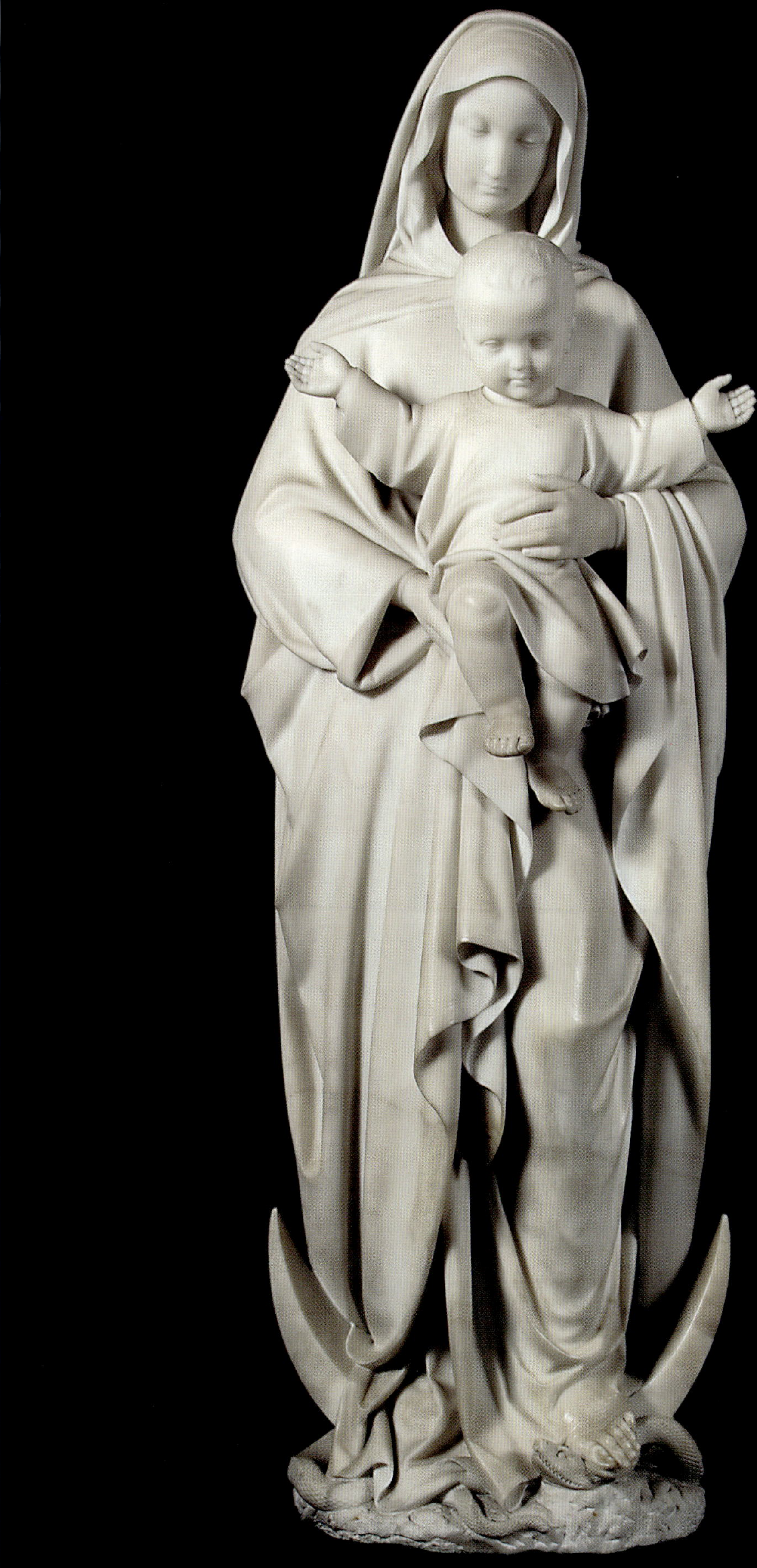

Karl Hoffmann, *Our Lady of Help*, 1855, marble, choir screen.

A Portrait for Newsham's Golden Jubilee

John Rogers Herbert, *Portrait of President Charles Newsham*, 1853

Among the series of portraits of Ushaw's presidents on display in the refectory and along the corridors of the college, the one of Charles Newsham (1791–1863) by John Rogers Herbert (1810–90) occupies a prominent position. It was presented to Newsham in 1853 by one of the most illustrious Ushaw alumni, Nicholas Patrick Wiseman, first cardinal archbishop of Westminster, on the fiftieth anniversary of Newsham's first entrance into the college's life.

It was probably the cardinal himself – well-acquainted with the painter since the time of his presidency of St Mary's College at Oscott (1840–47) – who suggested the name of Herbert to Fr Thomas Witham of Lartington Hall. Witham was one of Ushaw's greatest benefactors and he took care of the arrangements for covering the painting's costs. Not only was Herbert the painter of Wiseman's portrait at Oscott (1842), but he counted, after his conversion to Catholicism in the late 1830s, as one of the cardinal's most zealous allies in the turbulent years following the reestablishment of the Catholic hierarchy in England and Wales in 1850.

Herbert's childhood acquaintance with A.W.N. Pugin was probably responsible for his conversion; his involvement in the decoration of Pugin's New Palace of Westminster certainly consolidated their friendship. The link to the architect further motivated Herbert's involvement with Ushaw in a period during which, under Newsham's presidency and Pugin's guidance, the college was acquiring its distinct neo-gothic look. If for the commission of sacred art, designed to introduce new rituals and devotional practices to Ushaw, the college rigorously opted for works executed in Rome, for the portraits of its presidents it turned to English artists. In those years, Herbert undoubtedly appeared as a choice of great prestige.

At the time of this important commission, Herbert was a distinguished member of the Royal Academy of Arts and certainly the most revered Catholic artist in the country. Members of the Pre-Raphaelite Brotherhood had elected him as one of their precursors and sought his sponsorship for their official publication, *The Germ*. Nobody, however, would have regarded him primarily as a portrait painter. His reputation was instead attached to biblical subjects, painted with a style reminiscent of the one pioneered by the Nazarene movement in Rome. The essential simplicity with which Herbert approached Newsham's portrait reflects this standing and signals his departure from the academic codes governing the genre.

Herbert portrays Newsham in sober ecclesiastical attire, sitting at his desk, while dealing with Pugin's plans for the college's new chapels and buildings. The president, who for his ceaseless activities and lofty ideals had earned the title of Ushaw's 'second founder', is here depicted in his unadorned office, in a momentary pause from his work. Cast in this austere working environment, the mixture of modesty and gravity that shines through his composed posture acquires a devotional meaning, alluding implicitly to the Christian motto *laborare est orare* (to labour is to pray), which Herbert would later adopt as the title for one of his most admired paintings, now at the Tate Gallery in London.

STEFANO CRACOLICI

John Rogers Herbert, *Portrait of President Charles Newsham*, 1853, oil on canvas, 240 × 145 cm. Frame designed by A.W.N. Pugin.

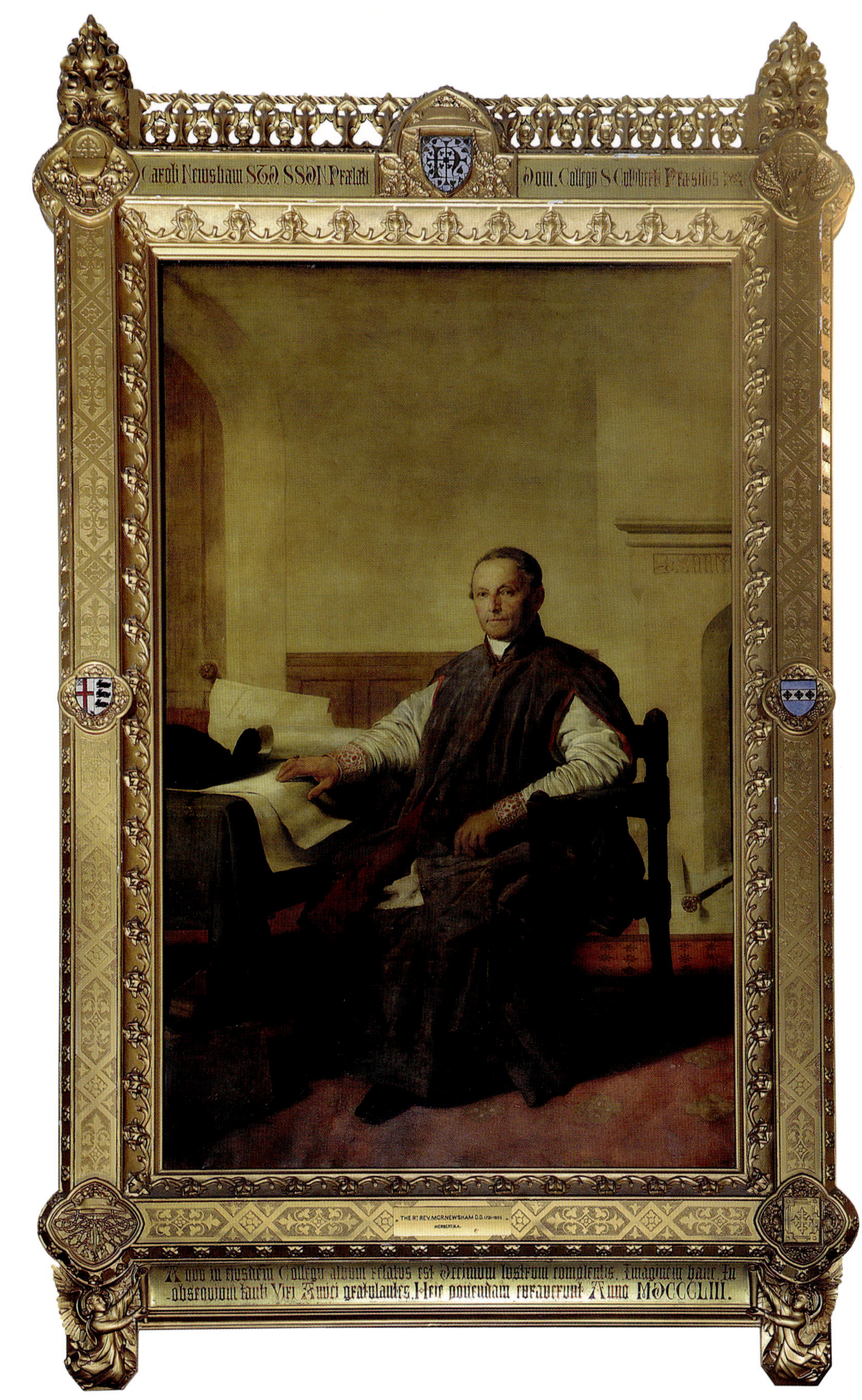
THE Rt REV. MGR NEWSHAM D.D.
HERBERT R.A.

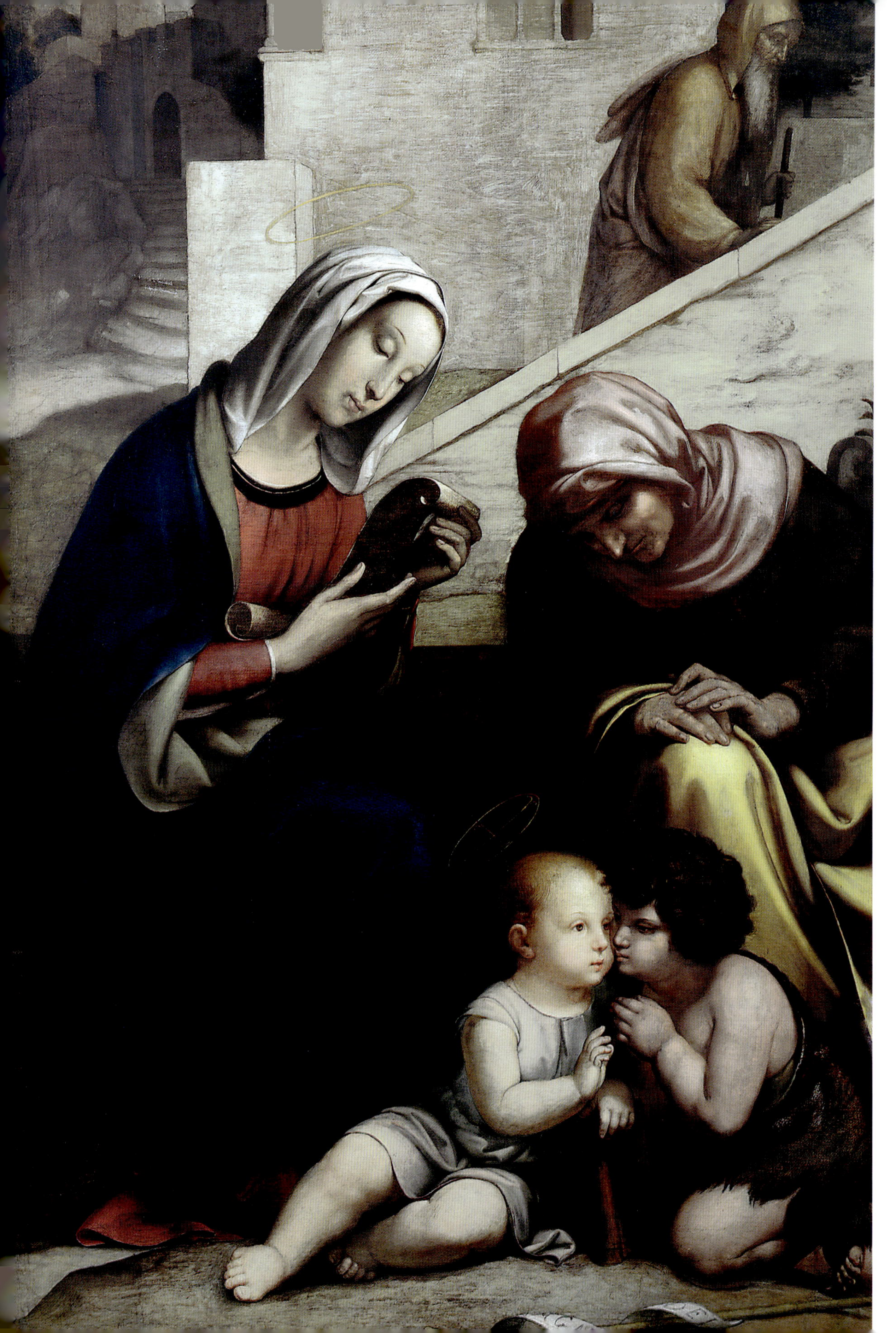

Ushaw and the Art of the Nazarenes

The Nazarene movement, 1854

Together with the artworks directly commissioned by Ushaw to Karl Hoffmann, Franz von Rohden and Alexander Maximilian Seitz, a number of additional pieces produced by the Nazarenes in Rome reached the college via private donations. President Charles Newsham's predilection for the Nazarenes generated among distinguished English Catholic collectors a new vogue for these kinds of devotional artworks. In Rome, Rohden, Hoffmann and Seitz formed with Overbeck an artistic circle exclusively committed to the production and dissemination of artistic objects destined for Catholic devotion.

Ms Elizabeth Orrell of Blackbrook gave to the college another Rohden painting, depicting the Holy Family, and a portrait of Pope Pius IX by Seitz. While the portrait is unfortunately missing, the charming *Holy Family*, or more accurately *The Virgin Mary and Elizabeth, with Jesus and St John* (1854), is still preserved. Ms Orrell exhibited this painting at the Manchester Great Exhibition in 1857 and another version of it, now at the Neue Pinacothek in Munich, was acquired in 1855 by Ludwig I, King of Bavaria; an original sketch of the motif is preserved at the Städelsches Kunstinstitut in Frankfurt. The painter has handled here an intimate subject particularly treasured in Nazarene circles.

Rohden's habit of producing several versions of his pictures is a sign of his relentless quest for the perfect composition. This can be especially followed at Ushaw by comparing the painting in the Oratory of the Holy Family with another astonishing version of the *Adoration of the Magi and the Shepherds* (1877), which joined the college through a private donation. The painting closely recalls an earlier version of Rohden's *Adoration*, dated 1853, now in a private collection in Los Angeles; but it differs quite markedly from the 1851 version at Ushaw in style and orientation, the portraits of Overbeck and Rohden's father both being absent.

Another exquisite work by Rohden, depicting the *Entombment of Christ* (1878), testifies once more to Rohden's allegiance to Overbeck's models. The two large pictures have been gloriously framed by the Florentine woodcarver Leone Antonio Bulletti (1824–84), who came to England to work at Alnwick Castle and then remained in the area, opening a woodcarving shop in Newcastle. Both frames are signed and dated by Bulletti. The one of the *Entombment* also includes the location: 'Royal Albert Hall – Christmas 1879'. The year before, Bulletti had moved to London to take up the role of first director and chief-instructor of the newly founded School of Art Wood-Carving, Royal Albert Hall, in South Kensington.

STEFANO CRACOLICI

Franz von Rohden, *The Virgin Mary and Elizabeth with Jesus and St John (The Holy Family)*, Rome 1854, oil on canvas, 102 × 67 cm.

One of Ushaw's Most Famous Alumni

The Wiseman collection, nineteenth century

Nicholas Patrick Stephen Wiseman (1802–65), cardinal and first archbishop of Westminster, was one of the most influential English Catholics of the nineteenth century. Educated at Ushaw College and ordained at the Venerable English College in Rome, Wiseman developed a reputation as an outstanding scholar and was appointed rector of the English College in 1828. Returning to England permanently 12 years later, he secured various episcopal positions until his appointment as Archbishop of Westminster following the restoration of the Catholic hierarchy in 1850. In this role, he personified and popularised the resurgence of mid-Victorian English Catholicism, introducing Italianate devotions to, for example, the Blessed Sacrament and the Blessed Virgin Mary. In spite of initial opposition to these reforms, his single-mindedness and determination eventually won over many detractors and his transformation of the English Catholic Church is unquestionable, the legacy of which is still evident today.

Given his leading role within the English Catholic Church – not to mention his prominent position in nineteenth-century English history more generally – it is not surprising that the Wiseman collection of archives and objects contain some of Ushaw College's richest treasures. Aside from his correspondence, which comprises over a thousand letters, there are some notable individual items.

The cardinal's link with Ushaw is evident in the programme, script and character sketch drawings for his play, *The Hidden Gem*, a drama set in ancient Rome that was written for the 1858 Ushaw College jubilee. It is revealing of Wiseman's intimate connection with Ushaw, dating back to his schooldays, and his personal bond with the president, Charles Newsham, who tutored Wiseman as a boy.

Wiseman's literary and scholarly achievements are also represented in the manuscript copy of his most popular work, the novel *Fabiola* (1855). Bound in half-red goatskin and red cloth sides with Wiseman's gold-stamped coat of arms, this is the first and only draft copy in existence – the author certifying as much on the frontispiece. *Fabiola* is set against the backdrop of Christian persecution in Rome during the fourth century and was allegedly written as a response to Charles Kingsley's anti-Catholic work, *Hypatia* (1853). It can therefore be read as a rallying cry for English Catholicism which had only recently been, to quote Wiseman from an earlier polemic, 'restored to its orbit in the ecclesiastical firmament, from which its light had long vanished'. It is, therefore, an absolutely integral document to understanding Wiseman's vision for the mid-nineteenth-century Catholic Church.

Nicholas Wiseman was famous as much for the force of his personality as his literary reputation and this is particularly evident in the portrait by Thomas Brigstocke which hangs in the refectory at Ushaw. This oil on canvas painting, measuring nearly three metres in height with an ornate gold-painted frame, portrays Wiseman resplendent in ecclesiastical robes. It is almost regal in its representation, a rather grandiose self-image which Wiseman effectively stage-managed himself during his lifetime. The young acolyte in the background was rumoured to be Raphael Merry del Val (later Cardinal Secretary of State to Pope Pius X) but was, in fact, the youthful Count Manuel de Torre Diaz, who was an Ushaw student during the 1850s and would later gift the college a gold and silver cope.

JONATHAN BUSH

Character sketches from Nicholas Wiseman's play *The Hidden Gem* (Ushaw, UC/H104).

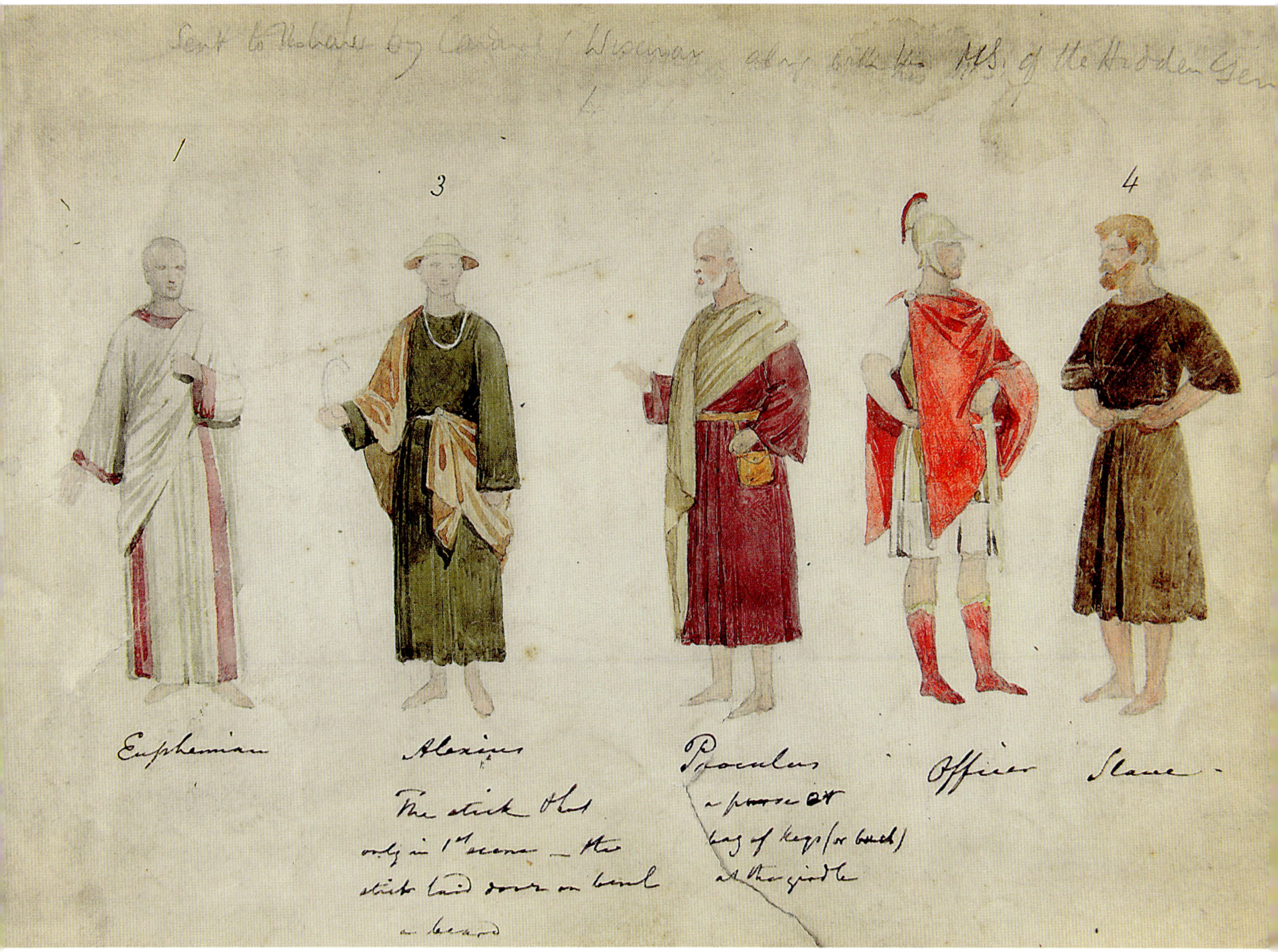

1

3

4

Euphemian

Alexius

The stick that only in 1st scene — the stick laid down on bench

Proculus

a ~~purse~~ or bag of keys (or bunch) at the girdle

Officer

Slave

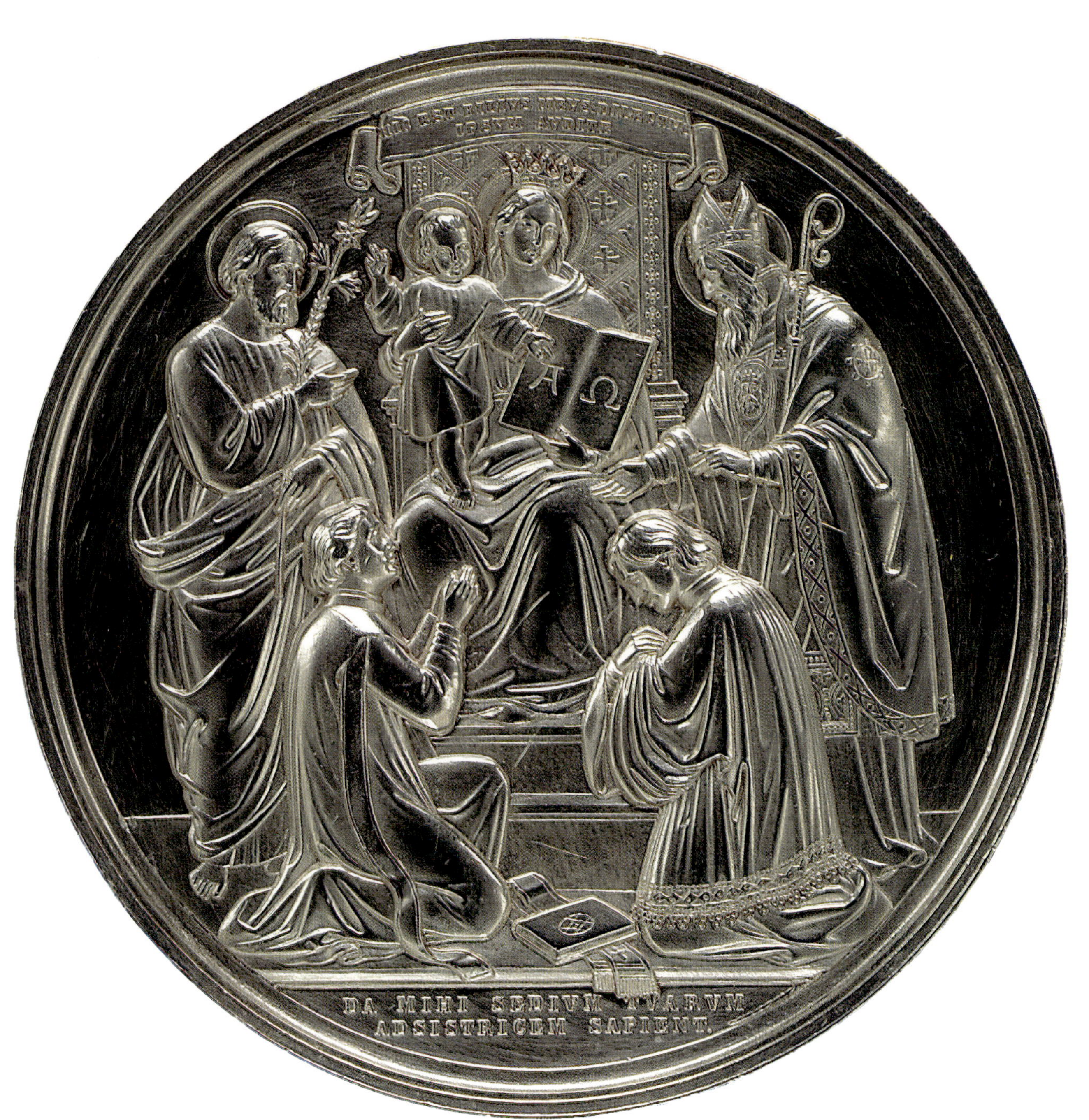
DA MIHI SEDIVM TVARVM
ADSISTRICEM SAPIENT.

Ushaw Prize Medal

Karl Friedrich Voigt medal, 1863

Ushaw was one of the first educational institutions in England to introduce prize medals as a reward for students. The initiative should be attributed, as with many others, to college president Charles Newsham following the success of the public ceremony that accompanied the prize-giving of books in 1837. Newsham and his collaborators were faced with the problem of how to 'brand' the college and, more practically, with the difficult task of finding a suitable patron and image for the obverse and reverse of the medal. In the years that followed, generic *bene merenti* medals from Rome, bearing the effigy of the Pope and a wreath of bay leaves, seemed to fit the purpose.

Everything changed, however, with the preparations for Ushaw's golden jubilee of 1858. The plan for a new prize medal, specifically struck for the college, emerged; it was supposed to embody the prestige of the institution and convey the distinctiveness of the occasion for the years to come. Newsham turned to Cardinal Nicholas Wiseman for advice. In an insightful letter, preserved in the college's archives, Wiseman replied with the suggestion of Cardinal William Allen, the founder of the English College in Douai, for the reverse. He also gave detailed indications for the image to be struck on the obverse, as well as adding the text of the inscriptions to be featured on both sides.

Rejecting the prototypes provided by English artists as too generic in their gothic style, Wiseman urged Newsham to consider the medal as a 'monument of art'. He recommended committing its design to one of the most devout and talented painters of the time, such as Edward von Steinle, Friedrich Overbeck or Ernst Deger. Following Wiseman's advice, Newsham turned to Rome and engaged the painter Alexander Maximilian Seitz (1811–88) for its design, and medallist Karl Friedrich Voigt (1800–74) for its execution. The prize medal soon became Newsham's new obsession and the debates over its design significantly delayed its completion, which was achieved only in 1863 – five years after the jubilee.

Nevertheless, after 1863 the prize medal was regularly awarded. Eight medals – four of silver and four of bronze – were presented each year as first and second prizes in the four highest classes of humanities: rhetoric, poetry, syntax and grammar.

In full agreement with Wiseman's instructions, the obverse of the medal depicts the Virgin Mary enthroned as the *sedes sapientiae* (seat of wisdom), with the infant Christ standing on her knee and pointing to a book displaying the Alpha and Omega; on her right and left are the two patrons of the college – St Joseph and St Cuthbert – presenting to her a lay and an ecclesiastical student respectively. The reverse bears in high relief the effigy of Cardinal Allen. The result certainly constitutes a masterpiece of its kind.

STEFANO CRACOLICI

Karl Voigt *Ushaw Prize Medal*, silver, based on a drawing by Alexander Maximilian Seitz, 1863. Obverse (shown) reads: *Hic est Filius meus dilectus, ipsum audite* (This is my Son, the Beloved: listen to him) [top], *Da mihi sedium tuarum adsistricem sapientiam* (Give me the wisdom that sits by thy throne) [bottom]. Reverse reads: *Guliel. Card. Alanus* (Cardinal William Allen) [title], *In mem. tanti viri Coll. apud Ushaw hoc praemium meriti excudi fec. MDCCCLVIII* (Ushaw College made this award of achievement to be struck in the memory of such a great man, 1858) [around].

Francis Thompson Unedited

Francis Thompson, 'To The English Martyrs', 1905–6. UC/P39/3

Francis Thompson (1859–1907), best known for his long poem of spiritual torment and pursuit 'The Hound of Heaven' (1890), was a student at Ushaw College from 1870 to 1877. Although he excelled in English and Latin, his behaviour was wayward and eccentric, and he left without taking holy orders, having been deemed by his spiritual advisers to be temperamentally unsuited to the priesthood. Even so, the Catholic liturgy at Ushaw and the natural beauty of the Durham countryside where he walked had a profound and lasting influence on his work.

Having failed as a medical student at Owens College in Manchester, Thompson spent several years as an outcast and an opium addict on the streets of London before being rescued by Alice and Wilfrid Meynell.

Among the Francis Thompson papers at Ushaw is a signed manuscript copy of Thompson's last major poem, 'To the English Martyrs'. An impassioned ode commemorating the Catholic martyrs of the English Reformation, the poem was commissioned by the *Dublin Review* and written by Thompson in the peaceful surroundings of Crawley Friary in West Sussex in the winter months of 1905–6.

The Ushaw holograph has a special importance, being a final draft in Thompson's elegant copperplate script and also a version that differs significantly from the printing of the poem in the *Dublin Review* and successive editions of the poet's works. The opening 46 lines have a powerful prophetic resonance, acknowledging 'the avenging wrath' of 'the malignant sun', and anticipating cataclysmic war, disease and disaster. The 'third year' of retribution with which the poem commences looks back to the earthquakes that shook parts of England and Wales in 1903.

Alarmed by this vengeful rhetoric, Meynell deleted the poem's apocalyptic prelude before publication, and so the Ushaw manuscript is the only surviving record of the poem as Thompson himself wished it to be read. It would be wrong to attribute the poem's disturbed vision to opium addiction (as Meynell possibly did), since its fundamental appeal comes largely from its steady alliance of radical political protest and unwavering Catholic faith. While honouring the sacrifice of the English martyrs, the poem repeatedly turns on England, denouncing its long abuse of liberty.

One of the aesthetic advantages of Meynell's editorial intervention is that the printed poem opens strikingly and memorably with the 'Red rain' and 'Red dew' of blood sacrifice falling on the gallows of 'Tyburn tree'. The 'black shadow' of Tyburn both recalls the Cross at Calvary and spreads over blighted England at the beginning of a new century. The ominous black bird with 'red-bedabbled breast and beak' completes this powerful symbolic depiction of death, destruction and eventual redemption. At the heart of the poem's procession of English martyrs is Thomas More, 'Dear Jester in the Courts of God', revered by Thompson for his 'holy ease' and irrepressible spirit.

It closes with an observation on freedom that is couched in a language of paradox and conceit reminiscent of the best of seventeenth-century religious verse: 'Hardest servitude has he / That's gaoled in arrogant liberty; / And freedom, spacious and unflawed, / Who is walled about with God'.

STEPHEN REGAN

The final page of the autographed manuscript of Francis Thompson's 'To the English Martyrs'.

That brazen walls disbed. Your hand,
Princes, put forth to the command,
And levy upon the guilty land
Your saving wars, on it go down—
Black beneath God's and heaven's frown;
Your prevalent approaches make
With unsustainable Grace, and take
Captive the land that captived you;
To Christ enslave ye and subdue
Her so-bragged freedom: for the crime
She wrought on you in antique time,
Parcel the land among you: reign
Viceroys to your sweet Suzerain!
Till she shall know
This lesson in her overthrow:—
Hardest servitude has he
That's gaoled in arrogant liberty;
And freedom spacious and unflawed,
Who is walled about with God.

Francis Thompson.

Index

Note: Page numbers in *italics* refer to an illustration.